EXCAVATIONS AT
GRIMES GRAVES
NORFOLK
1972–1976

Grimes Graves from the air.

EXCAVATIONS AT
GRIMES GRAVES
NORFOLK
1972–1976

FASCICULE 6

EXPLORATION AND EXCAVATION BEYOND THE DEEP MINES

Including Gale de Giberne Sieveking's excavations in the West Field

IAN LONGWORTH, GILLIAN VARNDELL AND JACEK LECH

With contributions by
Janet Ambers, Nick Ashton, Mike Cowell, Paul Craddock and Mike Hughes

and illustrations by
Stephen Crummy, Phillip Dean, Karen Hughes and Meredydd Moores

Published for the Trustees of the British Museum
by British Museum Press

First published in 2012 by British Museum Press
A division of The British Museum Company Ltd
38 Russell Square, London WC1B 3QQ

A catalogue record for this book is available from the British Library

ISBN 978 0 7141 2331 8

Designed and typeset in Plantin
by John Hawkins Design
Printed and bound in Hong Kong by Printing Express Ltd

The papers used in this book are natural, recyclable products made
from wood grown in well-managed forests and other controlled sources.
The manufacturing processes conform to the environmental
regulations of the country of origin.

Supported by the Marc Fitch Fund
additional support by the Francis Coales Charitable Foundation

Fig. 2 Site atlas of areas excavated and surveyed where known.

Valley base line

A

C oak

E oak

G forked pine (?)

tree

pit 7   pit 4   see fig. 9
B   pit 6
pit 3   pit 5
pit 3a
D   pit 13   see fig. 15 & 16
F
pit 14

see fig. 3
see fig. 10
see fig. 4
see fig. 5
see fig. 6

H

Pit 9

Pit 15

FL1
TH9
FL9
1971   1972
TH17
FL23
FL8   FL24

Pit 1   TH8

FL18

FL12
FL7   FL10
FL26
TH11
TH8
see fig. 7   FL3   FL2
TH3   FL13
TH1   FL14   T3   S12
A   see fig. 8   TH2   FL11   FL4   T4   FL85   The
B   T6   S19   T18   Grimshoe
D   Pit 8   S8   FL25   FL22   S16   Mound
F105   T1
E
Pit 12   Pit 2   T5   Greenwell
Pit
West Field   S14
Shaft W   FL17
T2   S15

see fig. 14

Pit 10
C   1926   see fig. 11   Longworth
Black Hole   FL21   Area 'C'
see fig. 12   FL15   Shaft   trenches
Pit 11   FL19   X
1928   FL16   Longworth
see fig. 13   Area 'A'
FL5   trenches
Pit 11*   Shaft U   FL6   Longworth
B   A   Area 'B'
trenches

The Forest Pits

N

0   100 m

	Sieveking
	Armstrong *et al.*
	Greenwell
	Mercer
	Longworth
	resistivity / mag. survey
+	phosphate survey point
FL8	floor
S16	section
T1	trench (museum)
TH18	trial hole
+	approx. position
Y□ □Z	line of sections (Armstrong)
	contour (m)
	contour (0.25 m)

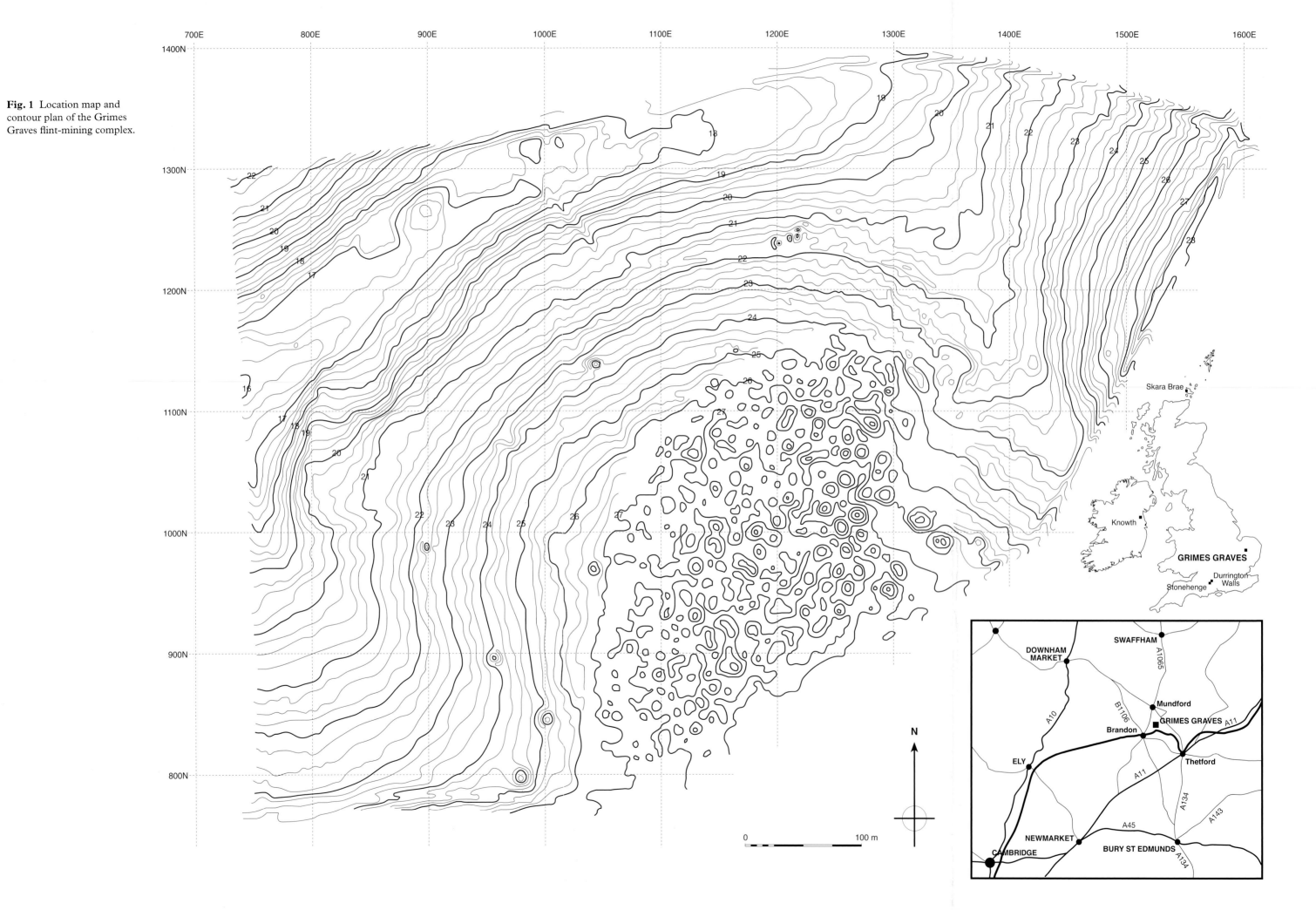

Fig. 1 Location map and contour plan of the Grimes Graves flint-mining complex.

Contents

Gale Sieveking at his home, 1974.

Gale de Giberne Sieveking
1925–2007

Unhappily Gale died before this volume could see the light of day. He was by any standard a man of great charm and vision; a source of many stimulating ideas, of which only a handful ever came to fruition, the rest lying beyond the powers that science and the financial resources of the time could support. His contribution to the re-excavation of Grimes Graves and the flint axe analysis programme that he promoted can now be seen to lie at the edge of what, in the early 1970s, could be achieved. As a mark of respect to a much-valued colleague and friend, the authors wish to dedicate this volume to his memory.

Sjeuf Felder at Grimes Graves, 1975.

Sjeuf Felder
1928–2009

As work on this volume was nearing completion we were saddened to learn of the death of Sjeuf Felder. It was Gale's idea to involve in the re-excavation of some of the deeper pits the Prehistoric Flint Mines Working Group of the Dutch Geological Society, Limburg section, of which Sjeuf was a tireless and enthusiastic member. His coal mining experience was brought to bear on the numerous problems, both academic and practical, that were encountered during this massive enterprise. He was co-organizer of several international flint symposia, and at Warsaw during the seventh of these was hailed as 'father of the conference'.

List of Figures

List of Tables

List of Plates

Acknowledgements

The authors wish to offer their grateful thanks to the many colleagues and friends who have contributed to aspects of the work at Grimes Graves recorded in this fascicule by direct contribution or critical comment as the progress of analysis has developed. We hope that we may be forgiven if some are not specifically named, for the roll call is indeed long. Their contributions have nonetheless been greatly appreciated.

In particular, we wish to express our profound thanks to the Institute of Archaeology and Ethnology, Polish Academy of Sciences, for their collaboration in making time and resources available to Professor Lech for his monumental work on the analysis of the chipping floors summarized in this volume.

Nothing could have been achieved without the permission of the then Ancient Monuments Branch of the Department of the Environment (now English Heritage), which allowed the British Museum to investigate a number of aspects of the Ancient Monument. Our thanks also go to the Forestry Commission, whose permission to access their plantations to the south of the Scheduled Monument enabled the extensive phosphate survey detailed in Chapter IIIA to be undertaken. We are also indebted to Peter Topping of English Heritage for providing and obtaining permission to use the air photo of the site, which forms the frontispiece, and their recent comprehensive ground survey, fig. 120.

We are, of course, well aware of the great debt we owe to our colleagues in the British Museum for their major contributions. In particular, the illustrators in the then Department of Prehistoric and Romano-British Antiquities, first under Philip Compton†, then Karen Hughes, who provided the detailed interpretative drawings used in this volume. Phillip Dean† and Meredydd Moores provided the bulk of the artefact drawings, with additions by Robert Pengelly. Stephen Crummy has managed to convert early vestigial field sketches and notes, as well as later plans and sections, into meaningful interpretations. We can only offer our apologies that their work has lain unpublished for so long. We are also grateful to Nick Ashton for his report on the Palaeolithic handaxe recovered from Shaft X (Appendix 4) and Roger Jacobi† for his advice on the likely date of the flintwork from cuttings 880/910 and 900/870.

On the scientific side we are grateful to Paul Craddock, Mike Cowell and Mike Hughes for their work both on the phosphate survey and on the flint analysis programme. They in turn would like to record their thanks to the dedicated work of other colleagues in the Museum, including Richard Greenwood from Scientific Research, for providing the initial phosphate diagrams. On-site volunteers also took part in the sampling programme and especial thanks must go to John McGarry, a professional surveyor, who laid out the grids for the survey. Thanks go to the Trainees provided by the North Sea Camp Detention Centre, Boston, Lincolnshire, and their masters, who made up much of the workforce for the survey. David Jenkins of the University of Bangor, North Wales, kindly provided an advance copy of his paper (Owen *et al.* 2001). The authors of the phosphate survey would also like to thank their wives for their assistance during the survey, including the field sampling. Antony Simpson kindly prepared fig. 117 for the flint analysis programme. Last but not least we would like to thank Janet Ambers for providing the report on the ^{14}C dating programme and much advice on its interpretation.

In the field, we would once again like to record our thanks to all those who helped during the excavations, in particular Chris Gingell, Philip Harding, John Burton, Richard Harrison, Ryszard Mazurowski and Elżbieta Sachse-Kozłowska.

During the many years of post-excavation processing we have received much valuable help from Dr Frances Healy, not least in the selection of further material for the flint analysis programme, along with Alan West of the Castle Museum, Norwich. Dr Healy has also kept us briefed on her current work devoted to refining the dating of the site. A special thank you must also go to Dr Mike Pitts for kindly allowing us to consult and use data from his corpus of flint axes housed in the National Monuments Record in Swindon.

Finally, our thoughts and consideration of a number of outstanding problems have gained from the knowledge and wisdom of the late Sjeuf Felder, Dr Marjorie de Grooth, Dr Jean Desloges, Cyril Marcigny and Simon Cleggett.

† Philip Compton died in February 2011. Phil Dean died in the autumn of 2009. Roger died in December 2009.

I Introduction

Excavation history before 1972

It has long been appreciated that activity associated with the mining of flint at Grimes Graves extended well beyond the area where the tops of the deep mine shafts remain visible today (figs 1 and 2; see also fig. 120). The site was well known to nineteenth- and early twentieth-century collectors as a source of flint specimens for their cabinets drawn from the many workshop sites scattered across the mine field. Much of this early interest, however, lies recorded in collections only where individual implements carry identification of their provenance. More systematic exploration and recovery began with work carried out for the Prehistoric Society of East Anglia by A.E. Peake in 1914, additional to the excavation of Pits 1 and 2, the two deep mines then examined (Peake 1915).

The reasons put forward for the 1914 campaign were several, as set out in the report produced at its close (Clarke 1915), and some may have been a rationalization after the event. However, foremost was the desire to confirm or deny the Neolithic date of the mines as advocated by the Revd W. Greenwell following his excavation of a deep mine between 1868 and 1870 (Greenwell 1870a and 1870b). During the years leading up to the campaign a number of antiquaries, including General Pitt-Rivers, Sir John Evans and Allen Brown, had compared the axe roughouts recovered from the site with implements from the French Palaeolithic. These observations culminated in a paper in *Archaeologia* in 1912 by Reginald Smith of the then Department of British and Medieval Antiquities in the British Museum, who argued that the flint mines both at Cissbury and at Grimes Graves should be viewed as of Palaeolithic (Aurignacian) date. In this argument the recovery of associated fauna was clearly one priority in order to establish whether the species were domesticated or wild and, of particular importance, whether any extinct species were represented. In addition to dating the mines, the work was also directed towards studying the miners themselves, their mining methods, how access was gained to the mines, whether the pits were worked at different dates, whether light could be shed upon how the mine field began, as well as the climate and environment of the times. From the material recovered it was hoped that it might be possible to discover evidence for any art (perhaps to help establish a Palaeolithic date) or pottery (which might have argued for the Neolithic) and to further study the implements produced. Were implements produced *in situ* or was the raw material itself traded, and was there any evidence for polishing? The aims were certainly ambitious and, not surprisingly, many were to remain to form the basis for future ongoing work at the site.

Excavation of Pits 1 and 2 confirmed many of Greenwell's observations, demonstrating that they applied equally at two widely separated locations across the mine field. The excavations had further documented the use of the polished axe as well as the antler pick in the working of the mines. In both pits pottery, which can now be identified as Grooved Ware (Longworth *et al.* 1988), was present.

A.E. Peake and E.T. Lingwood were to excavate another four pit tops in 1916 and 1917 (Peake 1917, 412 and 1919, 86–8), an unnumbered pit and Pits 3, 4 and 5, while the Revd H.G.O. Kendall examined a further pit top in 1919 (Kendall 1920a). None of these excavations was taken to a depth of more than 6 ft (1.8 m) and shed no further light upon the actual mining operations, although in the case of two, Peake recorded evidence of later occupation in the filled-up weathering cones, including a hearth, animal bones and, in one, coarse pottery.

It was left to A.L. Armstrong (who had acted as surveyor and draughtsman for the 1914 campaign, producing the site plan and section drawings) to undertake the task of examining the mine field in more detail during the interwar years between 1923 and 1939. Armstrong appears to have been motivated firstly by the desire to demonstrate how the mine field developed, but increasingly by the need to prove that Grimes Graves had at least its origins in the Palaeolithic, for a Neolithic date had been championed by W.G. Clarke in 1916 (Clarke 1917) and again in 1921 (Clarke 1921). Armstrong felt that the beginnings of mining on the site were likely to have started following the chance discovery of flint eroding to the surface. If so, then the development of the mine field could have followed a logical progression. In his presidential address to the Prehistoric Society of East Anglia in 1926, Armstrong (1927) followed the line of reasoning put forward by de Pauw and van Overloop for Spiennes, which had been discussed by H.W. Sandars (1910). The earliest mines would have been simple pits to exploit the flint where this lay at no great depth. Where the *floorstone* lay at a considerable depth, as had been demonstrated by Greenwell in his pit, and in Pits 1 and 2, then deep-galleried mines would have been needed, calling for a considerable outlay in time and labour, to say nothing of mining expertise. Between these two extremes would lie 'intermediate mines', deeper than the first 'primitive' mines but still not calling for the sophistication required to exploit the flint at greater depth. Armstrong therefore set about the examination of further mines, beginning in 1923 with the excavation of a number of shallow mines to the north of the visible mine field – Pits 3 and 4 (Armstrong 1924a) (unfortunately Armstrong numbered these beginning with 3, causing some confusion with those already examined by Peake). The *floorstone* lay here at a depth of 10.5–12.5 ft (3.2–3.8 m) below the modern surface. He then moved his attention to the area to the west. The excavations of Pits 8–12 were completed by 1933 (Armstrong 1927, 1932 and 1934), although only Pit 12 was published in any detail. These were for Armstrong 'intermediate' pits, with the beginnings of galleries radiating from their shaft bases. In 1934 Armstrong, with the assistance of Dr R.V. Favell, was to explore two further pits, Pits 13 and 14, which lay between the visible mine field and Pits 3–7 to the north, although neither was published. Nor were his excavations in 1937 and 1939 of Pit 15, a mine sited on the edge of the visible mine field in the same segment. Pit 15 was to prove the most exciting for Armstrong and the most debatable for subsequent commentators, for at its base at a depth of 19 ft (5.8 m) Armstrong was convinced that he had found preserved a 'ritual' group, including a 'goddess' carved in chalk as well as a chalk phallus and group of three natural flint nodules arranged to resemble male genitalia. But had some or all of these features been faked?

In addition to excavation of individual mines, survey and exploration was conducted to examine other aspects of the mine field. Many of the pits opened by Armstrong were not visible on the ground and had been discovered during systematic trenching of the surface at various locations. A series of exploratory trenches had already been cut as part of the Prehistoric Society of East Anglia's campaign in 1914. Armstrong's main aim was now to discover where flint extraction on the site was likely to have commenced. If the *floorstone* was the main target of the miners then it was necessary to establish where this could be found at or near the surface, and the most obvious areas to search lay to the north and west. At one point Armstrong found what he had been looking for. The section, which he published (Armstrong 1923, fig. 13), showed the *floorstone* lifted and doubled over by cryoturbation close to the modern surface. 'By following downwards the contorted layer the undisturbed stone would soon be reached and its presence once realized, primitive mining activities would naturally follow' (ibid., 125). His thesis apparently demonstrated, further work was undertaken 'to ascertain how far to the west the floorstone remained *in situ*', and to find primitive mining sites in the valley. Although some evidence for the position of these trenches survives in his field notebooks,

their exact locations remain to a great extent speculative.

If trenching had concentrated on establishing the boundaries of the *floorstone* layer and the quest for the early mining sites that had first exploited it, a second reason for excavation had been the exploration of chipping floors and the recovery of artefacts made from the mined flint. Of the ninety-eight floors that received a recorded number, nothing is known of the location of twenty-seven. Of the rest, thirty-seven lay within the visible mine field, fifteen to the south and east, fourteen to the north and only five to the west. These varied in size from as little as 3 x 6 ft (0.9 x 1.8 m) to Floor 88, described as stretching over an area of 126 yd (105 sq m) (Armstrong 1927, 105–7). These duly yielded a mass of flint débitage, including a range of implements in varying stages of completeness, which continued to fuel the debate over the chronology of the site. Other than implement typology, the floors, however, contributed three further elements to the debate: some yielded fauna; at least one (Floor 85) was said to show clear stratigraphy; and others yielded 'art'. In trying to evaluate Armstrong's work in these interwar years, it must be remembered that the work was strongly motivated by a desire to prove that the mining at Grimes Graves at least began in the Palaeolithic. In the debate that Reginald Smith had promoted, other than a comparison of lithic technology, two factors could be brought to bear to suggest a Palaeolithic date: the presence of extinct fauna in association with the 'palaeoliths' and examples of 'palaeolithic' art. Armstrong's excavations failed to provide the first, but appeared to provide the second. From Pit 15 came the chalk carved 'goddess', and from Floors 15, 16, 29, 32, 58, 70 or 75 and 85 came apparent engravings in the cortex of a number of flint flakes.

Nothing found in Britain before or since, with the possible exception of the Somerset 'god-dolly' (Coles and Hibbert 1968), resembles the 'goddess', and there is strong reason to suppose that this and other elements of the Pit 15 ritual group have been faked (Varndell 1991, 103ff.), while some of the engravings, if not actually fakes, show signs of having been enhanced (Varndell 2005). As regards the ritual group in Pit 15, did a helpful workman 'provide' the evidence that Armstrong so desperately wished to find? In the case of the engravings more suspicion must fall on Armstrong himself. The 'goddess' is crude, but some of the engravings call for a greater knowledge of the plausible than a rural labourer of the time is likely to have possessed. Their enhancement – nudging the evidence to offer more than it should – smacks more of calculated fraud. The 'engravings' had been recovered over the period 1915–27, the 'goddess' in 1939. In 1933 J.G.D. Clark and S. Piggott had written their paper in *Antiquity* exposing the lithic typology argument for what it was, a mistaken comparison of finished Palaeolithic implements with the roughing out phases of Neolithic artefact production.

The fauna recovered from the site was in keeping with a Neolithic date and the pottery recovered from the mines was also of that period. Greenwell's first judgement was exonerated and Armstrong or his supporters were perhaps pushed to make one final, mistaken and possibly unethical, attempt to restore credence to a Palaeolithic date. In practice, Clark and Piggott had already put paid to such pretensions.

In 1931 the site was purchased for the nation by the then Ministry of Works and in the post-war years two of the mines, 1 and 15, were capped, ladders introduced, and the public encouraged to visit. By 1970 these mines were beginning to become less than presentable, with remedial work required to cope with the inevitable wear and tear of public visits over the years. It was proposed, therefore, that a new mine be explored, which, when completely excavated, could be opened to the public as a replacement. At the same time this would provide an opportunity to excavate *de novo* a deep mine using all the techniques that modern science could bring to bear. In particular, evidence would be sought both as to the environmental conditions and chronological setting of the mine. For logistical reasons the pit chosen lay on the north-eastern fringe of the mine field, and its excavation was undertaken in 1971 and 1972 by Professor Roger Mercer.

Mercer found that the 1971 shaft (Mercer 1981) was surrounded by a circular dump of mined chalk that may originally have been up to 4 m high. This had been thrown onto a land surface virtually free of flint working except on the western side where the shaft had cut through an earlier working floor. Between the shaft and this circular dump on the eastern side lay a Late Neolithic working area and hearth. In the upper layers of the shaft two Iron Age crouched inhumations had been placed on their backs. The earlier, a young female, was associated with an etched chalk plaque; the second, an adult male, with two iron ring-beads. In addition, a massive deposit of mainly non-*floorstone* débitage associated with a sherd of Bronze Age pottery had been shot into the shaft at an advanced stage in its infilling.

Excavations by the British Museum 1972–6

Excavations by the British Museum in 1972–6 were undertaken in the hope of resolving a number of the still outstanding problems connected with the interpretation of the site. In 1959 the Museum had received the finds recovered by Armstrong from his excavations during the interwar years. Much of this had remained unpublished and was only sparsely documented. It was known that at least two major phases of activity could be recognized: a mining phase, when flint was being extracted on a massive scale during the Neolithic period, and a later occupation phase during the Bronze Age. But many questions still remained to be addressed. Firstly, with regard to the phase when flint was being actively extracted from the

site during the Neolithic – over what period of time did this extend? Was it continuous or were there distinct episodes? Who were the miners? Where were they living? Were different techniques used to extract the flint and, not least, what was the range of implement being made from the flint so extracted? Secondly, what was the nature of the Bronze Age occupation on the site? Could one build up a picture of the economy of the time and was the presence of flint on the site the reason for that occupation?

Obtaining samples for ^{14}C dating was seen as the key step forward for establishing the chronological range of the site, but given its size – Grimes Graves extends over a minimum of 20 ha – it was clearly only going to be possible to attempt to undertake a series of small-scale excavations at different strategically chosen locations. For the deep mines it was agreed with the then Ancient Monuments Branch of the Department of the Environment, in whose guardianship the site lay, that investigations would be confined to reopening mines which had previously been explored. Armstrong's work had, however, already established that flint had also been extracted elsewhere on the site by means of shallower mines and these too needed to be examined. Armstrong had also explored a Bronze Age midden which had been deposited in a hollow, probably the weathering cone of one of the deep mines, on the southern fringe of the site, which he had called the 'Black Hole'. Mercer's work was revealing a similar pattern. To select areas to sample for both the Bronze Age occupation and variations in flint extraction, extensive areas were subjected to magnetometer, resistivity and phosphate surveys, and a completely new aerial survey commissioned.

Many of the results of this research programme have now been published in a series of fascicules:

1 *Neolithic antler picks from Grimes Graves, Norfolk, and Durrington Walls, Wiltshire: a biometrical analysis* by Juliet Clutton-Brock (1984) looked at the vast collection of antler picks recovered from the site and the state of the deer herds from which they had been drawn, comparing these results with those from a site of comparable date in Wiltshire.

2 *The Neolithic, Bronze Age and Later pottery* by I. Longworth, A. Ellison and V. Rigby (1988) assessed the pottery so far recovered from the site.

3 *Shaft X: Bronze Age flint, chalk and metal working* by I. Longworth, A. Herne, G. Varndell and S. Needham (1991) dealt with the excavation of the site of a Bronze Age midden and its contents which had been shot into the top of a filled-in mine shaft.

4 *Animals, environment and the Bronze Age economy* by A.J. Legge (1992) analysed the evidence recovered from the

Bronze Age midden to establish the environment and economy during the Bronze Age occupation of the area.

5 *Mining in the deeper mines* by I. Longworth and G. Varndell (1996) pulled together the survey work undertaken by the Dutch mining specialists and their interpretation of how the deep mines were worked, the efficiency of the mining and the likely output in terms of raw material recovered, together with previously unpublished records of earlier exploration.

In this final fascicule the remaining exploratory work undertaken on the site will be examined, including the Museum's own explorations in the West Field together with initial results from a detailed study of areas of flint reduction excavated to the west of Shaft X south of the Deep Mine Field and in the top of Feature 112.

Topography and geology

The Grimes Graves flint mines lie on a low chalk rise in the Norfolk Breckland, with the visible deep mine shafts clustering at the top. To the west the hillside slopes gradually into a shallow dry valley, and more abruptly to the north (figs 2 and 120). The chalk bedrock is capped by sand, with a cryoturbated zone between where the materials are mixed. This mixture of shattered chalk, chalk-mud and sand is referred to as 'cryte' in the text. Periglacial processes moved material downslope into the dry valleys. The occurrence of sizeable flint nodules and fragments within it rendered its exploitation worthwhile; in the West Field this was chiefly by means of shallow workings. The deposits here are contorted and mobile; disturbance by rabbits has contributed to the likelihood of intrusions and mixing of material.

II Previous survey and surface excavation

A Exploratory surveys

During the Prehistoric Society of East Anglia's campaign in 1914 a series of exploratory trenches had been placed to explore peripheral areas outside the visible mine field, where both mining activity and reduction areas appeared to exist: I–III in the West Field, IV and V to the north, VI, XVII and XVIII to the east of the boundary of the mine field, and VII to the south-east. The position of all of these trenches had been recorded by Armstrong on the site plan published in the 1915 report (Peake 1915; see also fig. 2). The main stimulus for further exploration came from Armstrong's wish to establish the very beginnings of flint extraction on the site. He therefore set about establishing the boundaries of where the *floorstone* could actually be found erupting through the surface. In practice, the main mine field is sited on a hill of chalk. By extrapolating the level at which the *floorstone* occurred in the deep mines outwards to the edge – assuming this to be a roughly constant level – the most obvious areas to explore were the slopes of the dry valley to the north and west.

In 1922 work began by cutting sections along the southern slope of the valley, north of the mine field, with the help of Dr Favell and E.T. Lingwood (Armstrong 1923, 115). The position of six of these is recorded in one of the field notebooks (figs 3 and 4).

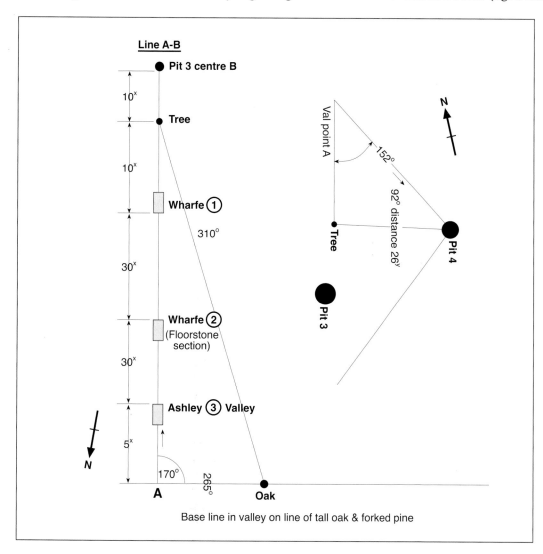

Fig. 3 Armstrong's 1922 sections along line A–B near Pit 3 (for location see fig. 2). *Note:* figs 3–17 are based faithfully upon Armstrong's notebooks; where he included no north point none has been extrapolated.

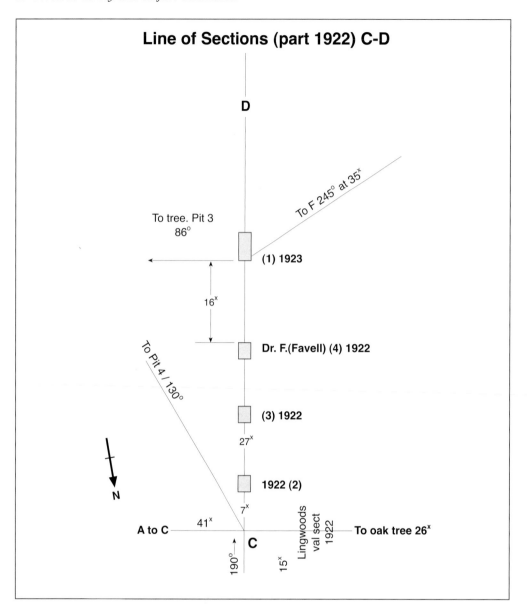

Line of Sections (part 1922) C-D

To F 245° at 35ˣ

To tree. Pit 3
86°

(1) 1923

16ˣ

To Pit 4 / 130°

Dr. F.(Favell) (4) 1922

(3) 1922

27ˣ

1922 (2)

7ˣ

N

A to C —————— 41ˣ —————— C —— To oak tree 26ˣ

190°   15ˣ   Lingwoods
                   val sect
                   1922

D

Fig. 4 Armstrong's sections cut in 1922 and 1923 along the line C–D north of the visible mine field (for location see fig. 2).

In 1923 the line of the possible outcrop was levelled through and pegged out along the north-east sector of the valley (ibid.) and further trenches cut, of which the position of some are known. 'No. 5 at the extremity of a line' picked up the lip of a pit (Pit 3), which was then excavated. After further exploration another pit (Pit 4) was located and also examined (Longworth and Varndell 1996).

One of the sections north of Pit 3 proved to be particularly significant. At this point Armstrong had calculated that the *floorstone* should have been at a depth of 5 ft 4 in (1.63 m) (assuming an unchanged level across the site). The section revealed, however, that at this point the *floorstone* had been lifted and doubled over by cryoturbation to within 6 in (15 cm) of the modern humus (ibid., fig. 13). This was precisely what Armstrong had hoped to find, marking for him the most likely area in which flint exploitation began. The alignment of these sections and a rough indication of their position

are indicated on an unpublished overlay to the 1914 plan. More detailed measured notes with some sketch sections are preserved in the field notebooks for 1923, allowing the position of the sections to be plotted with a fair degree of confidence (figs 5 and 6). At the same time further trial holes were dug by Lingwood on the south side of the mine field (ibid., 125), but no record survives of where these were placed, although excavation of Shaft X (Longworth *et al.* 1991, 19) may have recovered the position of one.

In the following year, 1924, Armstrong undertook further extensive exploration in the West Field, including two parallel lines of trenches dug 20 yd (18.3 m) apart, together with some cross-trenching (figs 7 and 8). In all, fifty-two trial holes were dug in a determined effort 'to ascertain how far west the *floorstone* remained *in situ*' and to seek out primitive flint workings in the valley that Armstrong now felt must surely exist.

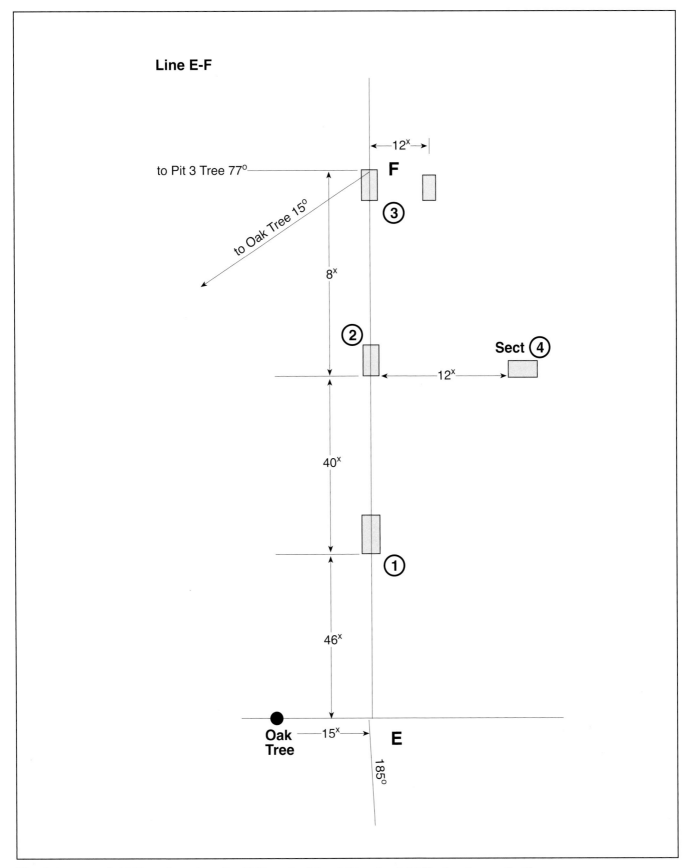

Fig. 5 Armstrong's 1923 sections along line E–F north of the visible mine field (for location see fig. 2).

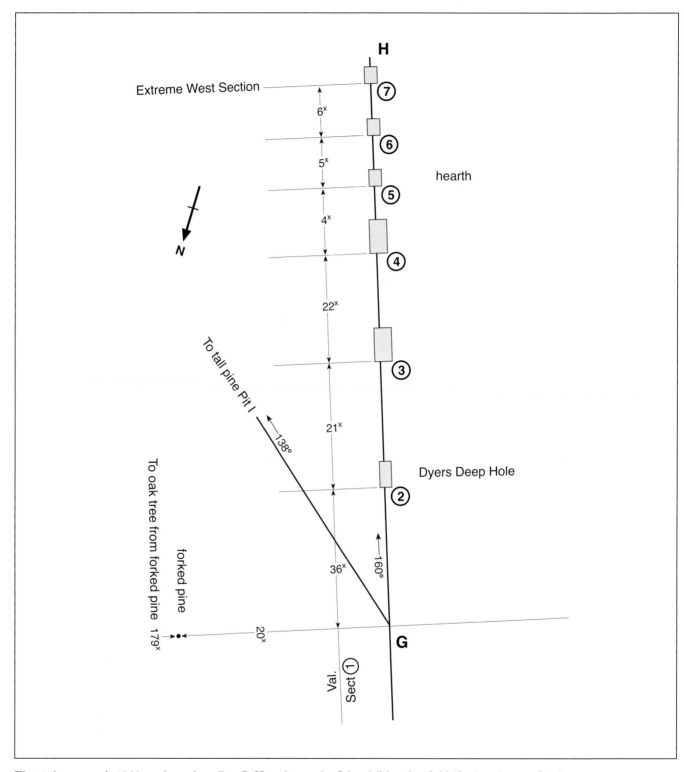

Fig. 6 Armstrong's 1923 sections along line G–H to the north of the visible mine field (for location see fig. 2).

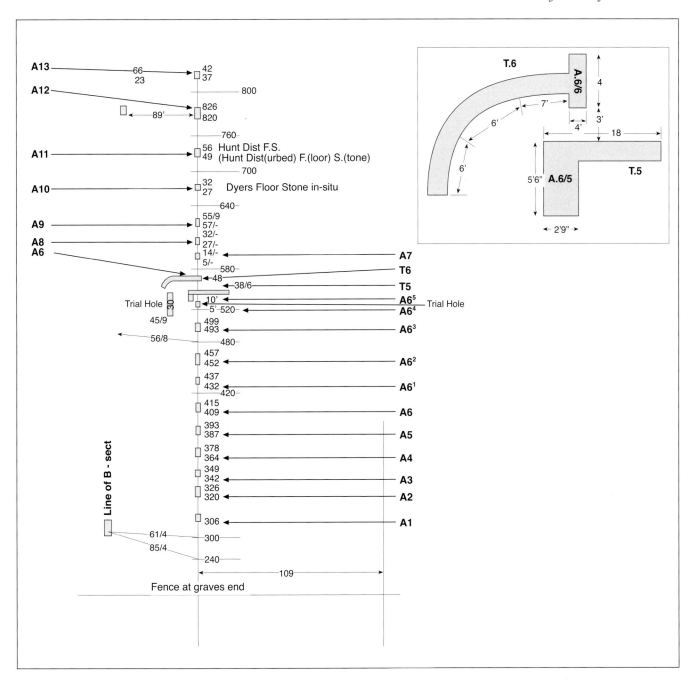

Fig. 7 Armstrong's 1924 sections along line A in the West Field (for location see fig. 2). Inset shows additional detail of what appears to be the cross sections T5–6.

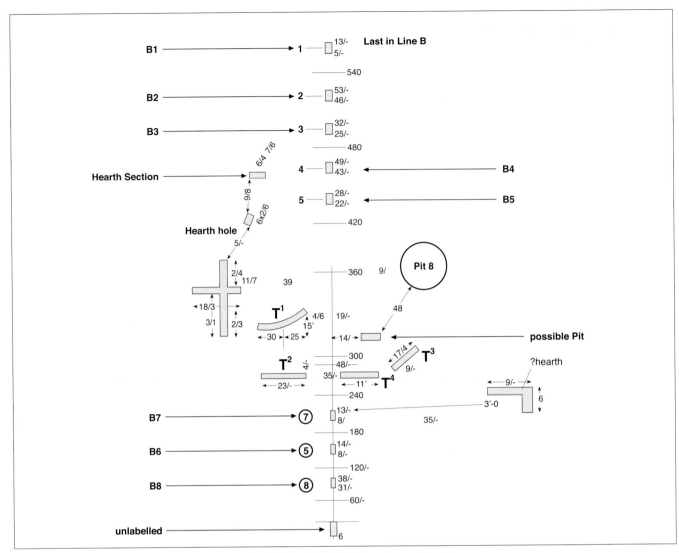

Fig. 8 Armstrong's 1924 sections along line B in the West Field (for location see fig. 2).

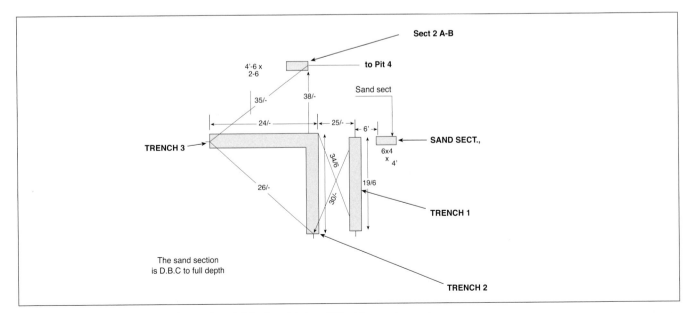

Fig. 9 Armstrong's 1924 Trenches 1, 2 and 3 in the vicinity of Pit 4 but unlocated.

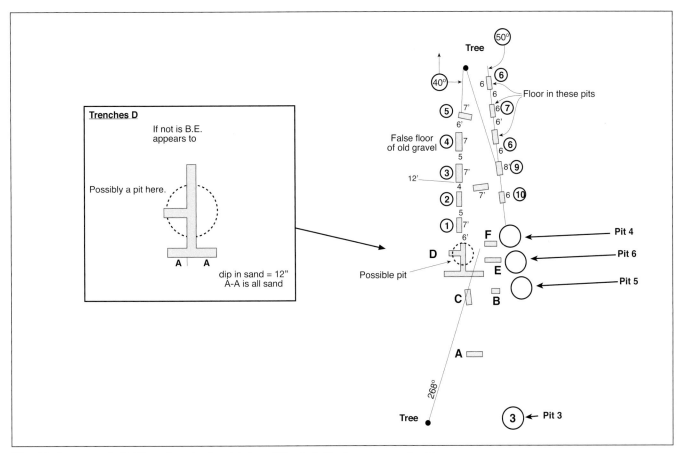

Fig. 10 Armstrong's 1925 sections in the vicinity of Pits 3–6 (for location see fig. 2).

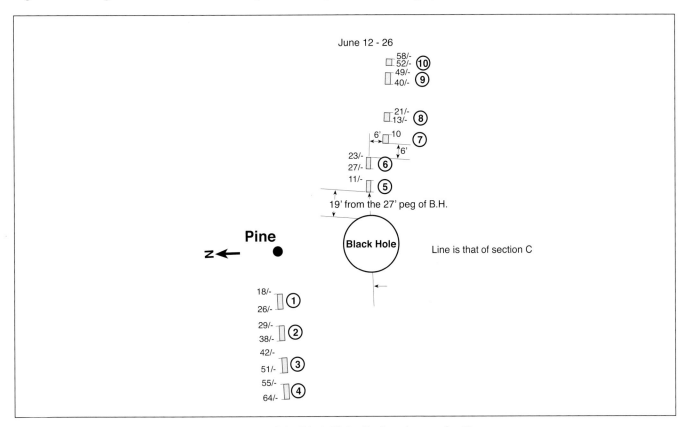

Fig. 11 Armstrong's 1926 sections in the vicinity of the Black Hole (for location see fig. 2).

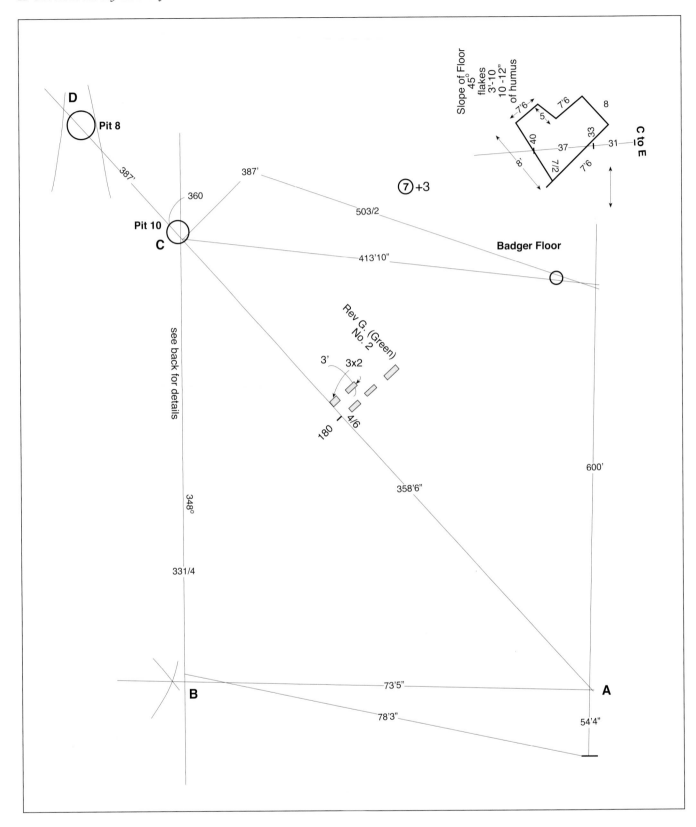

Fig. 12 A group of sections cut by Armstrong in 1928 south-east of Pit 10 in the West Field (for location see fig. 2).

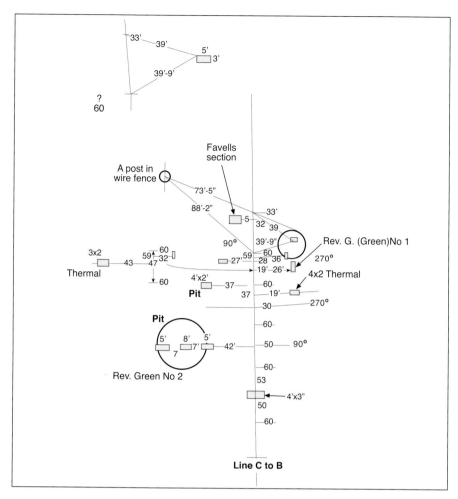

Fig. 13 Sections cut by Armstrong in 1928 south-east of Pit 10. The three trenches circled as pit incorporating Revd Green's no. 2 appear to be the same as the southern three sections in fig. 12 (for location see fig. 2).

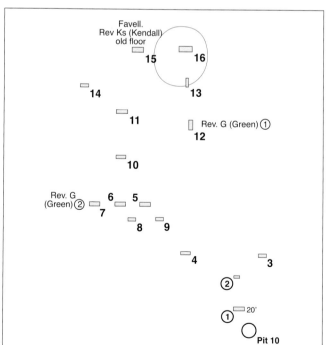

Fig. 14 Sketch plan of sections cut by Armstrong in 1928 south-east of Pit 10 showing some additional to those in fig. 13. This plan has no measurements and is obviously not to scale, but sections 5–9 are clearly those marked on fig. 12.

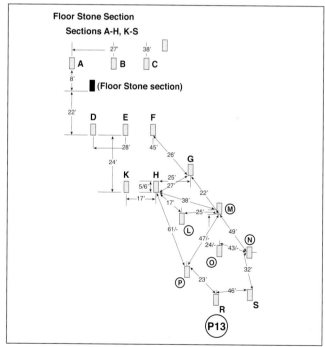

Fig. 15 Armstrong's 1934 sections near Pit 13 (for location see fig. 2).

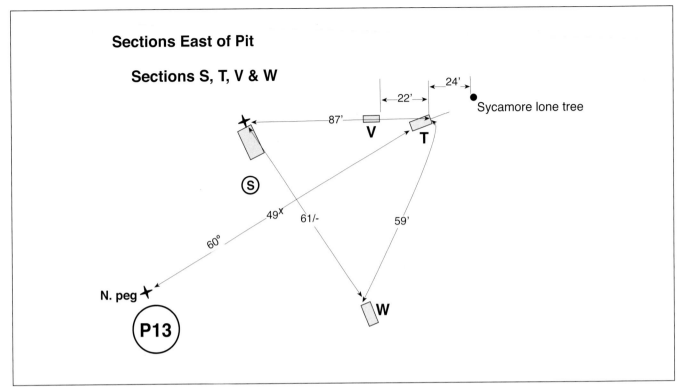

Fig. 16 Further cuttings made by Armstrong in 1934 near Pit 13, orientation uncertain (for location see fig. 2).

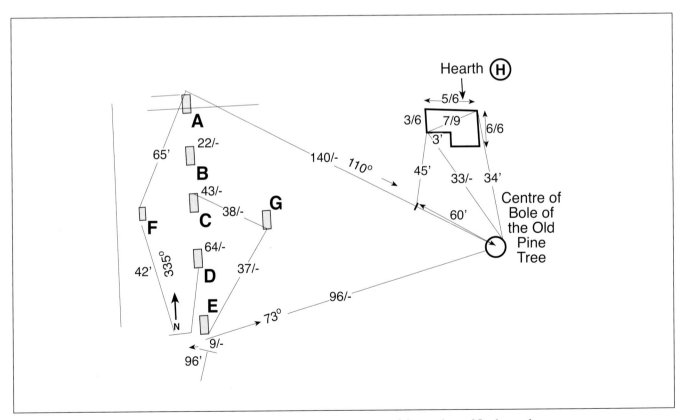

Fig. 17 Armstrong's 1934 sections made at the west end of the valley west of the trackway. Not located.

The orientation of these lines of trenches was published on a plan of minute scale (Armstrong 1924, fig. 4), but no sections were published, nor the position of individual trenches. It was noted, however, that the *floorstone* had been found at a depth of 6 ft 8 in (2 m), 222 yd (202 m) from the eastern fence around the visible mine field, but 'slightly contorted', and that the chalk above had been completely eroded. A further 10 yd (9 m) to the west 'it was present only as a folded and contorted mass of chalk and flint 5 ft 9 in (1.75 m) and upwards' (ibid., 191). Some 8 yd (7 m) further west no *floorstone* survived. Other trial holes had led to the discovery of Pit 8, and further exploration was undertaken in the vicinity of Pit 4 (fig. 9).

Traces of occupation were noted here and there in superficial levels and, although no pottery was present, this was thought to be of Iron Age date, i.e. the date then ascribed to the Black Hole deposits (ibid., 192ff.).

The surviving notebooks are of some help. The position of nineteen trenches is noted on line A together with four cross trenches, with a further nine in line B together with eleven cross trenches (figs 7 and 8).

In 1925 Armstrong turned his attention back to the area of Pits 3 to 6 to the north. Although never published, the position of two lines of cuttings is preserved in the field notebook for this year. From Pit 4 a set of five trenches was laid out, roughly continuing a line drawn through Pits 5 and 6 on a north-easterly axis. A converging line of four trenches was cut to the north and further cross trenches between and at both ends of this second line, making nineteen in all (fig. 10).

In the same year Armstrong cut two sections across a low bank to the south-east of the mine field near the Black Hole and Floor 16 (Armstrong 1927, 113), which marked the parish and estate boundary. The presence of 'Iron Age' pottery beneath this feature indicated for Armstrong a post-mining date. This exploration was followed up the following year, 1926, by further trenching between the Black Hole and Floor 88 (ibid., 111). The notebooks indicate ten trenches cut either side of the Black Hole, presumably along a south-west/north-east axis (fig. 11). In this year, further trenching in the West Field had led to the discovery of Pit 9. By 1926 Armstrong could claim that 162 sections had already been cut (ibid., 101).

In 1928 Armstrong's attention reverted to the southern sector of the West Field. Pit 12 was discovered and we know that a group of five trenches was cut south-east of Pit 10 (fig. 12) and a further twenty in its vicinity (figs 13 and 14).

In 1934 Dr R.V. Favell discovered Pit 14. In the same year Armstrong cut a further sixteen trenches north-west of Pit 13 to the north of the main mine field (fig. 15) and an additional four to the east (fig. 16). Another eight were

cut at the west end of the valley 'west of the trackway' (fig. 17). Thus by 1939 at least 216 exploratory trenches had been made, of which an approximate position can be established for 125. That this must be taken as a minimal figure is revealed by correspondence referring to the work of others such as Kendall (Armstrong Papers 45/21).

B Examination of workshop sites: the floors

Of the ninety-eight floors that received a number, nothing is known of the location of twenty-seven. Of the remainder, fifteen lay to the south or east of the Deep Mine Field, fourteen to the north and only five to the west. The bulk, however, thirty-seven, lie within the Deep Mine Field itself. The position of less than a third (i.e. twenty-nine) was recorded by their excavators on any form of map. Where this is known it has been included in fig. 2.

In most instances it is difficult to assess the actual status of individual 'floors' from the surviving records. The surface of much of Grimes Graves, with its naturally sandy topsoil layers, can only be described as 'fluid', and has been heavily worked and reworked by the action of rabbits. In this regime, concentrations of flint near the surface can represent little more than an amalgam of separate episodes artificially conflated over time. Many indeed seem to have come to the attention of earlier fieldworkers through the very disturbance in part created by them. Most records stress the recovery of flint implements, rather than describing the context, since this was the prime reason for their examination. Without the survival of chronologically sensitive material it is impossible in the majority of cases to be sure that the surviving material represents a single chronological horizon. For this reason the examination of further working areas which could be shown to be sealed or largely intact became one of the objectives of the Museum's own research campaign and was achieved both in the West Field and in Area A (see Chapter III).

Surviving records from the survey work carried out both before and after the First World War suggest that the task of transforming the mined flint into usable products was not always undertaken in a single location. The presence of quantities of large cortical flakes, for example on Floor 20, as opposed to smaller flakes devoid of cortex, seems to indicate that some areas were given over to a primary phase of reduction to create blanks which were then worked down to usable components on a different part of the site. J. Lech has been able to confirm this impression, demonstrating that much of the cortex of the blocks had been discarded before the selection of material to be worked on was transported to the working floors which he has analysed (see Chapter IVA).

Floor	Date	Dimensions (ft unless otherwise stated)	Position	Fig. 2	Reference
1	1914	10 x 8	Deep Mine Field	X	Clarke 1915, 99
2	1914	12 x 4	Deep Mine Field	X	Clarke 1915, 99–100
3	1914	11 x 21 > 27	Deep Mine Field	X	Clarke 1915, 100–104 Peake 1916, 275, 289–90
4	1914	14 x 7	Deep Mine Field	X	Clarke 1915, 104 Peake 1916, 290
5	1914	7 x 7	Deep Mine Field	X	Clarke 1915, 104
6	1914	'Smallest of all the floors'	Deep Mine Field	X	Clarke 1915, 104
7	1914	?	Deep Mine Field	X	Clarke 1915, 104–5
8	1914	?	Deep Mine Field	X	Clarke 1915, 105
9	1914	?	Deep Mine Field	X	Clarke 1915, 105
10	1914	8 x 4	Deep Mine Field	X	Clarke 1915, 105
11	1914	4 x 9	Deep Mine Field	X	Clarke 1915, 105 Peake 1919, 75–7
12	1914	10 x 5	Deep Mine Field	X	Clarke 1915, 105
13	1914	10 x 8	Deep Mine Field	X	Clarke 1915, 105–6 Peake 1916, 290
14	1914	6 x 4	Deep Mine Field	X	Clarke 1915, 106
15	1915–17	18 x 16+	S of Mine Field	X	Peake 1916, 271–4; 1917, 412–31; 1919, 77–82, 92–3
16	1915–17	29 x 24	S of Mine Field	X	Peake 1916, 274–87; 1917, 412; 1919, 82–5, 92–3 Armstrong 1921b, 434 Kendall 1925, 64
17	1915	6 x 5	S of Mine Field	X	Peake 1916, 287–8
18	1915	6 x 3	Deep Mine Field	X	Peake 1916, 288
19	1916	7 x 14	Deep Mine Field	X	Peake 1917, 409–10
20	1916	10 diam.	'Near the west border of the Graves'		Peake 1917, 410
21	1916	15	S of Mine Field	X	Peake 1917, 410
22	1916	32 x 22	E side of graves	X	Peake 1917, 409–10
23	1916	8 x 4	Deep Mine Field	X	Peake 1917, 409
24	1916	Small	Deep Mine Field	X	Peake 1917, 409
25	1916	Small	Deep Mine Field	X	Peake 1917, 409
26	1916	Small	Deep Mine Field	X	Peake 1917, 409
27	1916	Small	Nr Greenwell's Pit		Peake 1917, 409, 412
28	1916	18 x 8	Nr grass road, NE of Mine Field and 'about 230 ft from the nearest'		Peake 1917, 409, 412
29	1917		N or S of Pit 1 Deep Mine Field		Peake 1919, 75, 86
30					
31					
32					
33					
34					
35	1918	Small	100 yd NW of Mine Field		Kendall 1920a, 293; 1920b, 194
36	1918		W of Floor 23 Deep Mine Field		Kendall 1920a, 295
37					
38			Edge of pit, W of Pit 1 Deep Mine Field		
39			S of Pit 1 Deep Mine Field		
40			N of Deep Mine Field		
41			Nr Greenwell's Pit		
42		Large	SE of Deep Mine Field between section 7 and Tumulus Pit. Prob. joined with Floor 85	X	Richardson 1920, 249–50 Armstrong 1921b, 442; 1924b, 195
43			Nr Pit 1 Deep Mine Field		

Table 1 Floors known to have been previously examined.

44			Centre Deep Mine Field		
45					
46	1919	11 x 11	50 yd NE of Pit 1, N of Deep Mine Field		Richardson 1920, 243–58
47	1919	6 x 8	N of Deep Mine Field, 20 yd NE of Floor 52		Kendall 1920a, 290
48	1919–20	4–5 diam.	Between second and third line of pits, N of Deep Mine Field		Kendall 1920a, 292; 1925, 66
49	1919	3 x 3	N of Deep Mine Field		Kendall 1920a, 292
50	1919	'Not much larger than 49'	Deep Mine Field, 3 or 4 pits SE of Pit 1		Kendall 1920a, 292
51	1919		N of Deep Mine Fields, 50 paces N of Floor 52		Kendall 1920a, 292
52	1919	20 x 12	N of deep mines, 50 paces NE of corner of West Field		Kendall 1920a, 292ff.
53	1919		N of deep mines, 10 ft from Floor 52		Kendall 1920a, 299
54	1919	4 x 3	N of deep mines, E of Floor 53		Kendall 1920a, 299–300
55	1919	9 x 7	49 paces WSW of line of birches across end of West Field		Kendall 1920a, 300
56	1919		Between NW corner Pit and the pit NE of it		Kendall 1920a, 300
57	1919		12 yd SE of Floor 51		Kendall 1920a, 300
58	1919	6 x 8	63 paces S of corner of West Field		Kendall 1920a, 300–303
59	1919		'Among birches to NE of the wood'		Kendall 1920a, 303
60			Deep Mine Field E of Floor 4, W of Floor 44		
61					
62			On W edge of Deep Mine Field		
63			SE of Deep Mine Field, NW of Floor 42		
64					
65					
66					
67					
68					
69					
70	1920		Deep Mine Field N of Pit 2		
71	1920		Centre of North Field		
72	1920		North Field		
73	1920	6 x 4	16 paces NE of Floor 58		
74	1920		13 paces WNW of Floor 46		
75	1920	14 x 4 paces	On edge of West Field nearly opposite entrance of Pit 1		Armstrong 1921a, 84; 1921, A11 Kendall 1925, 64
76	1929		Deep Mine Field on edge of Pit SE of Floor 3		
77	1920		54 NW of centre of Floor 75		
78	1920		Deep Mine Field		
79	1920		N of Floor 42, E of Floor 81		
80	1920		Prob. N of Floor 42		
81			Deep Mine Field, SW of Pit 2, W of Floor 79		
82			Deep Mine Field, SW sector		
83					
84	1921		Deep Mine Field 'in a mound near S border and a little W of Floor 16'		
85	1920–22	109 sq yd	SE of Deep Mine Field, adjoining Tumulus Pit	X	Armstrong 1921b, 434–43; 1922, 548–58; 1923, 113; 1924b, 194–202; 1927, 99 Kendall 1925, 66
86			SE of Deep Mine Field	X	Armstrong 1927, 121–3
87					
88	1923–4	126 sq yd	15 yd W of Greenwell's Pit	X	Armstrong 1927, 105–7
89					
90					
91	1924				
92	1922				
93–8					

III The British Museum campaign

One of the principal aims of the Museum campaign was to try to locate areas of occupation that might shed light upon the cultural affiliations of the miners working the field. Given the intensity of the mining within the visible mine field, any short-lived occupation within this area would have been largely destroyed with at best small remnant patches still surviving. But any short-lived squatting and tipping of Bronze Age midden material into the tops of previously infilled mine shafts provided one context that could be explored. If occupation extended outside the visible mine field, then the assumption was made that this was more likely to survive to the south, given that there was no water on site and the nearest source, the River Little Ouse, lay in this direction. It also seemed likely that while pack animals and certainly human porterage would naturally form two of the modes of transport used to convey flint leaving the site, the possibility that water transport might also have played a part could not be ignored. The area to be covered was both vast and wooded, forming part of the Forestry Commission's Plantation. Any surface survey would have been presented with insuperable difficulties. A survey of the surviving phosphate content of the soil over the area offered the only viable option.

A The phosphate survey
M. J. Hughes, P. T. Craddock and M. R. Cowell

The aim of the phosphate survey was to locate areas showing evidence of past human habitation both on the site and in the surrounding forested area. The method used was to analyse samples of soil for phosphate compounds. This method of survey complements those involving electromagnetic measurements such as magnetometry, soil electrical resistance and ground-penetrating radar, as well as air photography and field walking (Craddock *et al.* 1985). Phosphate surveys and field walking locate areas of occupation, whereas the other methods by and large locate individual archaeological features. Magnetic susceptibility measurements can locate remains of burning and, together with the phosphate analysis, have been shown to define areas within a site of differing activities (Clark 1996, 99–117; Tite and Mullins 1971). Sampling for phosphate analysis is more time-consuming and cumbersome when compared with geophysical methods of site location, but it has the added advantage

of providing a sample of the actual buried archaeological features which can itself be very valuable. A brief history of phosphate survey and details of the actual techniques developed for use at Grimes Graves and other sites are archived at the British Museum.

Phosphate analysis depends upon the presence of the element phosphorus, which occurs widely and abundantly as an essential component in all living matter. It occurs, for example, in nucleic acids and in adenosine triphosphate (ATP), the predominant high-energy component of all living organisms, with a pivotal role in cell energetics. Phosphate in human and animal living matter is returned to the soil in rubbish, excrement, waste food and, ultimately, human and animal remains. The human body, for example, contains 600–800 g of phosphorus, mostly in the skeleton (Bell *et al.* 1968). While Hamond (1983) concludes that urine contributes the largest amount of deposited phosphate at a human habitation site, faeces and especially bone, both human and animal (food remains), also contribute significant amounts. Cook and Heizer (1965) estimated that a community of 100 persons in an area of 1 ha will add 125 kg of phosphorus to the soil annually. Whatever the main source, human habitation generally increases the level of phosphate in the local soil. From an archaeological viewpoint this would be useless if the time residence of the added phosphate was small, i.e. if it was easily dissolved and washed down through the soil profile. However, organic phosphate added to the soil is systematically broken down, releasing phosphate ions that are then bound chemically into inorganic phosphates by a process of phosphate fixation (Rowell 1994, Chapter 10). The phosphate reacts with calcium, aluminium or iron ions in the soil to give low-solubility hydroxyphosphates, which render much of the phosphate unavailable to plants in most mineralized soils. The three ions that bind phosphate are abundant in most soils: calcium especially occurs in soils on chalk regions; iron occurs both as free iron oxides and in clay minerals; and aluminium is a major component of clays. Clay-rich soils offer large surface areas on the clay minerals, to which phosphate can be attached, as do humic acids. Even the sandy soils of Grimes Graves contain a clay and humic component as well as free iron oxides. Inorganic forms of phosphate added by human habitation, for example bone, are slowly attacked and the phosphate immobilized in acidic soils as iron and aluminium phosphates.

A slow build-up therefore occurs of excess phosphate in the soil around a site of human and animal habitation as the organic phosphate is fixed into chemically immobile forms in the soil. Surveying an area for signs of habitation involves measuring the phosphate content of the soil in apparently sterile (non-occupied) areas to provide a background reference value, and in areas where habitation is suspected, to look for enhanced phosphate concentrations.

There has been debate over whether a survey technique should measure inorganic, organic or total phosphate (inorganic plus organic), and the relative merits of analysing for different chemical forms of phosphate in soil for archaeological applications (Eidt and Woods 1974; Bethell and Máté 1989). A number of archaeological surveys have determined 'available' phosphorus, i.e. that which is present in free ionic form (not bound up as insoluble phosphates) and available for plant growth and therefore of interest to agronomists. However, this tendency to follow agricultural patterns of investigation is at odds with the general recognition that much 'archaeological' phosphate is present in inorganic forms. Methodologically it is much easier to measure inorganic phosphate, and since this is the form to which all added phosphate will transform over time, it is logically the component to measure, as we have done. Organic phosphate includes more recently added components, such as fertilizers, which have not yet been mineralized, and whose effects need to be differentiated from earlier archaeological additions of phosphate. Analyses for organic phosphate are more difficult and prone to inaccuracy than inorganic since the measurement is often by difference. Thus total phosphate is measured by a destructive chemical attack on the soil sample with either dry-ashing (ignition in a furnace: see Bethell and Máté 1989) prior to acid treatment to extract phosphate from the residue, or by the use of a combination of strong acids (for example nitric and perchloric: see Conway 1983). The latter procedure is potentially hazardous and not to be undertaken by inexperienced personnel, while the former is a relatively slow process and would require unacceptable effort for large-scale surveys. Bethell and Máté also caution against over-interpretation: 'a broad distinction between inorganic and organic P is produced by this method' (1989, 22). In contrast, a good estimate of inorganic phosphate can be obtained by acid-leaching a soil sample with a relatively weak hot solution of a mineral acid. Hesse (1971) covers all the main methods of analysis for phosphate in soil, although principally from an agricultural perspective.

While aerial photography has proved an invaluable method of large-scale area investigation in field archaeology, this technique could not be used over large areas of potential occupation at Grimes Graves because the forest encroaches up to the monument's boundary. Field walking is hampered both by the forest cover and

by prevalence of struck flint all over the landscape, both ancient and relatively modern, effectively masking any true centres of early occupation. Other parallel scientific location experiments were carried out within the area of the monument itself, for example soil resistivity and magnetic surveys, where the open ground allowed the free movement of electrical cables required for such surveys, but such techniques are very difficult to carry out on a large scale within a forest environment. Even across open ground, the survey area envisaged was too large for geophysical techniques. The very large-scale survey, which eventually covered several square kilometres of forest, could only have been undertaken using phosphate analysis. The subsequent integration at other sites, based on the work at Grimes Graves, of three scientific surveying techniques in archaeology, namely phosphate analysis, magnetometry and resistivity, has been coined 'survey excavation' by Pryor (1984).

The initial aim of the survey was to locate occupation contemporary with the actual mining that it was hoped would have been buried beneath the spoil from the shafts as the mined area expanded. When this failed to find the putative Neolithic settlement the survey was extended to the areas around the mines in the woodland survey.

Past archaeological investigations at Grimes Graves had shown a marked concentration of Bronze Age occupation on the southernmost side of the site – for example, Armstrong's Black Hole deposits (Armstrong 1923), with its midden deposits of very dark (i.e. humus-rich) soil, bone, pottery and other artefact fragments. However, it would have been unwise to have assumed without systematic archaeological investigation of the entire area of the monument that occupation debris did not occur elsewhere. The survey therefore included the tops of filled-in mine shafts at the site, the area within the monument boundary, and in the surrounding forest (fig. 18) to locate and discover the extent of the Middle Bronze Age occupation.

All samples were collected on regular grids at 50-m intervals, except for some additional grids at 10-m intervals. An east–west baseline was laid out near the southern boundary of the monument, and a grid was surveyed-in using levels and ranging rods, with numbered 1 x 1 in section wooden pegs being driven in at the grid intersection points. Plate 1 shows the surveyor, John McGarry, setting out the grid, a task hampered by the presence of the trees. The surveying was carried out prior to the sampling teams beginning to collect samples, so that the latter collected samples wherever a peg was encountered, without the necessity of measuring distances etc. as they proceeded.

The 1972–6 British Museum excavations provided the opportunity to use the site as an experimental 'test-bed' for the applicability of this method for large-scale site survey in Britain. The specific programmes that were undertaken were of three types:

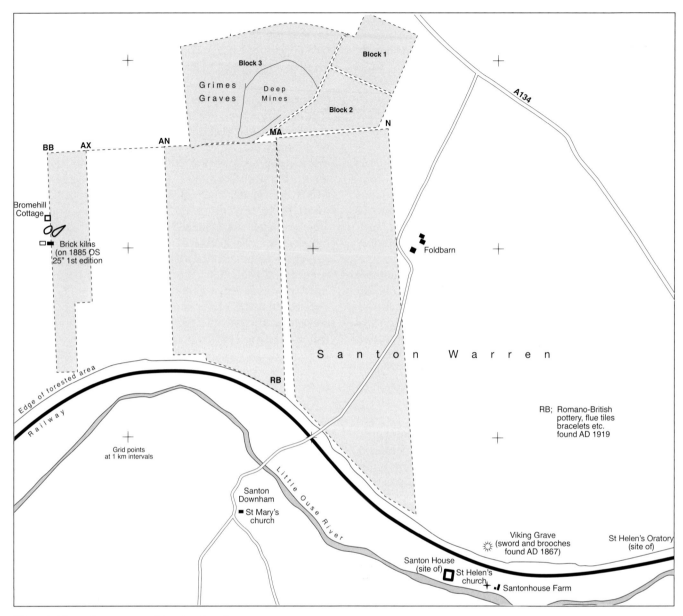

Fig. 18 Map of area covered by the phosphate survey.

1 Experiments to check the validity of the method under the soil conditions prevailing at Grimes Graves, which suggested the need to take a vertical series of soil samples to ensure that occupation layers were sampled.
2 Area survey of the tops of the filled-in mine shafts to look for evidence that the tops were used for occupation.
3 Large-scale survey of the Forestry Commission woodland surrounding the monument.

1 Experiments to check the validity of the survey method under the soil conditions prevailing at Grimes Graves

Area A1: Bronze Age midden material in the top of a filled-in mine shaft excavated in 1972 by Mercer (Mercer 1981, figs 20 and 21).

Areas A2 and A3: Two trenches cut across the tops of two filled-in mine shafts, one of which gave high and one low phosphate readings in the soil survey.

Grimes Graves is set within the light sandy soil area known as the Breckland; its soils are described in detail by Corbett (1973). They are very well drained because of the high sand content, and support well the growth of coniferous trees: much of the Breckland is Forestry Commission land with a mixture of Scots and Sicilian pine interspersed with deciduous stands. At the outset of the survey, it was felt necessary to demonstrate that phosphate of human origin could be retained by these light free-draining soils. Two types of test were therefore set up: in one case, definite occupation debris found during excavation at the site was tested for phosphate

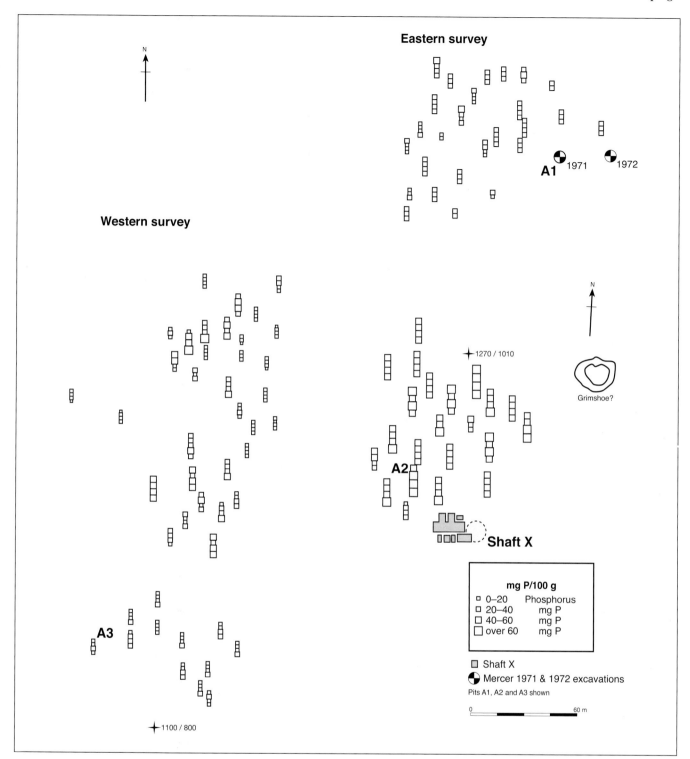

Eastern survey

Western survey

1270 / 1010

Grimshoe?

A2

Shaft X

mg P/100 g

▫ 0–20   Phosphorus
▫ 20–40   mg P
▢ 40–60   mg P
◻ over 60   mg P

◻ Shaft X
◕ Mercer 1971 & 1972 excavations
Pits A1, A2 and A3 shown

0   60 m

A3

1100 / 800

Fig. 19 Plan and results of analysis on soils from the tops of the filled pit shafts.

(Area A1 – see fig. 19 for location), while in the other, the test was approached via the phosphate results first. Two filled-in mine shafts that had been sampled and analysed, one having high phosphate concentrations in the soil, and the other apparently only 'background' values, were subsequently trenched in Areas A2 and A3 respectively.

Area A1

Mercer (1981) excavated a pit shaft at Grimes Graves in 1971 and, during the excavation of the surrounding surface, uncovered the top of a previously unsuspected mine shaft. Excavation revealed in the upper layers of the filling (ibid., 36ff.) massive deposits of Bronze Age occupation debris identical in type to that located by Armstrong in his Black Hole (Armstrong 1927). Associated with these layers of charcoal-rich occupation debris were sherds of pottery whose closest parallels are Deverel–Rimbury ware, and also some evidence of metal working. The midden debris was deposited in the shaft in a long series of individual tips; they clearly divide themselves into three phases separated by periods of accumulation of material that is relatively sterile. The section therefore provided an ideal test of phosphate analysis, being rich in occupation debris but interspersed with sterile material. Six soil samples were collected from a vertical section over 2 m in depth (the north face of Trench 8B, SE quadrant: Mercer 1981, fig. 21, lower left quadrant). The results were very satisfactory in that the two dark charcoal-rich lenses in the profile were extremely phosphate-rich (containing 430 and 550 mg P/100 g soil respectively), whereas the upper chalky soil and topsoil were much less enriched in phosphate. In contrast, control samples taken as a 50-cm vertical section a few metres further along the section over the edge of the pit, ranging from humic topsoil down to the top of the weathered chalk bedrock, with no occupation debris visible and apparently sterile soil, showed only 24–42 mg P, suggesting an enrichment factor of at least ten times in the occupation debris. In this case the 50-cm section acted as a 'background' control sample, i.e. it indicated the level of phosphate naturally present in the soil, which is always low in value but still measurable.

The results of this experiment demonstrate clearly that occupation-derived phosphate has remained in place in Grimes Graves soil over several millennia, and that where the deposits are rich, they can easily be detected by their relatively high phosphate content in contrast to the low content of sterile soils at the site. As a footnote to these results, it is one of the accidents of experimental work that in no other area surveyed subsequent to A1 were such high concentrations of phosphate encountered. After several seasons' work at the site failing to find such high values it was suspected that we had encountered in A1 the notorious 'unrepeatable result' unfortunately familiar to the scientific community, although a few values in the 100–200 mg P range did occasionally occur elsewhere. A consequence of the high values in A1 was that the earliest analytical work on the pit top survey (Sieveking *et al.* 1973) used only cold dilute acid to extract the phosphate, since this treatment was adequate to release enough phosphate from the A1 soils to clearly indicate human habitation. However, the pit top survey revealed lower amounts of phosphate where human occupation could be proved to have occurred, and the acid-extraction step was subsequently carried out more rigorously to ensure complete removal of acid-soluble phosphate from the soil.

Areas A2 and A3

One of the aims of the survey was to try to locate further examples of the rich occupation deposits of the type

found by Armstrong and Mercer, both sites being on the edge of the mined area. Since such debris was expected to occur in the top levels of the filled-in mine shafts, a programme of sampling these deposits was undertaken. After some forty to fifty such mine shaft tops had been sampled without finding any high values comparable to those found in A1, it was felt advisable to check by excavation two pit tops from the earlier survey (Sieveking *et al.* 1973). In one of these only 'low' phosphate values had been measured (Area A3), while in the other they were 'high' (Shaft W = Area A2). Further soil samples were taken after a trench approximately 7 m long and 1 m wide had been cut from the edge to the centre of the pit top debris where 'high' phosphate results had been obtained. Excavation revealed the presence of bone debris and, most significantly for the purposes of the test, a hearth with burnt material spreading out from its locus over a radius of tens of centimetres. The soil itself was darker than the normal soil colours of sterile features at the site, and the soil samples taken from the section, including special samples from the hearth material, all showed enriched amounts of phosphate (50–100 mg P). In contrast, Area A3 (the 'low' phosphate pit top), which was also excavated by a long metre-wide trench from the edge to the centre of the pit top, showed no bone material or other evidence of occupation, and many of the top layers consisted of clean sand with flints, i.e. sterile soil layers. Further samples taken from this trench showed only low concentrations of phosphate (14–33 mg P). The experiment therefore successfully demonstrated the link between occupation debris in the top of a filled-in mine shaft and distinctly enriched concentrations of phosphate in the soil which could be sampled by a series of cores.

2 Survey of the tops of filled-in mine shafts

Area B1: Includes the work of two separate seasons – 1972 (results reported in Sieveking *et al.* 1973) and 1975.

The principal aim of this survey of mine shaft tops was to try to locate pit fillings rich in occupation debris such as those already located elsewhere on the site (see section A above) and to search for any trends in their distribution. These could be of two origins, either on the original land surface between the pits, buried by later mining activities, or in the tops of the filled-in shafts, deposited long after mining had ceased. There are well over 400 such pits at the site, of which only a proportion could be sampled. The survey was carried out in two stages, in the 1972 and 1975 seasons on the western and eastern sides of the visible mined area respectively. In the earlier surveys a fairly detailed sampling programme had been undertaken, around and within the pit tops, by collecting samples at points that were approximately north, east, south and west of the centre (Sieveking *et al.* 1973, 195).

The steeply dipping tip lines of spoil and debris cluster closer together near the surface at the pit edge, and so it was more logical to sample at the pit edges. However, where the pit edge has slumped, these levels were buried under a depth of soil, and sampling the edge at several points at each pit lessened the chance of phosphate-rich levels being missed. In addition, samples were also taken from material lying on the intact original ground surface that remains between adjacent pits to try to locate contemporary Neolithic occupation. Comprehensive sampling was discontinued firstly because, in the Eastern survey, when evidence of occupation was actually detected, it often appeared in all four sampling locations, rendering the extra sampling redundant. Secondly, by sampling each pit at four locations, progress was very slow, and the often deep samples taken at the centre of the pit would be likely to contain material from the occupation debris layers near the surface. Thus, in the Western survey (see fig. 19; cf. Sieveking *et al.* 1973, 194, fig. 6) near to the excavation of Bronze Age occupation, only one series of cores per pit was collected, in the centre of the pit top depression.

The final result of the two surveys is shown in fig. 19. In the Western survey area, the southernmost pits seem generally lower in phosphate than the rest, many cores containing less than 20 mg P and showing no visual evidence of occupation debris. However, in the central and northern part of the Western survey, the phosphate results tend to be higher and also some clusters of pits occur with 40–60 mg P, suggesting some localized and perhaps brief occupation in those areas. The Eastern survey showed many apparently sterile pit tops at the northern end of the survey area, except the midden site excavated in 1972 by Mercer (1981, figs 20 and 21); and an area extending at least 100 m north of Shaft X, which showed many pits with 40–75 mg P, including the pit sampled in Area A2 shown by excavation to contain occupation debris. This seems to indicate the likelihood of some longer-term occupation in this part of the mined area, and accords with other evidence of human occupation during the Bronze Age in this general area of the monument, including Shaft X and Armstrong's Black Hole.

In summary, the survey within a segment of the visible mined area showed little evidence of occupation on the northern or south-western sides, but a zone with concentrated high phosphate values, indicating occupation debris, in an east–west strip across the centre of the segment examined, and mainly towards the east. It is striking that although over ninety pits were sampled in this programme, none revealed the combination of extensive dark charcoal-rich layers and high phosphate concentrations found in the single pit top excavated in 1972 by Mercer (1981). The survey showed that the areas rich in phosphate are limited just to the mine tops, not extending to the spaces between. The survey also suggests that where human occupation at the site could be detected, this was concentrated along the south-eastern part of the monument, including areas where a Bronze Age date had been established by excavation. The phosphate survey does not support the suggestion that as each pit was dug during the mining phase, occupation took place immediately adjacent, with rubbish being discarded in adjacent filled-in pit tops. In fact, no high phosphate values indicative of contemporary Neolithic occupation were found in the vicinity of the mines.

Results of tests carried out in association with the excavation areas

One of the main reasons for setting up a site laboratory in order to process the soil samples for measurement of the phosphate content was to have the results available during the excavation season to clarify points of interpretation of the soil features as excavation progressed. In addition, when excavation yielded evidence which suggested that layers or features spread beyond the area actually opened up for excavation, it was possible to take core samples to test these hypotheses, which yielded both visual evidence in the form of the sequence of soil strata with samples of each and also confirmatory chemical evidence in the phosphate tests.

Soil samples in areas of filled-in pit shafts yielding deposits of Bronze Age date

Since the south-eastern side of the mined area in general proved to contain most of the evidence for Bronze Age occupation on the site, it appeared promising to sample the soil along a transect running approximately north-east from Shaft X (fig. 20: S1–9), following the presumed line of the edge of the mined area, and parallel to the present fence and forest access track. A series of samples was taken at 10-m intervals and analysed. Clean sand was encountered immediately below the topsoil down to the lowest cores in all but three points along this north-east transect. The original ground level must fall away north-east of Shaft X, and the sands, which in the past were frequently carried across the Breckland by storms, seem to have filled the depression with a dune whose top is approximately level with the ground surface near the excavations. However, deep soil deposits, some containing flecks of charcoal, were encountered elsewhere at points S1, S3 and S4 at the south end of the transect, and marked the edge of the deep sand deposits. The phosphate results showed that all the sand deposits were sterile, very low in phosphate; generally higher concentrations of phosphate were found in the deeper cores, with the highest concentrations in one core (S3) at about 1.5 m below the surface. A small test cutting was dug at this position (1313/927) (Longworth *et al.* 1988, 36, fig. 13), and modern animal bone and other refuse were encountered, indicating the source of the high phosphate results. Unfortunately the cutting did not yield any archaeologically significant features, and

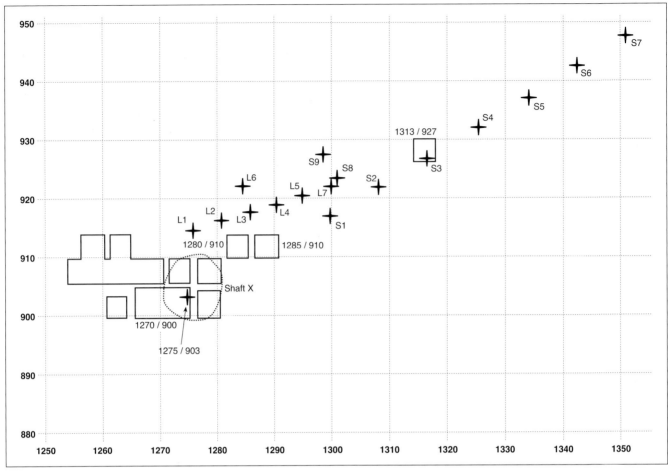

Fig. 20 Plan showing location of soil samples taken in relation to Bronze Age contexts.

one must regard it as one of the hazards of the phosphate method that it is not possible to indicate before excavation whether enriched levels of phosphate come from modern or ancient debris. However, the transect did demonstrate with a minimum of effort that deep deposits of sand lay to the north-east, and that cuttings in this area would yield very little.

In order to provide further information on the stratigraphy near Shaft X, a short 20-m transect was set out, sampling at 5-m intervals beginning at a point (site grid ref. 1275/915) near to the shaft (fig. 20: L1–7). The most extraordinary feature of the sampling was position L4, from which a vertical sequence of forty cores was collected, amounting to a total sampling depth of 8 m. This was very unusual: sampling elsewhere was often stopped by a flint, or because solid chalk appeared in the cores, indicating that natural deposits had been reached. In the case of L4 neither happened, and solid chalk still had not been reached when the last extension rod had been fitted. We were obviously sampling the fill of a previously unrecorded mine shaft. The sequence of layers in this series of cores compares closely with sections through excavated pit shafts, consisting of layers of sand

of different textures alternating with layers of more chalky and clayey sand. The phosphate results showed some enriched concentrations of phosphate in the top 120 cm of the filled-in mine shaft and the presence of charcoal, but apart from isolated sequences of cores lower down, at about 650 cm and 800 cm, with significant levels of phosphate, most of the cores were low in phosphate, as one would expect from the preponderance of sand below 1.5 m. At L1 the natural chalk was encountered at about 1.5 m, but nowhere else in L2–7.

Cutting 1270/900: Shaft X

Some of the results of tests associated with the 1972 excavation season have already been reported in Sieveking *et al.* (1973, 197–8). In this cutting, which contained a segment of Shaft X (fig. 20), there was much evidence of human occupation debris. Soil samples were taken to a depth of 1.6 m immediately adjacent to the cutting, in which pottery was first found at a depth of about 1 m. The phosphate results showed an erratic increase in phosphate content from the surface down to about 1 m (from 5 to 80 mg P), while below that level the phosphate exceeded 130 mg P, and the cores contained small fragments of bone. Hence the soil layers showing archaeological evidence of human occupation including bone also show a readily identifiable increase in phosphate content. Other minor areas tested in the 1972 season (see Sieveking *et al.* 1973, 198) did not show any significantly enriched concentrations of phosphate in the soil.

3 Large-scale survey of the woodland surrounding the monument

The Eastern, Central and Western Blocks of a large-scale survey covering the 1–2 km between the site and the River Little Ouse.

Block 1: a large flat area to the east of the site, which at the time of the survey was recently cleared open ground.
Block 2: an area to the south-east, adjacent to the monument boundary, which included an area surveyed at a closer (10-m) grid spacing.
Block 3: within the monument boundary but outside the visible mined area.

The area survey was divided into three major blocks (see figs 18 and 21 for their location) and the sampling interval of 50 m was chosen. Owen *et al.* (2001) have recently carried out a valuable series of tests to investigate the effects of sampling interval on phosphate surveys, although their principal aim was within-site investigation.

They stress that their finding of a considerable range of background variation in total phosphorus depending on the interval needs to be set in a local context with an adequate number of control samples. The practical limitations at Grimes Graves needed to be carefully weighed, namely the size of the area to be investigated (several square kilometres) and the specific problems to be answered, including the location of a possible settlement whose size in terms of spread of debris might be expected to be greater than 50 m. In the event the soil samples analysed in this part of the project amounted to about 8000 out of the total of about 10,000 for the whole project.

Eastern Block (figs 18 and 21; enclosed between survey lines A–N)
This was a long narrow block some 600 m wide x 2100 m long at its maximum, extending down to the River Little Ouse. Just to the east of the grid lie Field Barn farm and a minor road which cuts across Santon Warren. Fig. 22 shows a summary of the phosphate results: the average concentration of phosphate at each grid point has been calculated from the individual results on each soil core in the column of samples obtained. The average for each grid point has been plotted as a dot with increase in soil phosphate shown by increasing size. Survey lines A and N form the right and left boundaries respectively of fig. 22.

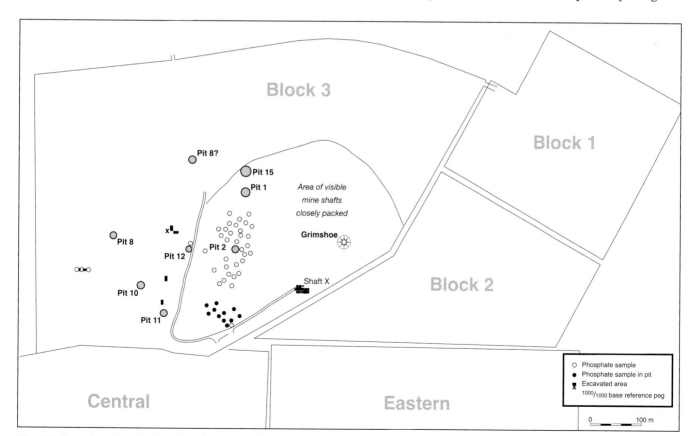

Fig. 21 Location plan for the phosphate sampling areas Blocks 1–3, Eastern and Central Blocks, and sampling points and features within the area of the monument.

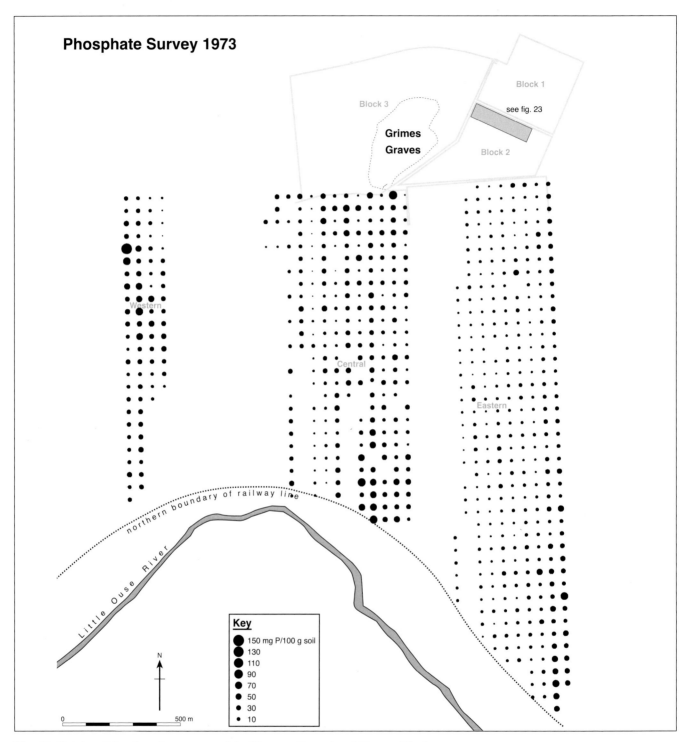

Fig. 22 Results of the phosphate survey of the Western, Central and Eastern Blocks.

Although care was taken to obtain data on a series of cores, in practice high phosphate values extended over a vertical series of cores, and averaging seems the most practical way of displaying the zones of enriched phosphate within the survey area. Test diagrams were produced using three-dimensional data to represent the concentration of phosphate in the vertical series of cores (analogous to fig. 19) and this confirmed an overall increase in phosphate throughout the vertical series of cores rather than being restricted to only one or two. Craddock (1984) used a similar approach to depicting three-dimensional phosphate data obtained at the Fengate, Cat's Water site.

It is clear that there is an anomaly with high phosphate values at the extreme south-east of this block. This anomaly fits very well with the presence just to the south of the south-east corner of the block (cf. fig. 18) of the site of Santon House and the nearby remains of the deserted medieval village, of which the only remaining building is St Helen's Church. A Viking grave lies slightly north of the church. The village itself may well have extended north of Santon House and the church, and refuse would therefore be expected to have been spread into the area of the south-east corner of the phosphate grid. The large area of enhanced phosphate is quite typical of the spread from a settlement site – see, for example, the field surveys of Provan (1971, fig. 2), which shows spreads of several hundred metres. This demonstrates that permanent settlement showed up clearly in the survey in these soil conditions using a 50-m grid.

Block 1 (fig. 21)

Samples were taken on a 50-m grid whose directions were laid out parallel to the sides shown in fig. 22. Out of fifty grid points, only three showed values of 50–80 mg P and these should be considered as very localized accumulations of phosphate material, with no obvious pattern. An area of 150 x 100 m in the south-west of the grid (bottom left corner of Block 1 in fig. 22) was sampled more intensively at 10-m intervals to follow up some of these localized accumulations. An unsystematic pattern emerged, though with one accumulation of higher phosphate values (*c.* 50 mg P) extending across a narrow spread of about 30 m. No obvious feature on the ground was linked with this, which suggests a very localized feature not associated with a settlement.

Block 2 (fig. 21)

As this area lies immediately adjacent to areas shown by excavation to have Bronze Age occupation, a section of Block 2 was intensively surveyed at 10-m intervals. Fig. 23 shows a phosphate grid for this 10-m interval sampling programme. The phosphate does increase towards the west end of the grid, where a few isolated areas with 50–70 mg P were found in approximate linear spreads, with one feature about 40 x 20 m and another 30 x 15 m, but the levels are not high enough to be sure

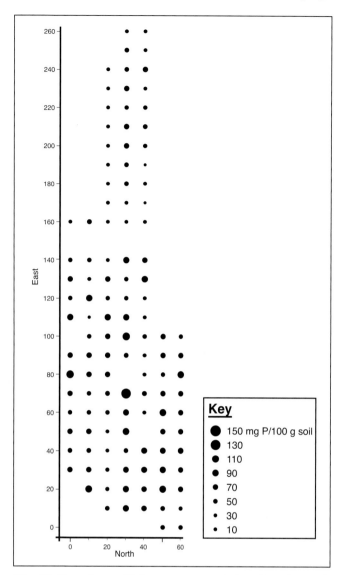

Fig. 23 Phosphate grid for an area sampled at 10-m intervals within Block 2, south of the perimeter fence.

that it indicates a substantial area of occupation. There were, however, more and closer-spaced occurrences of higher phosphate in this block compared to Block 1, so a general picture emerges that the incidence of phosphate accumulation increases towards the monument. For the rest of Block 2 sampled at 50-m intervals, most grid points were 20–30 mg P, with occasional values of 40–50 mg, and seemed to repeat the pattern at the 10-m interval survey. These figures can be compared to results from the Fengate, Newark Road site (Craddock *et al.* 1985) dated to the second millennium BC, on calcareous river gravels, ranging from 25–50 to over 50 mg P in silted ditches around two structures associated with family settlement probably of relatively short duration, with 'background' values of less than 25 mg P. By contrast, the much larger nearby Iron Age site of longer duration at Cat's Water had many samples of over 100 mg P.

Block 3 (fig. 21)

This includes the area within the present-day boundaries of the monument (fig. 18). The average concentrations of phosphate in the soil cores taken at 50-m intervals on a grid was about 20 mg P, which is effectively a 'background' non-occupation figure. Occasional isolated single vertical core series at a grid point gave values in the range 50–70 mg P, which may indicate a local accumulation of debris, but not an area with systematically enhanced phosphate. There is no evidence therefore from the phosphate survey of sustained occupation within the monument boundary, and to the north and east of the mined area.

Central Block (fig. 18: between survey lines AN and AA)

This 50-m grid was set out to abut the western edge of the Eastern Block (lines A–N). Grid lines AA and AN form the left (east) and right (west) sides of the grid respectively. Its north/south orientation is slightly different but the blocks are only about 50–100 m apart at the southern end. As with the Eastern Block, the southern edge was defined by the edge of the forested area near the railway line from Brandon to Thetford. The phosphate grid (fig. 22) shows a single point with particularly high phosphate at the north-east corner. This may be an isolated high value associated with a small feature. As it did not indicate a substantial area of human occupation it was not pursued further. The main feature of the grid is, however, a broad area of enhanced phosphate concentration (reaching over 80 mg P at its centre) near the south-eastern boundary of the grid. As this area is fairly substantial in extent, some archaeological feature would be expected. In fact, it corresponds very closely in location with the find in 1919 of Romano-British pottery, flue tiles (suggesting a building) and bracelets etc., and marked on the 25" OS map of the period (cf. fig. 18). Whatever the nature of this feature, it shows clear evidence of human occupation in the enhanced phosphate spread over several hundred metres of soil. No other enhanced areas of phosphate were indicated within the phosphate grid.

Western Block (figs 18 and 22)

Finally, although the 50-m survey of the forested area extended westwards as far as line BB (i.e. some 1000 m west of the south-west corner of the monument boundary – see fig. 18), sampling that began at the BB line and worked eastwards towards the western edge of the Central Block did not continue beyond the AX line. The area between AN and AX was therefore never sampled. Fig. 22 shows the phosphate grid between the lines AX (left) and BB (right): the main features are two areas of enriched phosphate 200–500 m south of the northern boundary of the grid, on the western side. These areas correspond closely with the location of Bromehill Cottage and the site of former brick kilns (fig. 18), as shown on the 1928 25" OS map of the area. The brick works is shown as a series of north/south structures with a kiln immediately north

of them. These were about 150 m south of Bromehill Cottage, and appear on the 1885 edition of the 25" OS map (sheets XCIII.9 and VII.9). Bromehill Cottage is some 300 m south of the northern edge of the grid in fig. 22, and its position corresponds almost exactly with the highest phosphate in this grid, abutting the western edge. The lower phosphate peak may correspond with areas of rubbish and disposal associated with the former brick works. Again, areas which have been known to be associated with human activity within the area surveyed have shown enriched phosphate in the soil. The rest of the grid is featureless, indicating no particular area of sustained human occupation.

Assessment

Craddock *et al.* (1985) have summarized the lessons to be drawn from a programme of analysis for soil phosphate spread over ten years, which began with the survey at Grimes Graves. The on-site value of the immediate availability of results to an excavation director is one of the prime reasons for setting up a field laboratory rather than taking the samples to an off-site laboratory. In the latter case, the survey technique might well produce interesting results but too late to be followed up by further sampling. The apparatus used for phosphate analysis can be inexpensive, and may be operated by someone with some laboratory expertise, for example science students from local schools.

As a location technique, it is inevitably slower than geophysics or aerial photography, as it involves laying down a grid, collecting and analysing soil samples, and interpreting the results. As an approximate calculation, it took about 144 operator-weeks or 3 man-years to collect and analyse the soil samples at Grimes Graves, using a labour force of up to 12 people at any one time to collect the soil samples. From experiments at Fengate and Maxey, and the results from the forest area at Grimes Graves, the collection of a series of cores may have been unnecessary, and could have saved approximately two thirds of the samples collected. However, the grid would still have had to be laid out and some coring done to assess the optimum depth for collection of the soil sample. This is with the benefit of hindsight, and cuts across the indications obtained from the initial experiments at Grimes Graves, which showed heavily stratified deposits that were phosphate-rich, interspersed with soil or sand of lower phosphate, though still enhanced above background. The stratigraphic information obtained by a sequence of cores (especially in the excavation of Shaft X) would have been lost with single-sampling.

The phosphate survey indicates that occupation of whatever date around the site may have been in small dispersed areas, rather than in larger, more concentrated settlements, with some evidence of increasing phosphate concentration as the site is approached from the south. The location by phosphate analysis of known features of archaeological significance within the area surveyed (for example the Romano-British site and deserted medieval village) indicates that such concentrations of human occupation can be detected even in the agriculturally poor sandy soils of the Breckland. It is, of course, not possible to determine from the phosphate whether these two localities were also occupied in prehistory.

The use of phosphate survey over a large area for primary location of sites of potential interest can only be justified under particular circumstances, such as those prevailing at Grimes Graves – dense vegetational cover or forestation. More detailed phosphate surveying within defined sites, as undertaken within the boundaries of the Grimes Graves monument, is most usefully employed to define areas of occupation prior to excavation. Within the monument the survey showed that, while areas showing evidence of occupation did occur, they were not widespread and cover relatively little of the overall area. Their preponderance along the south and east side of the visible mined area was indicated by the phosphate survey.

B The West Field

As already noted, much of the preceding work in the West Field had been conducted with the express purpose of proving the hypothesis that primitive mining would have begun from flint outcropping along the valley sides, but little in the way of precise information had accrued regarding the real nature of the flint deposits in this area, or the extent and precise nature of any exploitation which may have taken place. Equally, areas of reduction and finishing, although occasionally encountered and noted by Armstrong, had been of secondary interest. It was to bring some focus to these problems that Sieveking undertook further examination of selected portions of this area following extensive survey work.

1 Geophysical surveys

Surface indications of early mining over large areas in the West Field were found to have been largely masked by recent farming activity. To establish areas suitable for excavation it was therefore necessary to undertake large-scale geophysical surveys, employing both resistivity and magnetic techniques. The work was begun in 1972 and completed the following year. Results from the 1972 season were published in Sieveking *et al.* 1973, 185ff.

a The resistivity survey (figs 2, 24 and 25)
Some thirty-seven and a half 30-metre squares (A1–8, B1–8, C1–8, D1–7 and E1–7) were surveyed in 1972 and a further thirty-nine 30-metre squares in 1973 (F2–6, G2–6, AA1–2, OA1–6, OB1–3, OC1–2, OD1, OAA1–6, OBB2–6, OCC3–5 and OEE7–8). In addition, a small area (A9–10, B9, C9 and D9) was examined in the second year along the border of the scheduled site to the south.

Area S R1–6 was also surveyed to the north-east of Shaft X and Y1–3 outside the area of the scheduled monument to the south-east.

The resistivity survey was undertaken in the hope that sufficient contrast could be found between the high expected resistivity of the filling of any mine shaft and that of the likely low resistivity of the surrounding solid chalk.

b The magnetic survey (figs 2 and 24)
While buried shafts were likely to be magnetically sterile, it was hoped that areas of occupation might be recognizable as areas of enhanced soil magnetism. A first season was undertaken in 1972 by the late A.J. Clark and D. Haddon-Reece using the Ancient Monuments Laboratory 1-m base length Plessey fluxgate gradiometer and automatic reader. The results of this season were also published in Sieveking *et al.* 1973, 190ff.

The 1972 survey covered an area of ten 30-metre squares of the West Field. Much of this was devoted to an area immediately west of the visible Deep Mine Field, but with a smaller area examined further west at the break of slope. In 1973 a further six 30-metre squares were examined to the west of the first block investigated the previous year. In addition, an area of 1491 sq m in the region of Shaft X was examined, and a 30-sq-m area of boggy and tussocky ground in the north-east of the site, though here with negative results.

2 Areas examined

As an initial test of the results obtained from the 1972 resistivity and magnetic surveys, nine 3-metre squares were set to examine an area around Pits 8, 10, 11 and 12 (Sieveking *et al.* 1973). Cuttings 1013/995 and 1018/995, placed to examine a low mound discovered during ground survey, revealed this to be a modern feature, perhaps a spoil heap related to Armstrong's investigation of Pit 12. Cuttings 1007/1000 and 1007/1005 showed chalk block debris apparently derived from a pit which had not been detected by the survey techniques employed. Cuttings 1000/910 and 1000/905, set to examine anomalies in the resistivity survey, again revealed the presence of pits whose upper features had been truncated by modern land use. Only small portions of the pit edges were, however, revealed. Cutting 995/860, which had been opened to investigate an area within the resistivity survey where no mine shafts seemed to be present, again revealed mining activity suggesting difficulty in the interpretation of the survey data. Cuttings 845/912 and 845/917, set in an area further west to investigate minor features recorded in the magnetic survey, revealed a relatively recent modern ditch.

The results of further work during the resistivity survey had suggested the possibility of a 'boundary' of more or less continuous overlapping shallow mines forming an angle across the West Field, with perhaps larger and

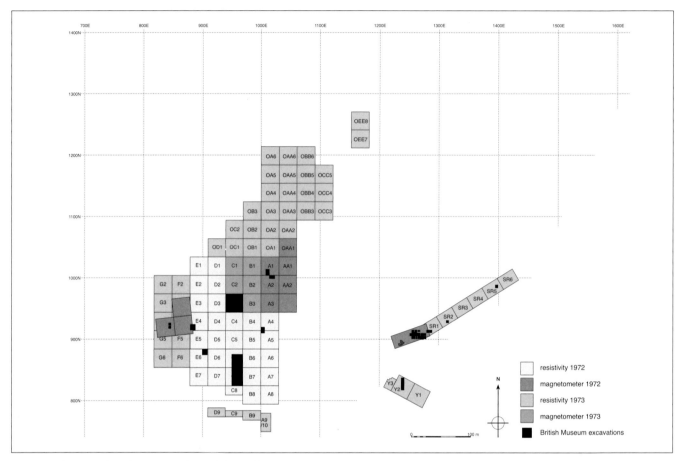

Fig. 24 Plan showing the extent of resistivity and magnetometer surveys carried out in 1972 and 1973, with grids marked.

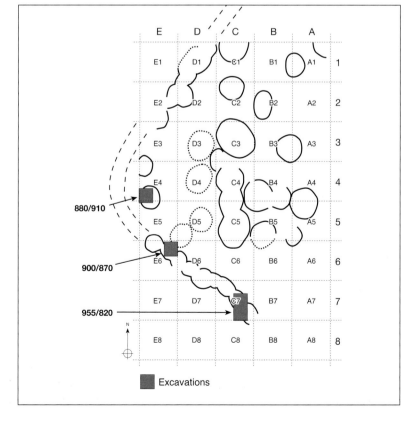

Fig. 25 Presence of features suggested by the resistivity survey in the West Field including an apparent line of continuous overlapping mines.

more isolated mines lying within (fig. 25). Three cuttings were therefore sited during the 1973 season to test these hypotheses: 880/910 to examine one of the isolated features, and 900/870 and 955/820 to examine the apparent line of mines forming the 'boundary' feature, but with negative results.

In five instances initial investigations during 1972 and 1973 seemed to pick up areas of flint working or short-lived occupation, but modern disturbance was also present. The unsatisfactory nature of these small-scale excavations suggested that large area excavation was more likely to offer an opportunity to see dug features and individual reduction sites in their entirety and in relation to each other. Successive campaigns in the years 1974–6 were devoted therefore to exploration of two areas of the West Field: 950/820, covering an area of some 1000 sq m, and 940/940, covering an additional 900 sq m. Over these areas the topsoil was removed mechanically.

Conditions in the West Field proved technically challenging. In practice, Sieveking's work came to be constrained not only by the nature of the deposits encountered, which made definition of individual features difficult, but (and largely as a consequence of this) also by time and finance available. Some features were not fully recorded and others could not be excavated to their entire depth (see Table 2). Sufficient, however, was achieved to establish that in the areas examined episodes of flint reduction had taken place, often small in scale but in one instance, Feature 112, of some magnitude. There was also abundant evidence for the mining of flint with the discovery in one instance of a split-level mine, Feature 105, comparable to Pits 3 and 3A (Longworth and Varndell 1996, 39), previously explored to the north of the visible mine field. Here the mine had been taken to a depth of some 4.7 m (see figs 58 and 59). In the northern segment explored, four galleries were found dug at the junction where cryoturbated deposits lay on top of solid tabular chalk. No doubt when the flint which could be extracted from these deposits had been exhausted, the mine had then been taken down through the solid chalk to where *floorstone* still remained *in situ*, with beginnings of a further three galleries in evidence at this level. Here, again, bone picks were employed like those used in the other mines of this type previously explored (cf. Legge 1992, 69ff.). Although no independent dating evidence was forthcoming from the mine, a date of 2580–2140 (BM-1060) had been obtained from an antler recovered from a niche in the upper level workings of Pit 3A, offering a probable chronological horizon for this type of mine. However, in the new dating programme now being undertaken by English Heritage, dates for individual bone picks now suggest that these are of Bronze Age date and by inference that the split-level mines belong to that period. As the programme continues more dates on bone picks augment the case for an Early Bronze Age date for at least some of these mines (Healy pers. comm.).

Other features proved on excavation to be relatively small open-cast pits dug to retrieve whatever remnant *floorstone* survived in the area near the surface. Of these, Features 6, 11, 14, 28, 32, 34 and 50 had a depth of only 1.5–2 m. Several, including Features 3, 5, 14, 24, 32, 34, 101 and 141, showed characteristic undercutting or niching at or near their base, where nodules had been sought or extracted. A few were somewhat deeper. Feature 3 had a maximum depth of 2.15 m, and two further pits, Features 24 and 141, had not been bottomed at 2.2 m and 1.9 m respectively. Feature 122 may also have been the top of a much deeper mine. In addition to these types of exploitation, Sieveking saw in Feature 7 an exploratory shaft designed to test for the presence or absence of useful flint in the area (Sieveking 1979). While this interpretation seems highly likely, its presence may well have arisen from an opportunistic utilization of a pre-existing solution hollow, which was then emptied and extended for this purpose.

Even after the turf and topsoil had been mechanically removed, it is clear that in the soft sandy surface deposits immediately beneath, ploughing and working by rabbits had left the upper layers of many features disturbed and susceptible to penetration by later material, as evidenced in cutting 940/940 by the presence of gunflints in these levels. Certainly the quantities of axe and discoidal knife roughouts from the disturbed levels at the surface demonstrate that many episodes of flint reduction have been lost to these processes, although some survived either *in situ* or redeposited in the filling of the pits. Evidence, too, was recovered for what appears to be a short-stay occupation in the earlier part of the Bronze Age, Feature 108 yielding over two hundred sherds, of which at least fifty-seven were Collared Vessel (Longworth *et al.* 1988, 24), the associated charcoal giving a ^{14}C determination of 1740–1620 (BM-1031).

Unfortunately no pottery or chronologically sensitive artefacts were recovered from contexts which could give a direct date for the digging of the shallow mines. Dating for these needs therefore to rely upon what ^{14}C determinations are available from antler and charcoal, and a consideration of the contexts of items such as the oblique arrowhead and discoidal knife, which can be taken as acceptable proxies for a Late Neolithic date.

If the interpretation of Feature 7 as primarily for prospection is correct then some interest was already being taken in this area of the West Field before work in the Deep Mine Field had ceased, for a ^{14}C determination for an antler from the floor of this feature yielded a date range of 2470–2300 on re-measurement (BM-3121). Dates derived from antlers taken from what appear to be primary contexts in three other features may also indicate some chronological overlap with the deep mines, unless these are residual from an earlier phase and merely incorporated by chance into the infilling (in any case they should reflect mining, presumably nearby). An antler from Feature 14, giving a ^{14}C determination of 2300–2040 (BM-1010), lay on a shallow layer of redeposited chalk at its base and is likely to have been deposited shortly after work had ceased in the pit. This is very similar to the date for a second antler of 2410–2200 (BM-1015) from a small pit, Feature 51, dug down from the base of the same mine. Similarly, a third antler from Feature 3, also probably from a primary context, has a similar date range, but extending later (BM-970). Confirmation of later mining comes from Feature 24, a mine almost certainly excavated to a point close to its original floor. Here a deposit of sand and chalk (layer 4) is clearly part of early backfilling. This contained discoidal knives and an antler yielding a ^{14}C determination of 2280–2060 (BM-1008). The remaining ^{14}C determinations are from contexts in the later infilling of the pits and provide only horizons *ante quem* for the actual mining itself. Antlers taken from secondary fills in Features 11 and 34 gave dates

of 2300–2140 (BM-1016) and 2200–1980 (BM-1062) respectively. Samples from the upper fills of Features 4, 6, 13, 32, 36 and 124 provide a comparable range. Although evidence from the sections for rapid deliberate infilling is not always robust, and therefore assessing over what period of time the infilling of each feature took place is largely a matter of conjecture, it is clear from the ^{14}C dates that many of the pits explored were incorporating material into their upper levels belonging to a time later than the floruit of the deep mines. Given the instability of the surface deposits and shallowness of most of the workings, it is unlikely that these dates do not also reflect active mining continuing into this later phase. It is also evident that some pits remained visible and provided useful loci for short-stay and flint-working episodes, which in the case of Feature 106 extended well into the Bronze Age (BM-1030).

Cutting and Feature number	Feature bottomed	Feature not bottomed	Knapping debris (in pit)	Knapping debris (surface)	Hearth/burnt area	Not defined	Bronze Age occupation
880/910 1					X		
2	X						
900/870 2					X		
4		X					
5					X		
950/820 1		X	X				
2						X	
3	X						
4		X					
5		X	X				
6	X						
7	X						
8						X	
9				X			
10		X	X				
11	X						
12					X		
13		X					
14	X						
15	X		X	X			
16				X			
17		X					
18		X	X				
19				X			
20		X				X	
21				X		X	
22		X					
23				X			
24		X					
25		X					
26		X					

Table 2 Features examined by Sieveking in the West Field.

27		X					
28	X						
29		X					
30						X	
31					X		
32	X						
33		X					
34	X						
35		X		X			
36		X	X				
37		X	X				
38				X	X		
39	X						
40	X						
41				X			
42					X		
43		X					
44							
45		X					
46				X			
47						X	
48		X					
49		X					
50	X						
51	X						
52			X	X			
53							
940/940 101	X		X	X			
102		X					
103		X					
104		X					
105	X		X				
106		X		X	X		
107		X	X				
108							X
109						X	
110		X					
111		X	X				
112		X	X		X		
113			?X				
114				X			
115		X					
116		X					
117	X		X				
118				X			
119				X			
120			X				
121		X					
122		X					
123						X	
124		X			X		
125		X					
126		X					
127		X					
128		X					

129		X					
130		X	X				
131						X	
132						X	
133						X	
134						X	
135						X	
136						X	
137						X	
138						X	
139						X	
140						X	
141	X						
142						X	
143						X	
144						X	
145						X	
146		X					
147						X	

3 Catalogue of features recovered

Abbreviations

BA	Bronze Age
BSV	Bucket-shaped Vessel
CV	Collared Vessel
EBA	Early Bronze Age
GW	Grooved Ware
MNB	Middle Neolithic Bowl
U	Unidentified
( )	Layer

Some lithic types (e.g. 'Axes (broken): one form 1' or 'Discoidal knives (broken): one, form Ind. stage II') are defined in Chapter IV.

Cutting 880/910 (figs 2 and 26)

Excavated in 1973, 11 x 11 m, revealed a hearth and a pit.

FEATURE 1
Hearth. (Radiocarbon sample BM-990)

FEATURE 2
An irregular pit 2.6 x 1.6 m filled with deposits of sand including burnt material, probably from F1. A quantity of Middle Neolithic Bowl sherds were recovered from it.

Contexts

1	Grey sand
2	Yellow/brown sand
3	Blackened sand
4	Brown loamy sand
5	Red/brown sand

Finds
Flint: Leaf arrowheads: two, (-).
Pottery: MNB: twenty-six, (-). BA (of which 1 BSV): three, (1).

Finds from within the cutting but unattributed to features
Pottery: MNB: fifty-four, (2). BSV: twenty-one, (2) (layer numbers do not appear on sections).

Finds from within cutting but lying outside the features
Flint: ? Arrowhead roughout: one (from superficial deposits).

Cutting 900/870 (figs 2 and 27)

Excavated in 1973, 9 x 9 m, and 910/870 added in 1974. 900/870 revealed two hearths and a pit.

FEATURE 1
Unrecorded.

Finds
Flint: Discoidal knives: one, form Ind. stage II (2).

FEATURE 2
Finds
Pottery: EBA: seven, (2).
Hearth material composed of blackened sand. (Radiocarbon sample BM-991)

FEATURE 4 (fig. 27)
Pit sectioned E–W by baulk, 3 m across, dug to a depth of 1.1 m but not bottomed. Filled with deposits of sand above crushed chalk.

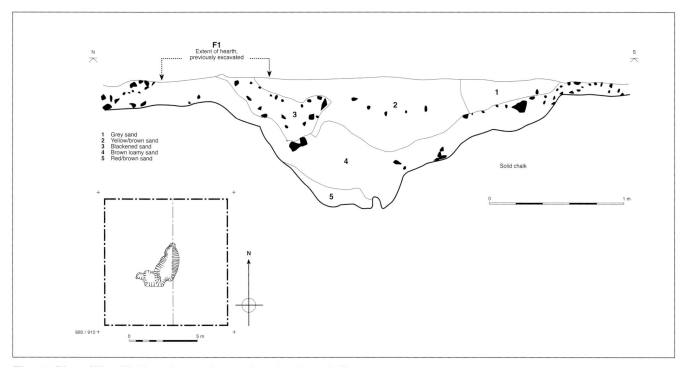

Fig. 26 Plan of West Field cutting 880/910 and section through Feature 2.

Fig. 27 Plan of West Field cutting 900/870 and section through Feature 4.

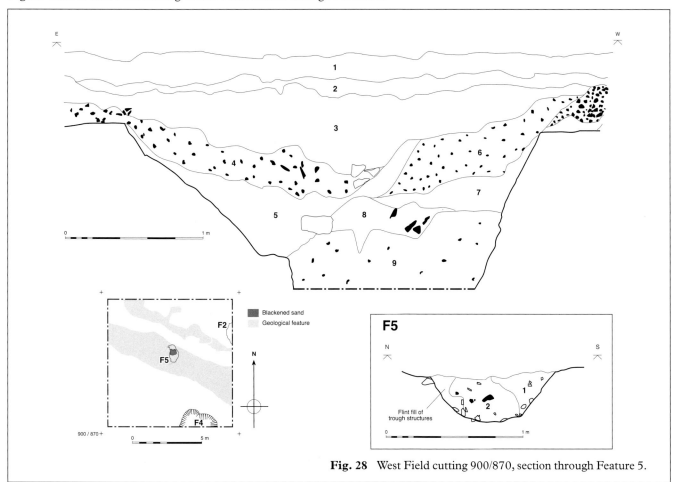

Fig. 28 West Field cutting 900/870, section through Feature 5.

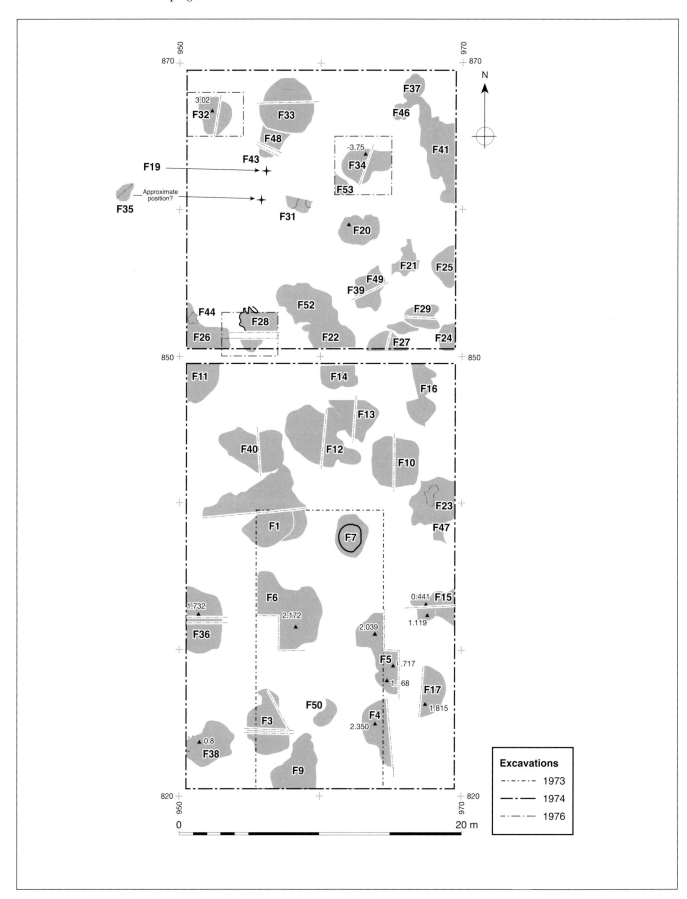

Fig. 29 Plan of West Field cutting 950/820 with individual features marked.

Contexts

1 Dark brown loamy sand
2 Yellow/grey sand
3 Grey/brown sand
4 Grey sand and flint
5 Brown loamy sand
6 Dark grey sand and flint
7 Chalk and sand
8 Dark red/brown sand
9 Crushed chalk and flint

Finds

Flint: Discoidal knives: one, form e stage III (-).
Roughouts: one, (2).

FEATURE 5 (fig. 28)

Small pit 0.425 m across and 0.15 m deep, containing hearth material and sand dug into trough structure. (Radiocarbon sample BM-989)

Finds from within cutting but not ascribed to features

Flint: Axes: one, form 9. Axes (broken): one, form 3.
Rods (broken): one. Scrapers: one, (2). Two more from extension of cutting 910/870 (2).

Cutting 950/820 (figs 2 and 29)

FEATURE 1 (figs 29 and 30)

Oval pit or hollow 3.8 x 3.6 m, sectioned along E–W line, opened 1973 and 1974, but not fully excavated and only northern part removed. Section drawn to 0.6 m. At depth greater than this, large flint nodules and cores with knapping debris.

Superficial layers of sand incorporate a layer of flint waste. Beneath, layers of chalk rubble overlie layers of flint nodules and cores with knapping debris above

further level of sand and gravel.

Contexts

1 Dark sand with flint
2 Dark sand
3 Flints
4 Medium dark sand
5 Closely packed chalk and flints
6 Similar to 5
7 Large flint nodules and cores with knapping debris
8 Knapping debris and small nodules in gravel
9 Dark brown sand with small flints and gravel with small chalk flecks

Finds

Flint: Axes (broken): two, forms Ind. (3), 3 (9).
Fabricators: one, (7). Roughouts: one, (-).
Antler: Substantial fragments: three (1).

FEATURE 2

No information.

FEATURE 3 (figs 29 and 31)

Irregular oval pit sectioned E–W, 3.8 x 3.0 m and at least 2.15 m deep with irregular base. Excavated 1973 and 1974. Bottomed.

Fill composed of deposits of sand and gravel with minor inclusions of rotten chalk; increasing amounts of chalk present in the basal layers. Large deposit of compact rotten chalk lying against S baulk. (Radiocarbon sample BM-970 from lower fill)

Contexts

1 Dark brown sand
2 Dark yellow sand with flint
3 Yellow sandy chalk
4 Red sand
5 Red sandy gravel
6 Yellow sandy gravel

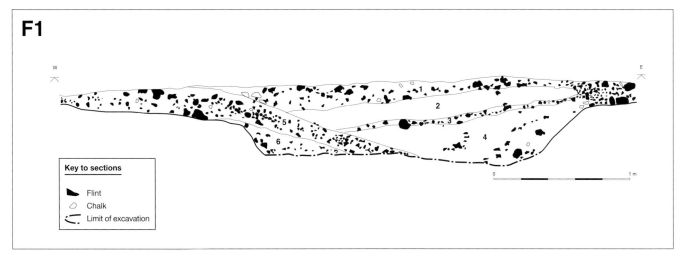

Fig. 30 West Field cutting 950/820, E–W section through Feature 1.

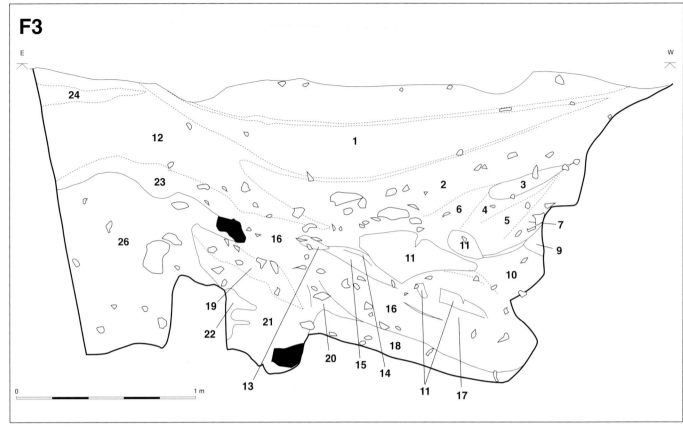

Fig. 31 West Field cutting 950/820, E–W section through Feature 3.

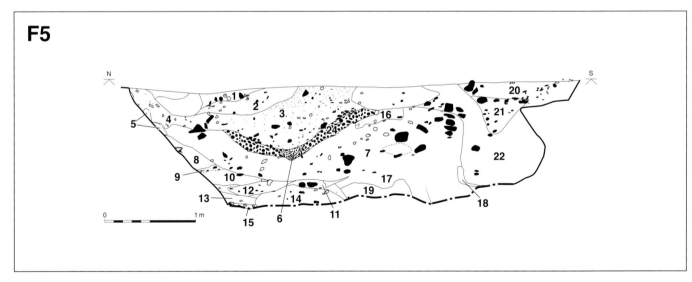

Fig. 32 West Field cutting 950/820, N–S section through Feature 5.

7   Dark yellow sand
8   Red sand
9   Yellow chalky gravel
10 Yellow sand with grit
11 Compacted rotten chalk
12 Dense gravel in orange sand
13 Yellow sandy chalk
14 Red sand
15 Yellow sand with grit
16 Dark brown sandy gravel
17 Red yellow sandy gravel
18 Sandy chalk
19 Orange gravel
20 Yellow chalky sand
21 Yellow gravelly sand
22 Compacted rotten chalk
23 Yellow sand
24 Dark gravelly sand
25 Dark sandy gravel
26 Compacted rotten chalk

Finds

Flint: Axes: one, form 10 (-). Axes (broken): two, forms: 10, Ind. (-). Discoidal knives (broken): one, form Ind. stage III (-). Picks: three, (-). Oblique arrowheads: one, (2). Scrapers: one, (-). Roughouts: one (reused), (2); three, (-). Hammers: one, (-).
Stone: Hammers: one, (-).
Antler: Substantial fragments: one (lower fill)

FEATURE 4

Irregular pit sectioned N–S, excavated 1974. Edge of pit and eastern half not fully defined. 4.76 m across, taken to a depth of 1.76 m but not bottomed. (Radiocarbon sample BM-1019 from [3])

Deposits principally of sand with some chalk inclusions.

Contexts

1   Dark brown sand with small flints
2   Flint layer
3   Dark brown sand to lighter sandy gravel becoming yellow/orange sand
4   Fine chalk lenses
5   Red sand
6   Series of tip lines: red/orange sand, rotted fine chalk, red gravelly soil, rotted chalk rubble with flints, dark orange/red sand, lighter chalky yellow sand
7   Lighter yellow sand
8   Yellow sand
9   Chalk rotted to light yellow with a little sand and flints, fairly compacted
10 Red/yellow sand with flints and chalk rubble
11 Orange/yellow gravel and flints
12 Red sand

13 Dark yellow gravelly sand
14 Chalk, sandy and rotted
15 Grey
16 Chalk and sand tip lines

Finds

Flint: Scrapers: one, (3). Roughouts: two, (16) (2).
Antler: Substantial fragments: two, (2) (3). (Radiocarbon sample BM-1019)

FEATURE 5 (figs 29 and 32)

Irregular pit sectioned N–S and E–W, excavated 1973 and 1974. Western part removed but not bottomed. Flint-knapping debris in upper layer.

Deposits of sand, chalk and gravel. Layer of flint-knapping debris (24), lay approximately halfway down the deposit as excavated, beneath deposits of gravel and above rotted sandy chalk. (Radiocarbon samples BM-992 [24]; BM-3119 [24])

Contexts

1   Medium brown sandy soil with gravel and flint nodules
2   Chalky/sandy soil with gravel and small flint nodules and small chalk lumps
3   Yellow/orange gravel with sand and small flint nodules merging into sandy chalk
4   Light brown/orange sand with small flint
5   Rotted chalk and sand
6   Lens of charcoal
7   Rotted sandy chalk
8   Red sand
9   Orange sand and flint
10 Light brown/orange sand with chalk flecks
11 Orange sand and flint
12 Lens of fine rotted chalk/light brown sand
13 Bright orange gravel
14 Fine rotted chalk with some larger pieces and flint
15 Dark orange sand
16 Chalky sandy lens
17 Bright orange sandy gravel
18 Grey ashy layer
19 Very compacted chalk with flint
20 Dark brown sand with flint nodules at base
21 Sandy chalky layer with chalk and flint
22 Yellow/orange sand with flint
23 Fine chalk rubble in sandy brown soil with flint nodules and flakes
24 Layer of flint-knapping debris at base of 3 in grey soil
25 Yellow sand and gravel with some chalk
26 Layer of burning/black sand
27 Dark sandy charcoal layer
28 Sandy chalk with gravel

Finds

Flint: Axes: one, form 3 (-). Axes (broken): one, form Ind. (22). Discoidal knives: two, form Ind. stage II (2); one, form f stage III (-). Discoidal knives (broken): one, form Ind. stage II (2); one, form c stage III (2). Picks: one, (-). Rods (broken): one, (-). Points: one, (24). Plane scrapers: one, (-). Plane scrapers (broken): one, (-). Roughouts: five, (20) (24) (-). Roughouts (broken): two, (22) (24).

Stone: Hammers: five (-).

Antler: Substantial fragments: three (4) (6) (20) + 1 (24) (radiocarbon sample)

FEATURE 6 (figs 29 and 33)

Irregular pit sectioned on staggered line N–S and E–W. Partially excavated 1973 and 1974 over eastern half. Bottomed at 1.6 m. Superficial deposits of sand lay above deposits of more compacted sand with chalky lumps, incorporating lenses of finer material. (Radiocarbon samples BM-1007 [1]; 993 [4]; 3120 [4]; 3006 [-])

Contexts

1　Red gritty sand with flints
2　Fine orange sand with small flints
3　Small compacted chalk lumps in sandy chalk fill with flints
4　Very compacted fine chalk lens
5　Fine light sand lens
6　Fairly compacted lens of light sand and small chalk lumps
7　As 3 but slightly less compacted and with more chalk

Finds

Flint: Axes: four, forms 5 (1), 4 and 7 (4), Ind. (-). Axes (broken): one, form Ind. (4). Discoidal knives: one, form c stage III (1); one, form Ind. stage I (4). Discoidal knives (broken): one, form Ind. stage II (-). Picks: two, (1) (2). Picks (broken): four, (1), (-). Plane scrapers: one, (4). Points (broken): one roughout, (1). Hammers: two, (1) (-).

Antler: Substantial fragments: fifteen, (1) (2) (4) (5) (-); fragments: (5); roe deer antler: one, (2).

Antler pick in fill and antler crown with flint ? at base.

FEATURE 45

Small pit in top of Feature 6 excavated 1974, either part of that feature or cut into it, sectioned E–W, 0.5 m deep. Filled with deposits of sand.

Contexts

1　Grey/dark brown sand with small stones and grit, possibly burnt
2　Light chalky sand with small flints
3　Dark red gritty sand with a few flints
4　Yellow/orange sand with gravel

FEATURE 7 (figs 29 and 34)

Deep oval pit, fully excavated 1973 and 1974. 2.3 x 3.2 m at top, becoming 1.0 m in diam., 4.1 m deep. Upper levels of dark brown sand and yellow sand overlay a deposit of decomposed chalk entering from the north. (Radiocarbon samples BM-1009 [10]; 3121 [10]; 994 [8])

Contexts

1　Dark brown sand and flint
2　Yellow sand and flint
3　Yellow sand and decomposed chalk with flint
4　Decomposed chalk
5　-
6　Red and orange sand
7　Lens of red sand
8　Orange gravel with chalk lens
9　Fine chalk/sand with small flints, incorporating tip lines i–v
10　Compacted chalk fill

Finds

Flint: Axes: one, form 3 (-). Axes (broken): two, forms 3 and Ind. (-). Discoidal knives: one, form Ind. stage II (-). Discoidal knives (broken): one, form Ind. stage I (8). Fabricators: one, (8). Scrapers: one, (-). Plane scrapers: one, (-). Roughouts: five, (8) (-). Hammers: one, (-).

Stone: Hammers: one, (-).

Chalk: Balls: one, (10) (Varndell 1991) [C156].

Antler: Substantial fragments: two, (4) (10).

FEATURE 8

No information.

FEATURE 9

Remnant area of flint-working debris, probably redeposited. Excavated 1974. Sectioned E–W by southern baulk.

Flint-working debris lay beneath compacted chalk rubble and above lighter sandy, chalky gravel.

Contexts

1　Compacted chalk rubble
2　Flint-knapping debris
3　Light chalky, sandy gravel covered by layer of large nodules
4　Orange/red sand with knapping debris

Finds

Flint: Discoidal knives: one, form Ind. stage I (2); one, form Ind. stage II (-). Fabricators: one, (2). Fabricators (broken): one, (-). Roughouts: four, (2) (-).

Fired clay: Fragments, including one curved object.

Antler: Substantial fragments: four, (-).

Fig. 33 West Field cutting 950/820, N–S section through Feature 6 and E–W section through Feature 45.

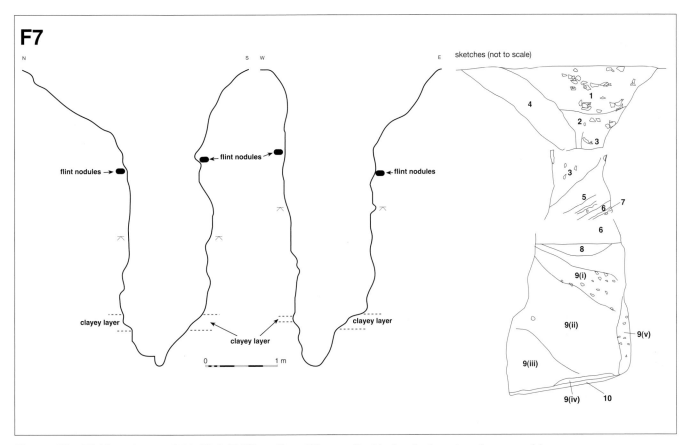

Fig. 34 West Field cutting 950/820, N–S, E–W profiles of Feature 7 with sketched sections (not to scale).

FEATURE 10 (figs 29 and 35)

Sub-rectangular pit sectioned N–S, 1.9 m across and 1.36 m deep. Eastern half excavated 1974. Probably in top of deeper feature, filled mainly with successive layers of sand. Dump of flint-working debris at a superficial level (2).

Contexts

1. Light brown sand
2. Flint dump in base of 1
3. Dark loamy sand with flint
4. Light sand with flints
5. -
6. Red/yellow sand
7. Light brown sand with nodules
8. Sand
9. Orange/red sand with flakes
10. Chalk
11. Yellow/brown sand
12. Yellow sand
13. Red sand

Finds

Flint: Axes: one, form 3 (3). Axes (broken): one, form Ind. (2). Discoidal knives: one, form Ind. stage I (1). Knives, other: one, (8). Roughouts: one, (2).

Antler: Substantial fragments: one, (10).

FEATURES 11, 26, 28 AND 42 (figs 29 and 36–8)

Large pit or series of pits in vicinity of peg 850. Partially excavated 1974 and 1976. Only part of northern edge defined. Bottom reached at > 1.7 m. In section Feature 44 appears either as part of this feature or is cut by it. Feature 42 is an area of burning on the edge of Feature 26, sectioned NW–SE.

Feature 11 filled with successive layers of sand incorporating minor chalk dumps (10, 14). (Radiocarbon sample BM-1016 [12])

Feature 26 filled with successive layers of sand over a dump of chalk (11).

Feature 28 filled with deposits of sand, gravel, chalk and cryte. (Radiocarbon sample BM-1063 [probably 21])

Contexts

FEATURE 11

1. Grey/brown sand and flint
2. Loamy sand
3. Grey sand with flint
4. Yellow/brown sand
5. Light brown sand and flint
6. Dark brown loamy sand
7. Light grey sand and flint

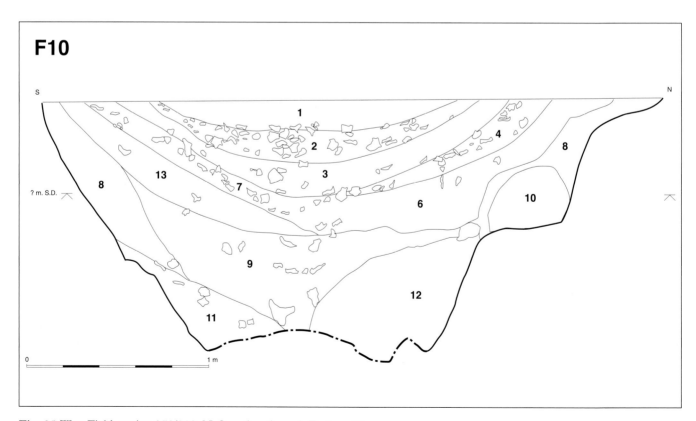

Fig. 35 West Field cutting 950/820, N–S section through Feature 10.

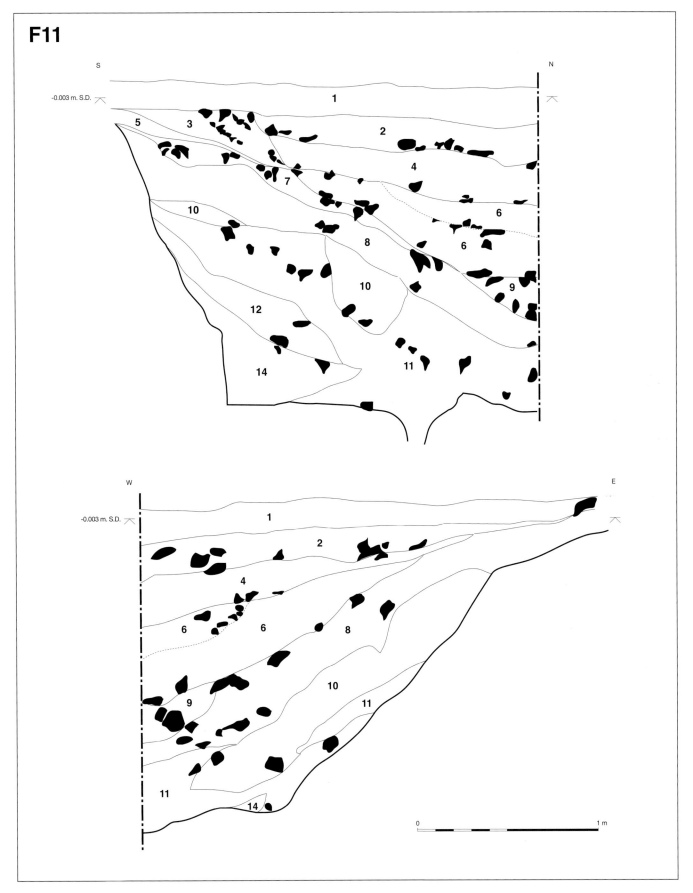

Fig. 36 West Field cutting 950/820, N–S, E–W sections through Feature 11.

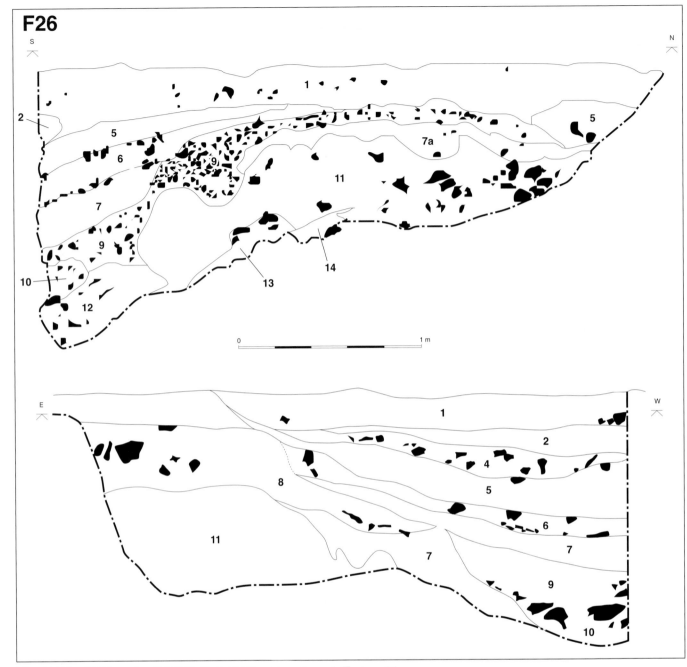

Fig. 37 West Field cutting 950/820, N–S, E–W sections through Feature 26.

8 Orange sand and flint
9 Dark grey sand and flint
10 Chalk
11 Red sand
12 Yellow sand
13 Yellow gravel
14 Sand/chalk

FEATURE 26
1 Dark sand
2 Dark grey sand
3 Brown sand and flint

4 Similar to 3
5 Light brown sand
6 Dark loamy sand and flint
7 Light loamy sand
7a Sand
8 Light brown gravel
9 Flint nodules in brown sand
10 Dark loamy sand, gravel and nodules
11 Chalk
12 Yellow sand with some flint and flakes
13 Flinty sand with gravel
14 Chalk with charcoal

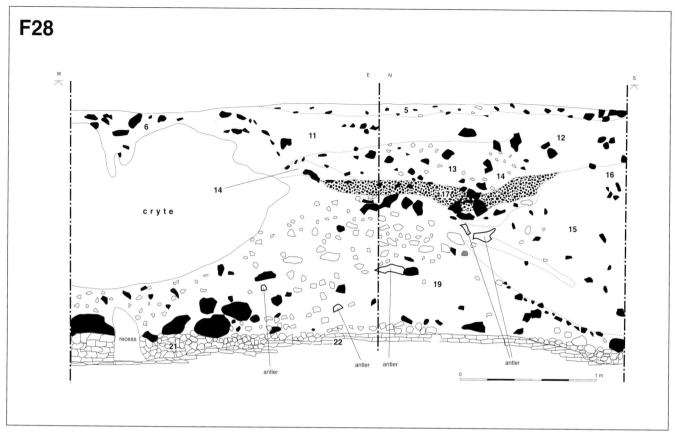

F28

Fig. 38 West Field cutting 950/820, N–S, E–W sections through Feature 28.

FEATURE 28

1   Dark sand
2   Light reddish sand
3   Black (burnt) sand with flake
4   As 3, not in section
5   Light brown sand with flake
5a Light brown sand with flake and much flint rubble
6   Yellow sand and gravel
7   Chalky sand with chalk lumps and flint
8   Chalky tip
9   Chalk dump not in section
10 Light yellow sand and gravel not in section
11 Lens of chalky sand with chipping not in section
12 Dark red brown sand with flake
13 Lens of chalky sand with chipping
14 Yellow chalky sand with flake
15 Grey cryte fill with chalk
16 Chalk tip with pocket of orange sand and flake
17 Dark (burnt) chalky sand with chipping
18 Brown sand with much flake and roughouts
19 Orange sand with flake and flint rubble
20 Loose brown sand not in section
21 Chalk rubble
22 Primary fill

Finds

FEATURE 11

Flint: Axes: one, form 3 (-). Roughouts: one, (2).
Antler: Substantial fragments: three, (12).

FEATURE 26

Flint: Roughouts: one, (6).

FEATURE 28

Flint: Axes: one, form Ind. (2). Axes (broken): two, forms 3 (-), Ind. (5). Discoidal knives: two, form d stage II (2) (5). Points: one, (17). Knives, other: one, (3). Borers: one, (2). Roughouts: three, (2) (17) (18). Roughouts (broken): one, (18). Hammers: one, (17).
Stone: Hammers: three, (2) (5) (18).
Pottery: GW: two, (5) (12). CV: one, (14). U: (crumbs) (17).
Antler: Substantial fragments from (21) (-).

FEATURE 12 (fig. 29)

Fire/charcoal spread in shallow depression in sand, SW of Feature 13. Excavated 1974, sectioned N–S, base not defined. (Radiocarbon sample BM-1005 [11])

Contexts

1 Charcoal/sand
2 Pink and grey burnt sand
3 Grey sand and flint pebbles
4 Yellow/grey sand and flint
5 Red/brown sand
6 Similar to 2
7 ? Natural
8 Similar to 3
9 Red/brown sand and flint
10 Charcoal/sand and flint
11 Charcoal/charcoal and sand
12 Yellow sand and flint
13 Pale sand and gravel
14 Yellow sand
15 Charcoal/sand wash

FEATURE 13 (figs 29 and 39)

Broad, sub-triangular pit 2.8 x 3.7 m and 1.03 m deep. Excavated 1974. Sectioned N–S, eastern half removed. Probably fill of larger feature.

Feature filled with successive layers of sand. (Radiocarbon sample BM-1022 [3])

Contexts

1 Orange/brown sand
2 Dark loamy sand
3 Charcoal and sand, black layer
4 Yellow/brown sand and nodules
5 Chalk rubble, quite hard
6 Red sand
7 Lens of dark brown loamy sand in 5
8 ? Natural/redeposited

Finds

Flint: Discoidal knives: one, form f stage III (4). Scrapers: one, (4). Roughouts: one, (4).

FEATURES 14, 22, 51 AND 52 (figs 29 and 40)

Feature 14 is a deep, flat-based pit, undercut at the base, sectioned by northern baulk, 2.25 m across and 1.65 m deep. Probably southern part of a pit whose northern half is represented by *Feature 22*. Excavated 1974, this was sectioned E–W by southern baulk of northern trench and excavated down to 1.28 m but probably not bottomed. (Radiocarbon sample BM-1010 from Feature 14 [25])

From base of Feature 14 a small circular pit was dug, *Feature 51*, 0.82 m in diam. and 0.65 m deep. (Radiocarbon sample BM-1015)

Feature 52, also excavated in 1974, is a group of flint nodules and cores in a dump of chalk rubble on northern edge of Feature 22 and extending into its fill.

Feature 14 consisted of deposits of sand incorporating three deposits of chalk. Feature 22 had deposits of sand incorporating a large deposit of chalk blocks. In Feature 51, chalk rubble lay on natural with red sand above.

Contexts

FEATURE 14

1 Dark loamy sand
2 Grey/brown sand with flint
3 Red/yellow sand
4 Sand (red/grey)
5 Natural dark red/grey sand
6 Dark red sand

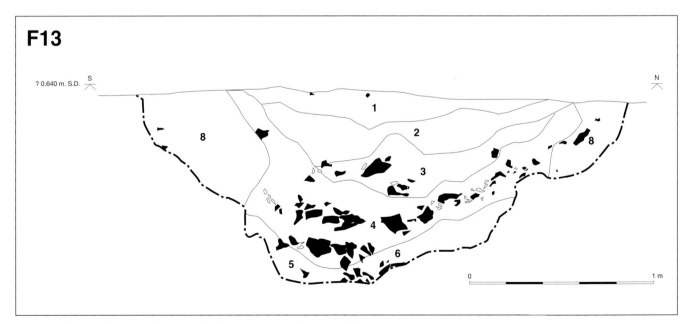

Fig. 39 West Field cutting 950/820, N–S section through Feature 13.

Fig. 40 West Field
cutting 950/820,
E–W section through
Feature 14, E–W
section through
Feature 22 and N–S
section through
Feature 51.

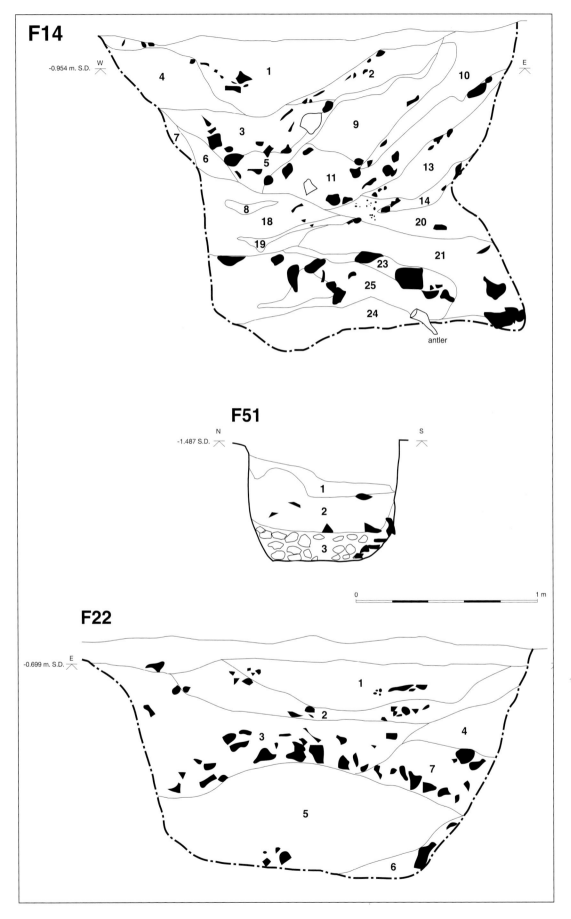

7   Natural
8   Dark brown loamy sand
9   Crushed chalk
10 Red sand
11 Crushed chalk
12 Light yellow sand with flint and flakes
13 Red sand
14 Orange sand
15 Red sand and a little flint
16 Yellow sand and gravel with a few flakes
17 Chalk
18 Grey/yellow sand
19 Dark loamy sand
20 Chalk
21 Red sand
22 Yellow sand
23 Red sand
24 Chalk
25 Red sand

FEATURE 22

1   Dark loamy sand
2   Orange sand and flint
3   Red sand and flint
4   Yellow sand
5   Chalk blocks
6   Sand/chalk
7   Dark loamy sand

FEATURE 51

1   Gravel (probably decayed chalk)
2   Red sand
3   Chalk rubble

Finds

FEATURE 14

Flint: Axes (broken): one, form Ind. (5). Discoidal knives: one, form c stage III (5). Knives (other): one, (8). Scrapers: one, (5).
Antler: Substantial fragments: one, (25).

FEATURE 22

Flint: Roughouts: one, (4).
Antler: Substantial fragments: one, (5).

FEATURE 15 (figs 29 and 41)

Shallow, flat-based irregular pit 0.6 m in diam. and 0.9 m deep, excavated in 1974, covered by dumped chalk. Sectioned N–S and E–W.

Filled with compacted sandy chalk. On W edge lay knapping debris composed mainly of large flakes, cores and nodules.

Contexts

1   Compacted chalk lumps with flints in sandy chalk soil

2   Knapping debris in dark, sandy soil
3   Fairly compacted sandy chalk with tip lines

Finds

Flint: Axes: one, form 10 (2).
Antler: Substantial fragments: two (lay just outside feature).

FEATURE 16 (fig. 29)

Remains of chalk dump in sand hollows, excavated 1974, half-sectioned NNW–SSE, eastern half removed. Flint-working debris at base of dump but uncertain whether in the basal layer or sealed by it. No section drawing survives. (Radiocarbon sample BM-1017 [7])

Contexts

1   Dark brown loamy soil and chipping (sieved)
2   Yellowish crushed chalk, rather sandy, with some flakes
3   Yellow/white crushed chalk with some flint (no flakes)
4   Yellow sandy chalk, some flakes
5   Flint cores and nodules (planned)
6   Yellow sand
7   Chipping floor
8   Yellow sand and chalk

Finds

Flint: Discoidal knives: one, form b/c stage II (3). Picks (broken): one, (7). Rods (broken): one, (3). Fabricators: one, (2). Fabricators (broken): one, (7). Scrapers: one, (7). Roughouts: five, (2) (3) (7).
Antler: (7) (radiocarbon sample)

FEATURE 17 (figs 29 and 42)

Oval pit, sectioned NNE–SSW, excavated 1974, eastern half removed 3.5 m across and taken to a depth of 1.15 m. Probably top of deeper feature.
Filled with deposits of sand.

Contexts

1   Medium brown sand
2   Medium to light brown sand with gravel and flint
3+4 Fine rotted chalk with dark sand on top
5   Orange sandy gravel
6   Rotted sandy chalk
7   Orange sandy gravel
8   Rotted yellow sandy chalk
9   Yellow sand with small gravel
10   Dark orange sandy gravel
11   Red sand
12   Orange sand
13   Rotted sandy chalk
14   Rotted sandy chalk
15   Rotted sandy chalk lens over brown sand lens

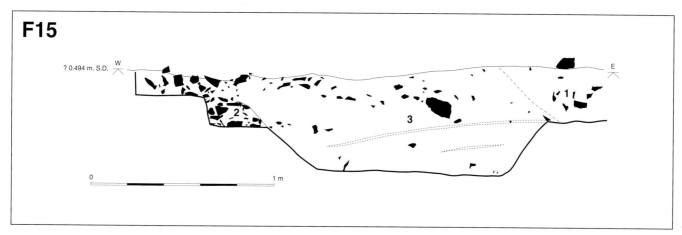

Fig. 41 West Field cutting 950/820, E–W section through Feature 15.

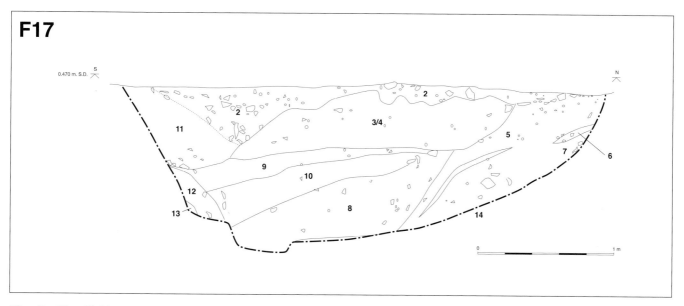

Fig. 42 West Field cutting 950/820, N–S section through Feature 17.

Finds

Flint: Axes: one, form Ind. (3). Axes (broken): one, form Ind. (2). Discoidal knives: one, form f stage II (2); one, form Ind. stage II (3). Fabricators: one, (6). Roughouts: one, (7).

Antler: Substantial fragments: one, (6).

FEATURE 18 (figs 29 and 43)

Top of feature containing chalk rubble sealing chipping debris. Excavated 1974. Location unknown. (Radiocarbon sample BM-1023 [2])

Chipping debris with large flint nodules also recorded.

Contexts

1   Dump of chalk rubble in brown sand
2   Chipping debris with large flint nodules in dark brown sand
3   Small chalk rubble in sandy matrix with small flints

Finds

Flint: Axes: two, forms 4 and Ind. (2). Scrapers: two, (1) (2). Roughouts: two, (2). Other: one borer/notched blade, (2).

FEATURE 19 (fig. 29)

Small residual area of dumped chalk rubble associated with antler and flint-working debris. Excavated 1974. (Radiocarbon sample BM-1012 [1])

61

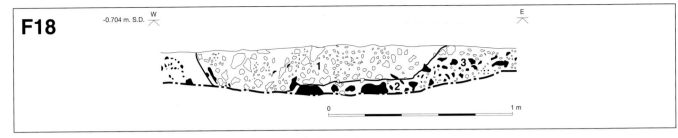

Fig. 43 West Field cutting 950/820, E–W section through Feature 18.

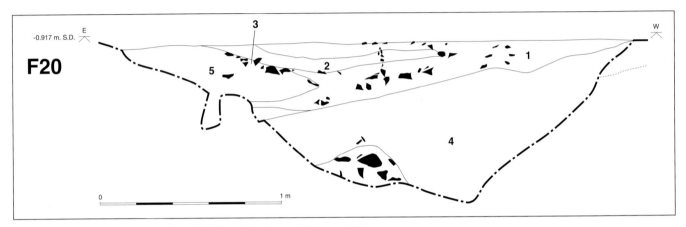

Fig. 44 West Field cutting 950/820, E–W section through Feature 20.

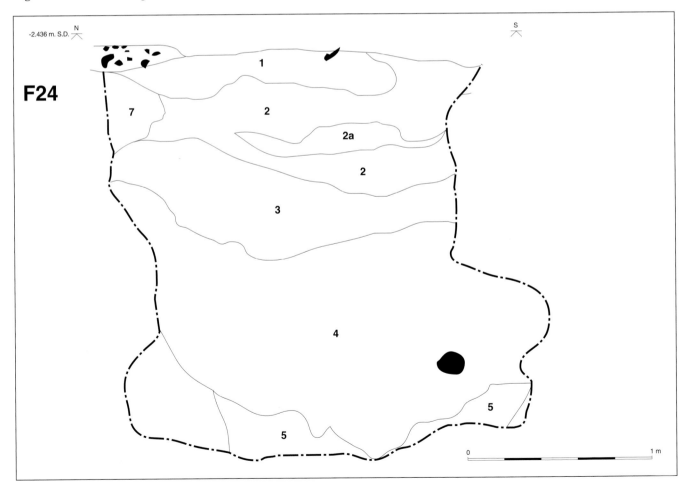

Fig. 45 West Field cutting 950/820, N–S section through Feature 24.

FEATURE 20 (figs 29 and 44)

Irregular oval pit containing burnt material, 3.0 m across and taken to a depth of 0.8 m. Excavated 1974, sectioned E–W. Probably top of a larger feature.

Upper deposits of sand overlay deposit of chalk (4), tipped in from the west.

Contexts

1 Darkish brown sand
2 Burnt sand
3 Flint
4 Chalk
5 Yellow/red sand

Finds

Flint: Rods (broken): one, (5). Oblique arrowheads: one, (2). Roughouts: two, (3) (5).
Antler: Substantial fragments: one, (2).

FEATURE 21 (fig. 29)

Flint-working debris associated with surviving spread of chalk rubble and burnt material. Excavated 1974, sectioned E–W.

No section drawing survives.

Contexts

1 Burnt soil with a little burnt sand
2 Flints including cores and flakes on chalk
3 Flint nodules in chalk and sand

Finds

Flint: Axes: two, forms Ind. (2) and 2 (3). Axes (broken): one, form 3 (2).

FEATURE 22

See Feature 14.

FEATURE 23

No information.

Remains of chalk dump associated with flint-working debris, lying between Features 10 and 47. Examined and planned in 1974 but not excavated. (Radiocarbon sample BM-1018 [1])

FEATURE 24 (figs 29 and 45)

Pit, 2.1 m across and 2.2 m deep, excavated 1974, sectioned by eastern and southern baulks of northern trench.

Filled with successive deposits of chalk with some sand. (Radiocarbon sample BM-1008 [4])

Contexts

1 Crushed chalk
2 Sand and chalk
2a Crushed chalk
3 Crushed chalk
4 Sand and chalk
5 White chalk rubble
6 Red lens in 4
7 Dark sand

Finds

Flint: Axes: one, form Ind. (4). Discoidal knives (broken): one, form b/d stage II (4); one, form Ind. stage I (5). Roughouts: two, (4). Roughouts (broken): one, (2).
Antler: Substantial fragments: two, (4) (5). Fragments: (1) (4). Fragment of ? roe deer antler: one, (3).

FEATURE 25 (figs 29 and 46)

Irregular pit sectioned N–S by eastern baulk of northern trench, 2.75 m across. Excavated 1974 to a depth of 0.75 m. Sides uncertain. Probably top of larger feature.

Filled with deposits of chalk and sand, overlying flint nodules.

Fig. 46 West Field cutting 950/820, N–S section through Feature 25.

Contexts

1 Turf
2 Top soil
3 Stony layer
4 Dark loamy soil
5 Chalk 'pellets' in loamy sand
6 More consolidated chalk 'pellets' with less loamy sand
7 Chalk
8 Sand (not seen in section)
9 Flint nodules
10 Very thin layer of chalky sand with flakes (barely seen in section)
11 Chalky with flint (planned but not lifted)

FEATURE 26
See Feature 11.

FEATURE 27 (fig. 29)
Pit excavated 1974, edges uncertain but at least 2.8 m across, sectioned N–S and by southern baulk of northern trench. NE quadrant removed. Taken to depth of 1.45 m but not bottomed.
 Filled with deposits of sand and chalk.

Contexts

1 Dark loamy sand
2 Yellow/brown sand
3 Crushed chalk
4 Yellow sand
5 Red sand and chalk
6 Chalk/sand lens
7 Red sand
8 Yellow/red sand
9 Lens of red sand
10 Yellow/red sand
11 Chalk fill
12 Lens of yellow sand

Finds

Flint: Discoidal knives (broken): one, form Ind. stage II (3).
Antler: Fragments: (8).

FEATURE 28
See Feature 11.

FEATURE 29 (fig. 29)
Irregular pit in SE corner of northern trench, excavated 1974. Sectioned E–W and taken to depth of 0.8 m.
 Filled with deposits of chalk and sand.

Contexts

1 Crushed chalk
2 Dark loamy sand
3 Red/brown sand
4 Chalk
5 Red sand
6 Chalk/sand

Finds

Flint: Scrapers: two, (2).
Antler: Fragments: (1) (2) (3).

FEATURE 30
No information.

FEATURE 31 (figs 29 and 47)
Shallow double depression with burnt material, excavated 1974. 1.9 m across and 0.35 m deep sectioned E–W, northern half removed.

Contexts

1 Darkish loamy sand and flint
2 Burnt sand with flint
3 Darkish loamy sand
4 Yellow sand (probably natural)

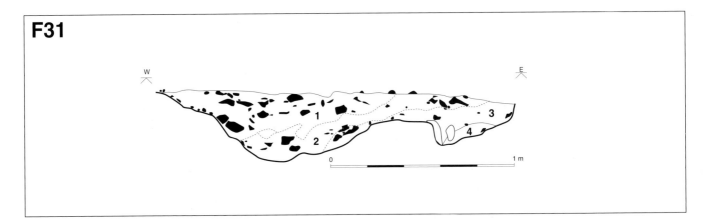

Fig. 47 West Field cutting 950/820, E–W section through Feature 31.

F32

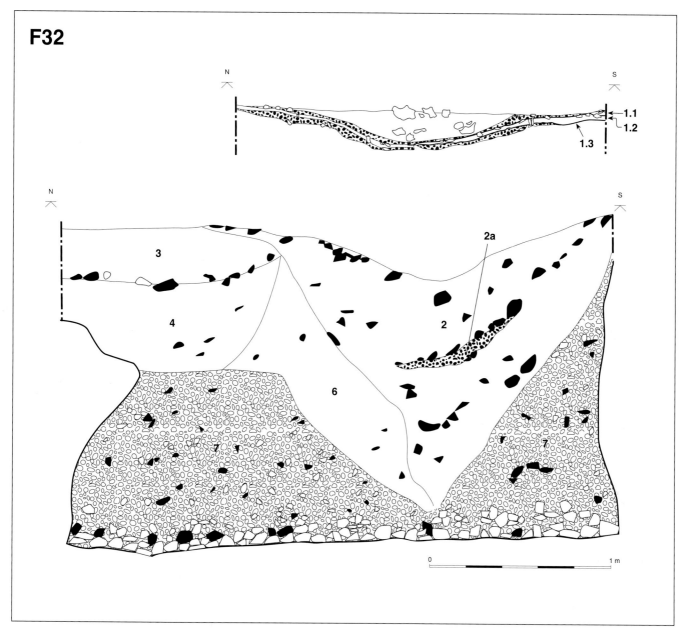

Fig. 48 West Field cutting 950/820, N–S section through Feature 32.

Finds
Antler: Fragment: (1).

FEATURE 32 (figs 29 and 48, and plate 2)
Nodule dump lying in top of large pit, excavated 1974 and 1976, sectioned N–S. Only northern and south-western sides defined. < 2.65 m across and at least 1.7 m deep. Some undercutting at base on north, west and southern sides. *Floorstone* nodules *in situ* in pillar in NW quadrant.

Pit is filled with deposits of sand and chalk tipped in from N and S above main fill of deposits of chalk rubble. (Radiocarbon sample BM-1064 [4])

Contexts
1	Nodule dump
1.1–3	Showing successive layers in dump
2	Clean brown sand with flakes
2a	Dark grey/brown sand (ash) with much chipping
3	Chalk dump
4	Orange sand and flint
5	Chalk tip
6	Loose chalk fill/cryte
7	Dense chalk rubble in cryte

Finds

Flint: Axes (broken): two, forms 1 and 6 (2). Discoidal knives: two, form Ind. stage I (2) (3). Fabricators: one, (2). Knives (other): two, (2) (2a). Scrapers: three, (2). Roughouts: one, (1). Roughouts (broken): seven, (2) (2a).

Antler: (4) (radiocarbon sample).

FEATURE 33 (fig. 29)

Round pit excavated 1974, *c*. 3.8 m across, sectioned E–W, taken to depth of 0.8 m but not bottomed. Edges difficult to define. Southern half removed. Relationship with Features 43 and 48 not established.

Filled with deposits of sand above chalk.

Contexts

1 Darkish loamy sand
2 Dark yellow sand with flint
3 Yellow sand
4 Chalk

Finds

Flint: Axes (broken): two, forms 3 and Ind. (2). Oblique arrowheads: one, (1). Roughouts (broken): two, (2).

Pottery: CV: 21, (1).

FEATURE 34 (figs 29 and 49, and plate 3)

Large irregular pit excavated 1974 and 1976, sides defined except in east where pit enters baulk, 3.5 m long, 2.4 m across, bottomed at 1.83 m. Undercutting at base. (Radiocarbon sample BM-1062 [3])

Contexts

1 Dark grey/brown sand with flakes
2 Orange/brown sand with flakes
3 Cryte
3a Dense chalk rubble and flakes in chalky sand
3b Large flint nodules and flakes in chalk rubble
4 Clean brown sand
5 Clean dark orange sand with some flint
6 Loose chalk rubble in brown sand
7 Cryte with chalk rubble and flint nodules

Finds

Stone: Hammers: one, (1).
Antler: (3) (radiocarbon sample).

FEATURE 35 (figs 29 and 50)

Shallow depression excavated 1974, sectioned NW–SE, 1.47 x 1.07 m across and taken to a depth of 0.28 m. Two levels of flaking debris extended from outside the depression. May lie in top of deeper pit.

Flaking debris lies beneath deposit of sand.

Fig. 49 West Field cutting 950/820, NE–SW section through Feature 34.

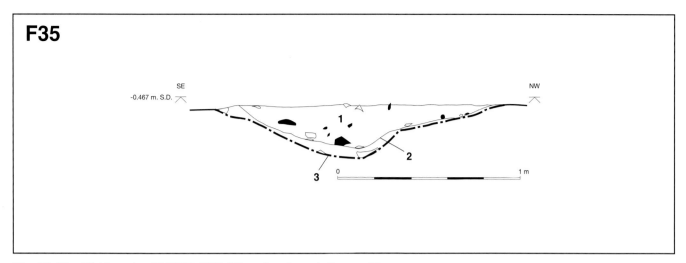

Fig. 50 West Field cutting 950/820, NW–SE section through Feature 35.

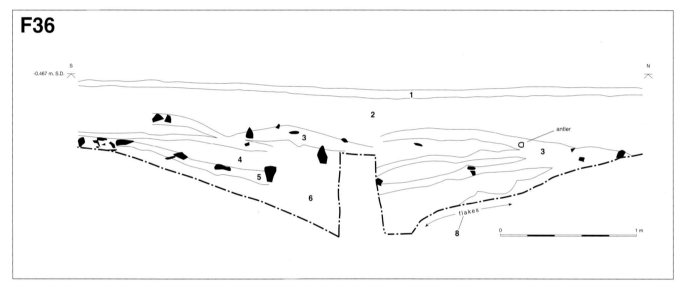

Fig. 51 West Field cutting 950/820, N–S section through Feature 36.

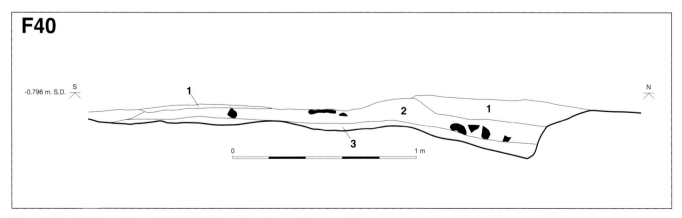

Fig. 52 West Field cutting 950/820, N–S section through Feature 40.

Contexts

1 Dark sand
2 Upper flint-working layer
3 Lower flint-working layer

FEATURE 36 (figs 29 and 51)
Circular depression excavated 1974, 4.4 m across and taken down to a depth of more than 1.0 m. Eastern half removed. Sectioned by N–S baulk and E–W by standing baulk. Deepest layer of flaking debris overlies ? fill of deeper feature. (Radiocarbon sample BM-1024 [7])
   Filled with deposits of sand.

Contexts

1 Turf
2 Topsoil
3 Gravel
4 Dark brown flinty sand
5 Flint nodules in dark brown sand and gravel
6 Dark brown mottled sand
7 Brown sand with flints
8 Flint chipping

Finds

Flint: Axes (broken): one, form Ind. (5). Discoidal knives: one, form e stage II (4). Picks: one, (4). Rods: one, (4). Roughouts: four, (4) (6) (7).
Antler: Fragments: (8).

FEATURE 37 (fig. 29)
Dump of flint-working debris in top of presumed pit excavated 1974, 2.15 x 1.45 m. Relationship with Features 41 and 46 not established.

Finds

Flint: Axes: one, form 10 (1). Axes (broken): one, form Ind. (1). Discoidal knives (broken): one, form Ind. stage I (1).
Antler: Fragments: (2).

FEATURE 38 (fig. 29)
Area of flint-working debris *in situ* excavated 1974, probably truncated by ploughing. Small area of burning noted on western edge yielded charcoal sample for dating (BM-1006).

Finds

Flint: Rods: one. Rods (broken): one. Roughouts: two. Roughouts (broken): one.

FEATURES 39 AND 49 (fig. 29)
Small oval pit filled with dark loamy sand (Feature 39) cut into top of Feature 49. Sectioned ENE–WSW, 1.6 m in diam. and 0.46 m deep. Feature 49, chalk filled top of an irregular pit, partially excavated 1974.

Contexts

FEATURE 39

1 Dark loamy sand

FEATURE 49

1 Crushed chalk
2 Sand and crushed chalk

Finds

FEATURE 49

Flint: Roughouts: one, (1).

FEATURE 40 (figs 29 and 52)
Irregular shallow scoop excavated 1974, 3.05 m across and 0.35 m deep, sectioned N–S, eastern half removed.
   Filled with deposits of chalk and sand.

Contexts

1 Greyish crushed chalk
2 Red sand
3 Chalk

No other contexts documented.

Finds

Flint: Roughouts: one, (2).
Antler: Fragment: (2).

FEATURE 41 (fig. 29)
Irregular dump of chalk rubble with some flint-working debris and fragment of antler, planned but not sectioned in 1974, adjoining Features 37 and 46.

FEATURE 42
See Feature 11.

FEATURE 43 (figs 29 and 53)
Small pit excavated 1974, sectioned E–W, 1.6 m across but not bottomed. Relationship to Feature 48 not established.
   Filled with deposits of sand.

Contexts

1 Flaking floor in darkish loamy sand
2 Darkish loamy sand with larger flints
3 Dark sand with burnt flints
4 Dark yellow sand
5 Sand (almost black) with burnt flints

Finds

Flint: Discoidal knives: one, form e stage II (2). Points (broken): one (? roughout), (2).

FEATURE 44 (fig. 29)
Flint nodules in patch of dark silt, excavated 1974. Part of fill of Feature 26 or cut into that feature.

F43

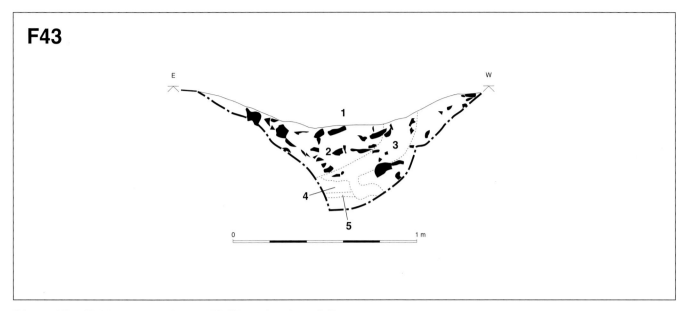

Fig. 53 West Field cutting 950/820, NW–SE section through Feature 43.

F50

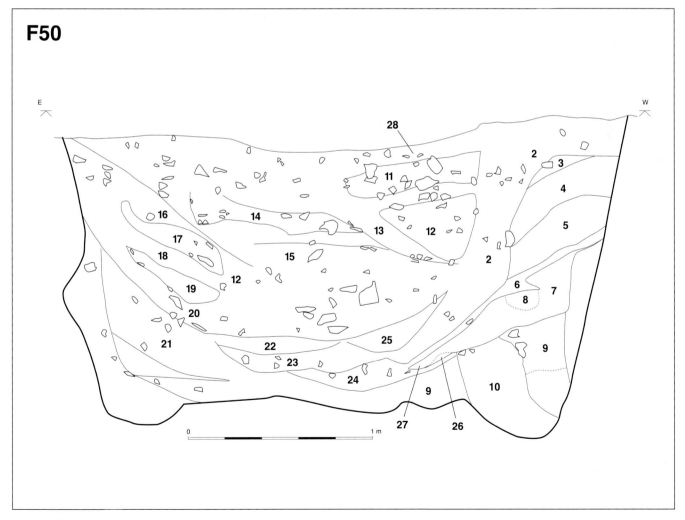

Fig. 54 West Field cutting 950/820, E–W section through Feature 50.

Contexts
1 Dark loamy sand with flint nodules and flakes
2 Yellow sand with flints

FEATURE 45
See Feature 6.

FEATURE 46 (fig. 29)
Small area of flint-working debris lying in dark sand to NW of Feature 41, lifted in 1974 but not further explored.

FEATURE 47
No information.

FEATURE 48 (fig. 29)
Sand-filled pit excavated in 1974, sectioned E–W, excavated to a depth of 0.5 m but not bottomed. Relationship with Features 33 and 43 not established.

Contexts
1 Yellow sand with flints

FEATURE 49
See Feature 39.

FEATURE 50 (figs 29 and 54)
Pit extending NE of Feature 3 but relationship not established. Only partially excavated 1974, 3.05 m across and 1.7 m deep. Base irregular.

Filled with deposits of sand and rotten chalk; some antler fragments recovered from superficial level.

Contexts
1 Dark sandy gravel
2 Pink sand
3 Pink sand with gravel
4 Dense gravel
5 Dense gravel with iron staining (manganese?)
6 Yellow sand with gravel
7 Yellow sand
8 Compacted rotten chalk
9 Compacted rotten chalk
10 Light yellow sand
11 Rotten sandy chalk
12 Light chalky sand
13 Yellow sand
14 Red/yellow sandy gravel
15 Red/yellow gravelly sand
16 Yellow sand
17 Slightly compacted rotten sandy chalk
18 Yellow gravelly sand
19 Fairly compacted rotten sandy chalk
20 Red/yellow gravelly sand
21 Fairly compacted rotten sandy chalk
22 Yellow sand
23 Dark red sand

24 Red gravel
25 Yellow sandy rotten chalk
26 Compacted rotten chalk
27 Yellow sandy gravel
28 Yellow gravelly sand

FEATURE 51
See Feature 14.

FEATURE 52
See Feature 14.

FEATURE 53 (fig. 29)
Group of nodules and flakes SW of Feature 34.

Cutting 940/940 (figs 2 and 55)

FEATURE 101 (figs 55 and 56)
Circular pit 3.7 x 3.0 m and 1.28 m deep, sectioned E–W, N–S and NE–SW, excavated 1975 and 1976. Chipping debris in top probably redeposited. Some undercutting at base. Later than Feature 124 and probably later than Feature 125.

Filled with successive deposits of sand, cryte and chalk rubble.

Contexts
1 Ploughsoil
2 Loose chalky fill with sand
3 Flint chipping floor
4 Brown sand
5 Chalk rubble and flint nodules with sand
6 Pale brown cryte with small chalk rubble
7 Sand with minor rubble
8 Very small chalk rubble
9 Pale brown sand
10 Pale brown sandy cryte
11 Clean orange sand
12 Brown sand and small rubble
13 Clean brown sand
14
15 Brown sand with small rubble
16 Very pale brown cryte and a little rubble
17 Thin band of small chalk rubble
18 Brown sand
19 Brown sand
20 Sandy cryte with small chalk rubble
21 Brown/orange sand
22 Brown sand with a little rubble
23 Brown sand
24 Pale brown cryte
25 Brown sand
26 Sand with small flint flakes
27 Pale yellow cryte and small chalk rubble
28 Orange/brown sand

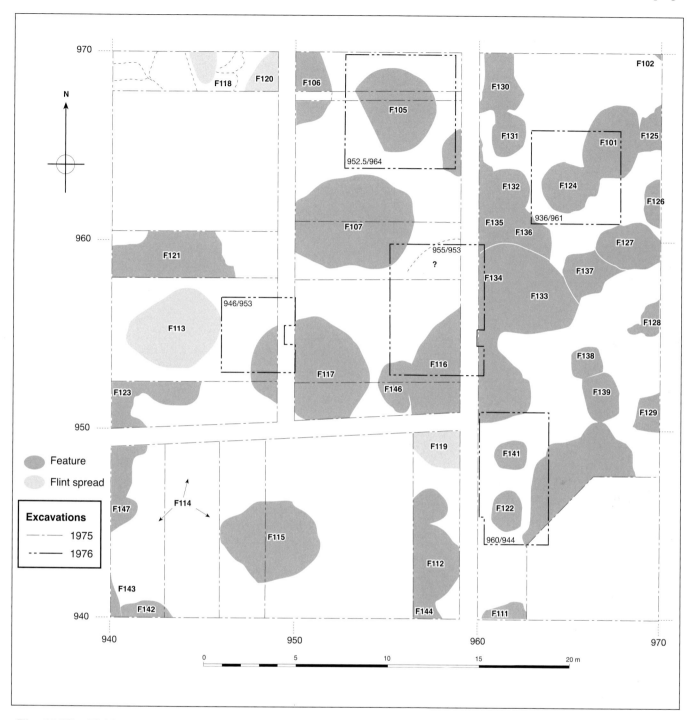

Fig. 55 West Field cutting 940/940 with individual features marked.

29 Pale yellow cryte fading into sand at basal end

30 Chalk rubble in cryte

31 Chalk rubble and flint

32 Brown earth

Finds

Flint: Knives (other): two, (3). Scrapers: one, (3). Borers: two, (3). Roughouts: five, (3) (6). Gunflints: 4, (3).

FEATURE 102 (fig. 55)

Excavated 1975. SW corner of ill-defined pit extending beneath baulk in NE corner of the trench.

FEATURES 103, 104 AND 110 (fig. 57)

Complex of pit tops excavated 1975 and 1976, sectioned E–W and NE–SW, 104 and 110 being ill defined. Contextual information was drawn from finds bags.

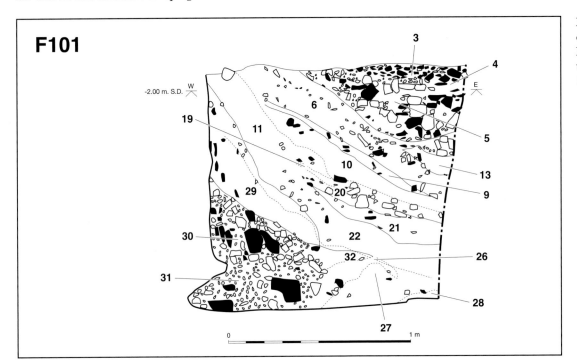

Fig. 56 West Field cutting 940/940, E–W section through Feature 101.

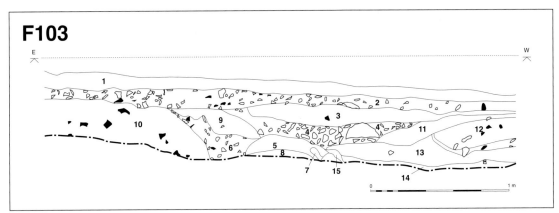

Fig. 57 West Field cutting 940/940, E–W section through Feature 103.

Contexts

FEATURE 103
1 Ploughsoil
2 Chalky fill with dark sand
3 Medium dark sandy soil
4 Medium to small chalk rubble in cryte
5 Clean sandy cryte
6 Cryte with chalk rubble
7 Lens of grey sand with small chalk rubble
8 Clean dark orange/brown sand
9 Clean grey sand with small chalk rubble
10 Clean orange/brown sand
11 Dark sand with chalk rubble
12 Orange sand with chalk rubble and flints
13 Clean orange/brown sand
14 Chalk rubble in grey sand
15 Small chalk rubble in cryte

Finds

FEATURE 104
Flint: Axes: one, form 4 (3). Roughouts: six, (4) (5) (7) (12).

FEATURE 105 (figs 55 and 58–60)
Two-level mine excavated 1975 and 1976. Northern half removed, sectioned E–W, 4.55 m across top and 4.7 m deep. Sherds of Bronze Age pottery including Collared Vessel from the topmost layer. At upper mining level 4 Galleries I, II, V and VI. At lower level, Galleries III and IV together with beginnings of third. *Floorstone* found *in situ* at this lower level. (Radiocarbon samples BM-1061 [39] and 3134 [39])

Contexts
1 Dark sand with chalk lumps and scattered flint
2 Chipping floor in pea chalk, probably *in situ*, covering oval area 2.2 x 1.8 m

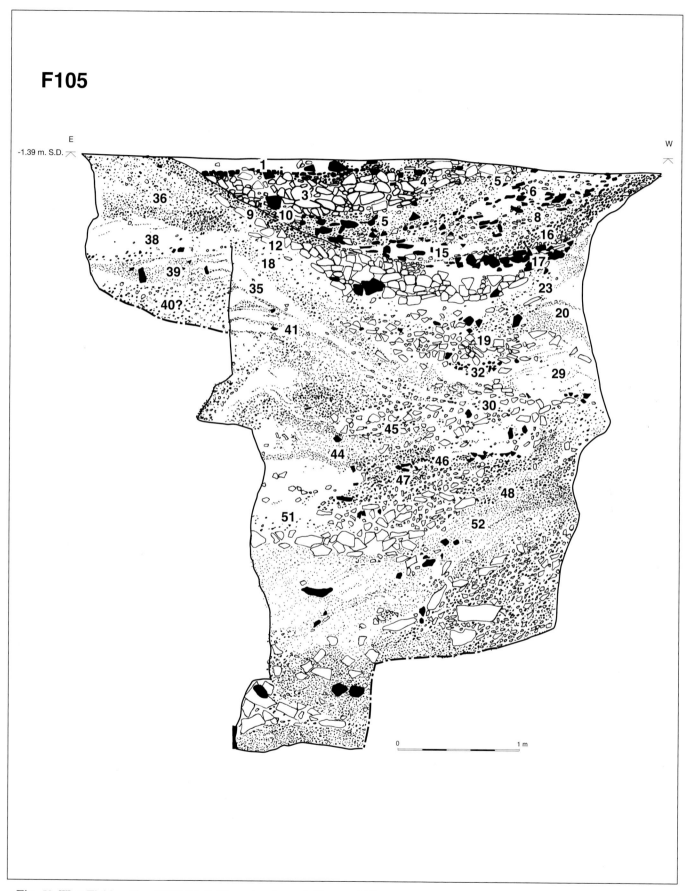

Fig. 58 West Field cutting 940/940, E–W section through Feature 105.

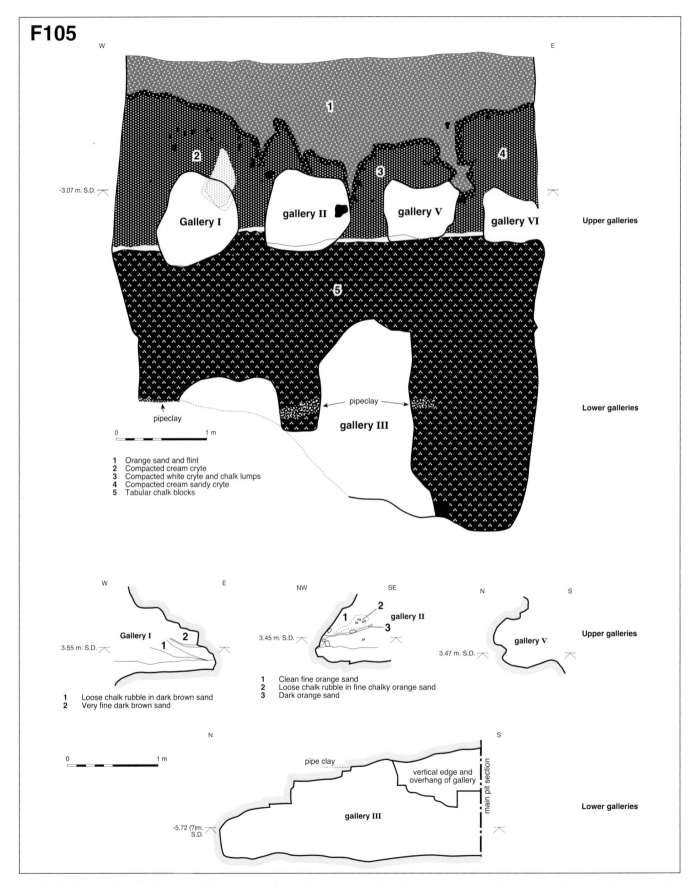

F105

W   E

1

2

-3.07 m. S.D.

4

Gallery I   gallery II   3   gallery V   gallery VI   **Upper galleries**

5

pipeclay   pipeclay   **Lower galleries**

pipeclay

gallery III

0   1 m

1   Orange sand and flint
2   Compacted cream cryte
3   Compacted white cryte and chalk lumps
4   Compacted cream sandy cryte
5   Tabular chalk blocks

W   E   NW   SE   N   S

Gallery I   2   2   **Upper galleries**

3.55 m. S.D.   1   3.45 m. S.D.   1   gallery II   3   gallery V

3.47 m. S.D.

1   Loose chalk rubble in dark brown sand   1   Clean fine orange sand
2   Very fine dark brown sand   2   Loose chalk rubble in fine chalky orange sand
                                3   Dark orange sand

N   S

0   1 m

pipe clay   vertical edge and
                      overhang of gallery   **Lower galleries**

gallery III   main pit section

-5.72 (?)m.
S.D.

Fig. 59 West Field cutting 940/940, E–W section through Feature 105 showing position of galleries on two levels with profiles of Galleries I, II, III and V.

F105 (plan)

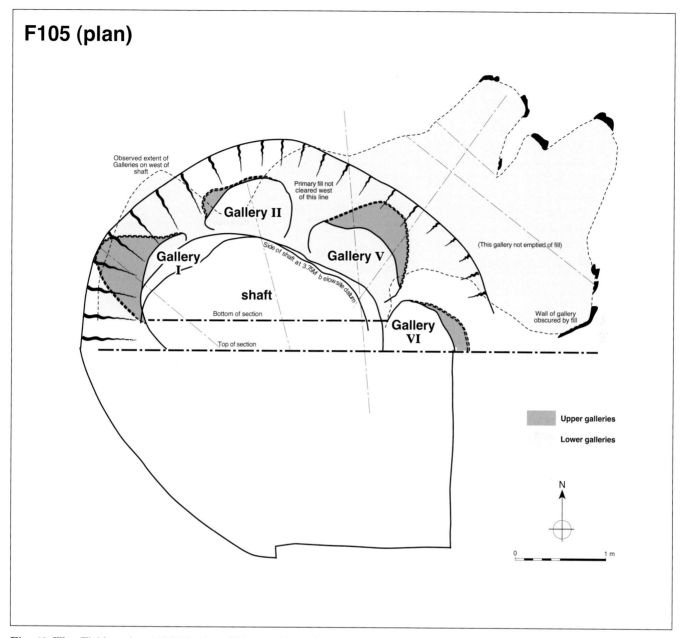

Fig. 60 West Field cutting 940/940, plan of Feature 105 with upper and lower galleries marked.

3 Large chalk rubble in dark sandy matrix
4 Large chalk rubble in chalky grey matrix
5 Cream cryte, sandy with small chalk lumps
6 Dark grey/brown sand with chalk lumps and scattered flints
7 Orange/brown tip lines with a few chalk lumps
8 Dark grey/brown sand with small chalk lumps and scarce flint
9 Small chalk lumps in white chalky matrix and scattered flints
10 Flint-flaking debris
11 Small and medium chalk rubble in dark brown sandy soil with some flaking debris forming small heap on SW edge of pit

12 Heavy chalk rubble in fine light brown chalky sand with large flint nodules
13 Cream cryte tip in SW corner with scattered flint
14 Creamy cryte tip in SW corner
15 Small tip of compacted cream cryte with chalk lumps, flint lumps and flakes on west edge of southern side
16 Small tip of broken weathered chalk from the west in white chalky matrix
17 Tip of flint nodules, flakes and roughouts in matrix similar to 16 and 12. Probably contemporary with floor to NW and therefore later than the pit
18 Small chalk lumps in sandy cryte with scarce flint
19 Medium chalk rubble in matrix of orange sand with

chalk flecks with large flint nodules at base – a tip
extending round east edge of the pit

20 Series of tip lines alternating dark brown sand and
fairly compacted cream sandy cryte

21 Medium brown sand with chalk lumps and
scattered flint

22 Fairly loose chalk rubble in light chalky sand and
scarce flint including flakes

23 Fairly loose sandy cream cryte with small chalk
lumps with some flint-knapping debris

24 Orange-orange/red sand with chalk lumps and
scattered flint including flaking debris

25 Reddish brown sand with chalk lumps with large
amounts of flint including knapping debris

26 Small chalk lumps in light chalky sand with
scattered flints

27 -

28 Dark brown sand with scarce flint and small chalk
lumps

29 Very compact cream sandy cryte with small chalk
lumps

30 Chalk rubble in light chalky matrix, scarce flint with
some knapping debris

31 Small chalk rubble in light chalky sand, some flint
including flakes

32 Flint chipping floor in fine brown chalky sand

33 Clean orange sand with natural flint

34 Fairly compact cream sandy cryte with little chalk
and scarce flint

35 Fine chalky sand with chalk lumps

36 Fairly compact chalky cryte with chalk lumps,
scattered flint including knapping debris

37 Fairly compact chalky cryte with larger lumps of
chalk

38 Fairly compact cream sandy cryte with small chalk
flecks and a few scattered flints

39 Fine dark brown sand with cryte flecks with a few
scattered lumps of chalk and flint

40 Fairly compact chalky cryte with chalk lumps

41 Alternate bands of dark brown sand and orange
sand with scattered chalk lumps

42 Clean orange sand

43 Loose dirty chalk rubble and mixed sands

44 Series of orange sand and chalk tips

45 Large chalk rubble in loose white chalky sand

46 Chipping floor in fine loose dark brown sand with
fine chalk particles possibly *in situ*

47 Very loose chalk rubble

48 Fine clean dark brown sand with flint-flaking debris

49 Very clean loose white chalk rubble

50 Tips of chalk rubble and scattered flints

51 Tip of fairly compact cream sandy cryte with chalk
lumps

52 Fine clean dark brown sand

Finds

Flint: Axes: four, forms 3 (6) (8) (14) and Ind. (9).
Axes (broken): two, forms 2 (53) and Ind.
(46). Picks: four, (15) (19) (25). Discoidal
knives: one, form b stage III (6); one, form Ind.
stage II (44). Fabricators: one, (36). Points:
one, (6). Knives (other): one, (4). Scrapers:
nine, (2) (3) (6) (17). Plane scrapers: one, (8).
Worked blades/flakes: ten, (2) (8). Roughouts:
thirty-three, (2) (6) (8) (9) (10) (12) (15) (16)
(17) (25). Roughouts (broken): four, (6) (8)
(18) (30). Gunflints: thirty, (2).

Stone: Hammers: eight, (3) (8) (10) (47) (52) (55).
Hammers (broken): three, (19) (34) (55).
Rubbing stones: two, (2) (53).

Pottery: CV: nine (1).

Fired clay: Fragments: six, (6).

Antler: Picks (broken): two, (39) (44). Fragments: (4)
(5) (9) (14) (39).

Bone: Picks: three, (Gallery 3). Pick fragments: two,
(Gallery 3). Fragments: three, (Gallery 3);
one, (48).

FEATURES 106 AND 120 (figs 55 and 61)
Probably three segments of same circular pit either side
of standing N–S, E–W baulks, excavated 1975 and 1976.
Taken down to a depth of 0.73 m but not bottomed.
Heavy chipping debris in upper level (2), and hearth
material in lower (layer 8) chipping horizon.

Filled with deposits of sand, chalk and cryte. Feature
120 consists of flint chipping debris, probably equivalent
to upper level (2) in Feature 106. (Radiocarbon sample
BM-1030 [8])

Contexts

1 Dark brown sand with small chalk rubble
2 Upper chipping unit in chalky sand
3 Grey chalk
4
5 Yellow cryte
6 Chalk rubble in dark brown sand
7 Chalk rubble in chalky grey sand
8 Lower chipping unit in grey sand
9 Orange sand
10 Yellow/brown sand
11 Chalk rubble
12 Chalk and flint rubble in yellow sand
13 Dark sandy soil with small chalk flecks
14 Grey chalky cryte
15 Chalk rubble in yellow sandy cryte

Finds

FEATURE 106
Flint: Discoidal knives: one, form Ind. stage I (1). Knives,
other: three, (2). Scrapers: two, (2). Worked

F106

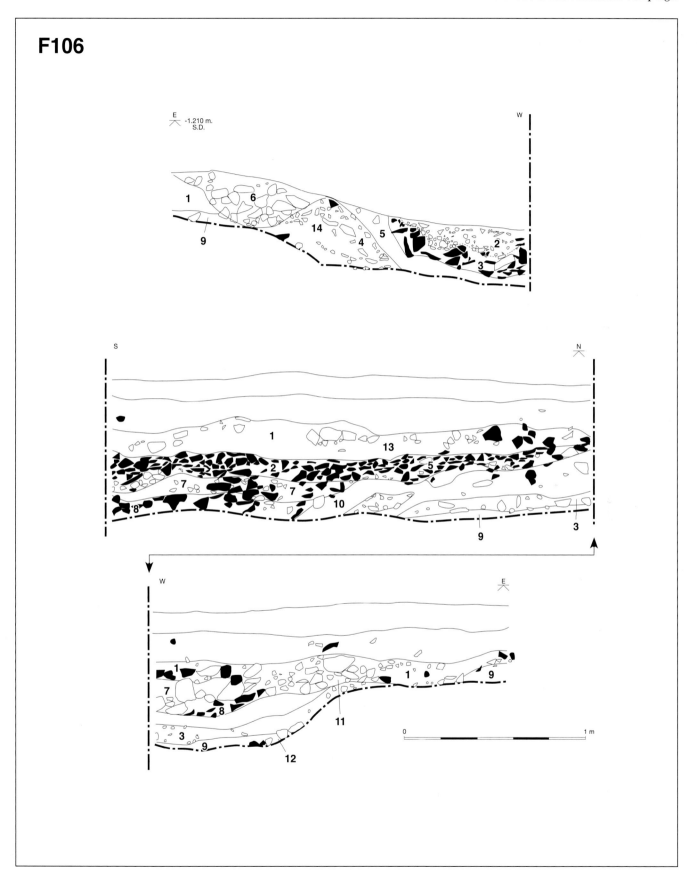

Fig. 61 West Field cutting 940/940, NE–NW, NW–SW and NE–SW sections through Feature 106. Original field drawings contained errors of orientation.

flakes/blades: two, (2). Notched pieces: one, (2). Roughouts: one, (2). Gunflints: thirteen, (1) (2).
Stone: Balls: one, (2).
Bone: Fragments: (2).

FEATURE 120
Flint: Worked flakes/blades: two. Roughouts: one. Gunflints: four.

FEATURE 107 (figs 55 and 62)
Large oval pit, sectioned E–W, excavated 1975 and 1976, 6 m across, the long access taken down to a depth of more than 0.56 m but not bottomed.
  Filled with sand and chalk rubble.

Contexts
  1   Dark brown sand with flint and chalk
  2   Flint nodules and small chalk rubble in dark chalky sand
  3   Chalky sand with small chalk rubble
  4   Cream sandy chalk
  5   Flint nodules and large chalk rubble in sandy chalk
  6   Clean chalky sand
  7   Cream sandy chalk with chalk rubble
  8   Flakes and small chalk rubble in clean chalky sand
  9   Chalk
  10 Chipping debris. Large cores and flakes on base of pit
  11 Small chalk rubble in white chalky fill

Finds
Flint: Roughouts: one, (3). Gunflints: two, (3).
Pottery: Three sherds, possibly Iron Age, (1) (2).

FEATURE 108 (fig. 63)
Occupation material (1) in shallow oval depression, 2.72 m across, excavated 1975 and 1976, sectioned E–W. (Radiocarbon sample BM-1031 [1])

Contexts
  1   Very dark sand with small chalk rubble, merges with:
  2   Dark sand mottled orange with small chalk rubble
  3   Orange sand

Finds
Flint: Axes (broken): two, forms 1 and 3 (1). Picks (broken): one, (1). Rods (broken): one, (1). Fabricators: one, (1). Scrapers: one, (1). Worked flakes/blades: one, (3). Roughouts: three, (1). Hammers: one, (1).
Stone: Hammers: two, (1).
Pottery: GW: two, (1). EBA: two hundred and forty sherds including at least fifty-seven CV; one thumb pot; one ? Beaker sherd, (1).
Fired clay: One ball; one disc fragment; one unclassified; one fragment, (1).

Antler: Fragments: (1).
Bone: Fragments: (1). Mandible fragments, (1).

FEATURE 109
Same as Feature 117.

FEATURE 110
See Features 103 and 104.

FEATURE 111 (fig. 55)
Pit partially excavated 1975 and 1976, sectioned E–W by baulk, northern segment removed.

Contexts
  1   Dark sand
  2   N edge of area of flint chipping
  3   Chalk rubble with flints in dark sand
  4   Dark sand
  5   Dark sand with small chalk pebbles and scattered flints

FEATURE 112 (figs 55 and 75–6)
Chipping floor in (2) truncated by ploughing in top of pit, excavated 1975 and 1976. Sherds of Collared Vessel and of other Early Bronze Age pottery, lifted as two, with further Collared Vessel sherds from (3). Sectioned N–S. (Radiocarbon sample BM-1032 [3])

Contexts
  1   Dark sandy ploughsoil
  2   Dense chipping unit in top of pits F112 and F145, in dark sand with scattered lumps of chalk
  3   Dark sand mottled with dark orange sand with scattered chalk lumps and some flint, charcoal, pottery
  4   Dark sand mottled with orange sand, with scattered flint and chalk lumps
  5   Chalk rubble in dark sandy matrix
  6   Dark sand with chalk lumps and a few scattered lumps of flint

Finds
Flint: Axes: three, form Ind. (2). Discoidal knives: five, form Ind. Stage I (2). Plane scrapers: one, (2). Gunflints: three, (2). Roughouts: one, (2).
Pottery: CV: seven, (2); seven, (3). EBA (unspecified): three, (2).
Antler: Fragment: (-).

FEATURE 113 (fig. 55)
Area of flint-knapping debris, excavated in 1975 and 1976. Probably top of deeper feature.

Contexts
  1   Dark sand with chipping and flint lumps (contains flint units I, II and III)

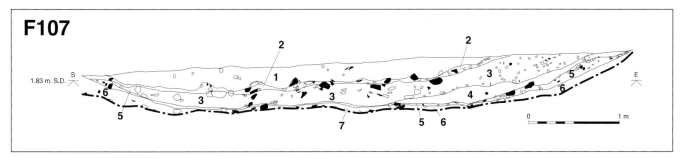

Fig. 62 West Field cutting 940/940, E–W section through Feature 107.

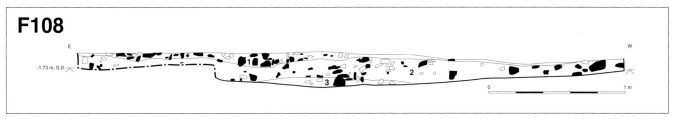

Fig. 63 West Field cutting 940/940, E–W section through Feature 108.

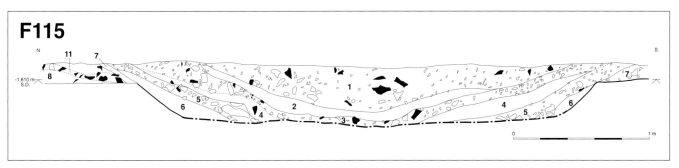

Fig. 64 West Field cutting 940/940, N–S section through Feature 115.

2 Tabular chalk rubble in dark sand with flint debris
3 Dark sand with flaking and small chalk rubble
4 Dark orange sand with knapping waste and bone

Finds
Flint: Discoidal knives (broken): one, form d stage II
(4). Scrapers (broken): two, (4). Borers: one, (4).
Roughouts: three, (1) (1.III) (3). Roughouts,
broken: one, (1). Hammers: two, (1).
Stone: Hammers: two, (1) (1.II).

FEATURE 114 (fig. 55)
Area of flint-knapping debris (units I–III) lay above area
of chalk rubble (2) overlying layer 3 including charcoal
and Bronze Age pottery in hollow.

Contexts
1 Flint-knapping debris
2 Large chalk rubble in dark sand with scattered flint
and flakes
3 Clean orange/brown sand with scattered flints and
chalk rubble

Finds
Flint: Axes: one, form 3 (3). Axes (broken): one, form 1
(1.II). Discoidal knives: one, form f stage II (2.II).
Fabricators: one, (1.I). Points: one, (1.II). Knives,
other: one, (1.I). Scrapers: three, (1.II). Borers:
three, (1.I) (1.II). Borers (broken): one, (1.I).
Gunflints: four, (1.II). Roughouts: eleven, (1)
(1.I) (1.II). Roughouts (broken): six, (1.I) (1.II).
Hammers: one, (1.III).
Stone: Hammers: one, (2).
Pottery: CV: eight (3).
Bone: Substantial fragments: one, (-) (long bone).

FEATURE 115 (figs 55 and 64)
Top of oval pit, sectioned N–S, excavated 1975 and 1976,
4.04 m across. Topmost layers only removed.
Filled with deposits of sand and chalk rubble.

Contexts
1 Dark sand with chalk and flint
2 Clean dark sand
3 Dark sand with chalk rubble and flint

4 Clean dark sand
5 Dark sand with chalk rubble
6 Clean dark sand
7 Small chalk rubble in dark sand
8 Clean dark sand
9 Chalk rubble in sandy cryte matrix. Some flakes
10 Undulating cryoturbated surface (probably natural)
11 Tip of large flint nodules in dark sand

Finds
Flint: Gunflints: one, (5).

FEATURE 116 (fig. 55)
Large oval pit excavated 1975 and 1976, sectioned N–S, E–W, upper layers only removed. Cuts Feature 146. Relationship with Features 134 and 140 uncertain.
Filled mainly with sand.

Contexts
1 Dark brown sand with chalk rubble and flint
2 Grey sand with small chalk rubble and flint
3 Fawn/light brown sand
4 As 3 but with chalk flecks
5 Clean medium brown sand
6 Gritty medium brown sand
7 Small chalk rubble
8 Clean medium brown sand
9 Clean orange/brown sand, ? natural
10 Light chalky sand with chalk flecks

FEATURE 117 (fig. 55)
Large circular pit, sectioned N–S, E–W, excavated 1975 and 1976, 0.8 m deep, part of southern quadrant removed. Dense chipping debris on floor and up the eastern side.
Filled mainly with sand above large deposit of knapping debris.

Contexts
26 Dark brown mottled light sand with small chalk lumps and flakes
27 Grey sand with small chalk rubble
28 Dark brown sand with chalk flecks and scattered flints
29 Dark brown sand mottled with black (? ashy) with small chalk rubble
30 Medium/dark brown sand with scattered chalk rubble and scattered flint
31 Flint-knapping debris in dark brown/grey sand
32 Medium/dark sand with chalky flecks
33 Small chalk rubble in grey chalky matrix
34 Grey sand with small chalk flecks
35 Light grey sand with chalk rubble
36 Clean orange/brown sand (presumed natural)

Finds
Flint: Discoidal knives: one, form Ind. stage I (26).

Scrapers: one, (31). Borers: one, (26). Worked flakes/blades: five, (31). Other: one round scraper or discoidal knife, (26). Gunflints: one, (31).

FEATURE 118 (fig. 55 and plate 4)
Area of flint-knapping debris.

Finds
Flint: Discoidal knives: one, form Ind. stage I. Knives, other: one. Worked flakes/blades: one.

FEATURE 119 (fig. 55)
Area of flint-knapping debris.

Finds
Flint: Roughouts: one.

FEATURE 120
See Feature 106.

Area of flint-knapping debris in pit.

Finds
Flint: Worked flakes/blades: two. Roughouts: one. Gunflints: four.

FEATURE 121 (fig. 55)
Top of pit excavated 1975 and 1976, sectioned E–W, excavated down to a depth of 0.84 m. (Radiocarbon sample BM-1033 [2])

Finds
Flint: Roughouts: one. Gunflints: one. Both from superficial deposits.

FEATURE 122 (figs 55 and 65)
Dump of chalk rubble, excavated 1975 and 1976, 2 m in diam. in top of deeper feature, taken down to a depth of 1.8 m. Sides uncertain and not bottomed.
Filled with deposits mainly of chalk rubble and cryte with some sand.

Contexts
1 Chalk rubble with sandy chalk fill
2 Orange sand with brown/orange sand and small chalk rubble tip lines
3 Chalk dust and small rubble/pale brown cryte
4 Chalk rubble and cryte
5 Cryte and chalk rubble
6 Brown sand with a little cryte
7 Brown cryte with sand and chalk ? tips
8 Pale brown cryte with chalk rubble
9 Chalk rubble with brown sand
10 White cryte
11 Chalk rubble with pale brown sand
12 Brown cryte/sand with chalk rubble

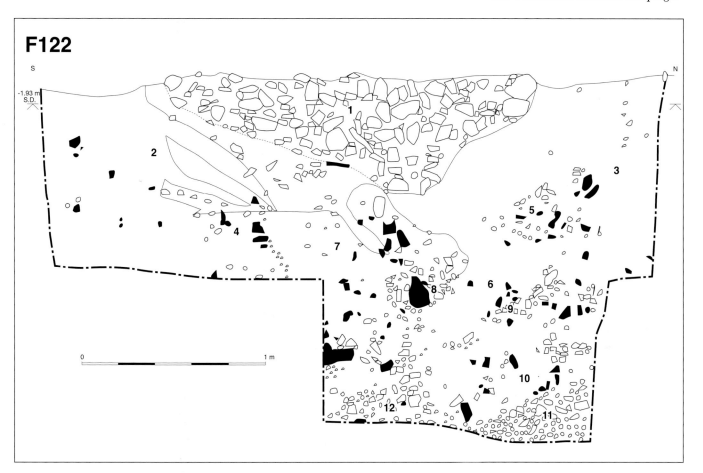

Fig. 65 West Field cutting 940/940, N–S section through Feature 122.

FEATURE 123 (fig. 55)
Top of feature recorded 1975 and 1976 but not excavated.

FEATURE 124 (fig. 55)
Circular pit excavated 1975 and 1976, sectioned NE–SW, 2.64 x 2.56 m, not bottomed but taken down to a depth of 1.08 m. Earlier than Feature 101. (Radiocarbon samples BM-1034 [2]; 3155 [2])

Filled with deposits of sand, chalk rubble and cryte.

Contexts
1 Fine grey sand with chalk
2 Black charcoal area with ash
3 Ashy grey sand and burnt chalk
4 Dark grey/brown sand with chalk rubble
4a Brown sandy earth with small chalk rubble
5 Chalk rubble and sand
6a Brown cryte with small chalk rubble
6b Small chalk rubble
6c Pale brown cryte
8 Brown sand with flint nodules
10 Sand and cryte
11 Brown sand/cryte
14 Very pale cryte

15 Dark brown sand
16 Pale brown/grey cryte

FEATURE 125 (fig. 55)
Pit excavated 1975, sectioned N–S, edges not defined and not bottomed. Earlier than Feature 101. Filled with deposits mainly of sand, some chalk rubble.

Contexts
1 Dark humic ploughsoil
2 Dark sandy soil with small chalk rubble and flint
3 Clean orange/brown sand
4 Natural cryte
5 Dark sandy soil with chalk and flint
6 Yellow/orange sand
7 Tip of chalk and flint
8 Dark yellowish sand
9 Grey/brown sand with chalk and flint
10 Grey sand
11 Yellow sand
12 Chalk rubble
13 Chalk rubble and flint
17 Grey/brown sand with chalk and flint
18 Orange sand with flint
19 Black-stained orange sand

FEATURE 126 (fig. 55)

Top of deeper feature excavated 1975 and 1976, sectioned N–S by baulk. Sides and bottom not defined. Filled with deposits of sand above chalk rubble and cryte.

Contexts

  1 Dark humic ploughsoil
  5 Dark sandy soil with chalk and flint
 24 Fawn sand with chalk and flint
 25 Chalk rubble and flint in sandy matrix
 26 Chalk rubble in compacted sandy chalk matrix
 27 Redeposited cryte with chalk rubble
 28 Small chalk rubble in compacted sandy chalk matrix

FEATURE 127 (fig. 55)

Top of deeper feature excavated 1975 and 1976, sectioned N–S by baulk. Sides and bottom not defined. Filled with deposits mainly of sand above chalk rubble.

Contexts

  1 Dark humic ploughsoil
  5 Dark sandy soil with chalk and flint
 20 Dark sand
 21 Chalk rubble in dark sand
 22 Fawn sand with chalk and flint
 23 Fawn sand with scattered chalk and flint
 25 Chalk rubble and flint in sandy matrix

FEATURE 128 (fig. 55)

Top of deeper feature excavated 1975, sectioned N–S by baulk. Sides and bottom not defined. Filled with deposits of sand and chalk rubble.

Contexts

  1 Dark humic ploughsoil
  5 Dark sandy soil with chalk and flint
 31 Medium dark brown sand with chalk and flint
 32 Chalk rubble in grey sandy matrix
 33 Small chalk rubble in grey sand
 34 Chalk and flint in light grey sand
 35 Chalk and flint in dark brown to dark grey sand
 36 Light fawn sand with chalk and flint

FEATURE 129 (fig. 55)

Top of deeper feature excavated 1975 and 1976, sectioned N–S by baulk. Sides and bottom not defined. Filled with deposits of sand and chalk rubble.

Contexts

  1 Dark humic ploughsoil
 40 Dark brown sand with chalk and flint
 41 Chalk rubble in loose dark sand
 42 Lens of light fawn sand and chalk
 43 Chalk rubble

FEATURE 130 (fig. 55)

Top of deeper feature excavated 1975 and 1976, sectioned N–S, E–W by baulks. Sides and bottom not defined. A deposit of flint chipping debris lay over deposits of chalk rubble and cryte.

Contexts

  1 Dark humic topsoil
  2 Loose chalky fill with sand
  3 Chipping debris
  4 Small chalk rubble
  5 Cryte
  6 Chalk rubble
  7 Orange/brown sand
  8 Orange/brown sand (probably natural)
  9 Dark sandy soil with small chalk rubble and flints

FEATURE 131 (fig. 55)

Top of deeper feature recorded 1975 and 1976. Appears to cut Feature 130.

FEATURE 132 (fig. 55)

Top of deeper feature recorded 1975 and 1976. Appears to cut through top of Feature 136.

FEATURE 133 (fig. 55)

Top of deeper feature recorded 1975 and 1976. Appears to cut through top of Feature 134.

FEATURE 134 (fig. 55)

Top of deeper feature recorded 1975 and 1976, sectioned N–S by baulk. Appears to be earlier than Feature 133.

FEATURE 135 (fig. 55)

Top of deeper feature, recorded 1975 and 1976, sectioned N–S by baulk. Appears to be cut by Features 134 and 132.

FEATURE 136 (fig. 55)

Top of deeper feature, recorded 1975 and 1976, sectioned N–S by baulk. Appears to be cut by Features 132 and 134.

FEATURE 137 (fig. 55)

Top of deeper feature, recorded 1975 and 1976, sectioned N–S by baulk. Appears to be cut by Features 127 and 133.

FEATURE 138 (fig. 55)

Top of deeper feature, recorded 1975 and 1976, relationship to Feature 139 uncertain.

FEATURE 139 (fig. 55)

Top of deeper feature, recorded 1975 and 1976, relationship to Feature 138 uncertain.

FEATURE 140 (fig. 55)

Top of deeper feature, recorded 1975 and 1976, sectioned N–S by baulk.

FEATURE 141 (fig. 55)

Irregular oval pit, excavated 1975 and 1976, 1.62 m across and 2.55 m long, multiple sections, bottomed at more than 1.9 m. Some *floorstone in situ* at base, with some evidence of niching.

FEATURE 142 (fig. 55)

Top of feature, recorded 1975 and 1976, sectioned E–W by baulk.

FEATURE 143 (fig. 55)

Top of feature, recorded 1975 and 1976, sectioned N–S by baulk.

FEATURE 144 (fig. 55)

Top of feature recorded in 1975 and 1976, sectioned N–S. May have been cut by Feature 112.

FEATURE 145

Adjoining Feature 122 but no other data.

FEATURE 146 (fig. 55)

Top of deeper feature excavated 1975 and 1976, sectioned E–W. Appears to have been cut by Feature 116.

Contexts

11 Chalk rubble
12 Chalk rubble in white chalky matrix
13 Chalk rubble in medium brown sand
14 Small chalk rubble in white chalky matrix
15 Small chalk rubble in light orange sand
16 Chalk rubble in dark sand
17 Clean orange/brown sand (natural slip)
18 Clean orange/brown sand

FEATURE 147 (fig. 55)

Top of feature recorded 1975 and 1976, sectioned N–S by baulk. Filled with deposits of chalk rubble.

Finds from the West Field not attributed to features

Finds were also retrieved from contexts outside the features in the main West Field cuttings. These were largely from superficial layers including ploughsoil:

Cutting 950/820

Flint: Axes: three, form 2 (1); one, form 3 (1); one, form 4 (1); one, Ind. (1). Axes (broken): three, form 3 (1); one, form 9 (1); three, Ind. (1); two, form 1 (2); one, form 10 (2); one, Ind. (2). Picks: one, (2). Picks (broken): two, (1) (2). Rods: one, (2). Rods (broken): three, (1) (2). Discoidal knives:

one, form f stage II (1); three, form Ind. stage II (2); four, form Ind. stage I (2). Discoidal knives (broken): two, form Ind. stage II (1). Scrapers: five, (1) (2). Borers (broken): one, (2). Fabricators: eight, (1) (2). Fabricators (broken): two, (2). Arrowheads: one, (2) (roughout). Roughouts: eighteen, (1) (2). Roughouts (broken): twelve, (1) (2). Hammers: one, (1).

Stone: Hammers: six, (1) (2).

Cutting 940/940

Flint: Axes (broken): one, form 3 (ploughsoil). Discoidal knives: one, form Ind. stage I (2) (ploughsoil). Discoidal knives (broken): one, form Ind. stage II (ploughsoil). Plane scrapers: two, (2) (-). Borers: one, (-). Roughouts: fourteen, (ploughsoil) (2). Hammers: one, (-).

Stone: Hammers: one, (-). Hammers (broken): two, (-).

Cutting 940/950

Flint: Axes (broken): one, form 1 (2). Discoidal knives (broken): one, form Ind. stage II (2). Knives (other): one, (2). Borers: one, (2). Fabricators (broken): one, (2). Roughouts: one, (2).

Pottery: CV: one, (2).

Cutting 950/950

Flint: Discoidal knives: one, form Ind. stage I (4). Borers: one, (2). Roughouts: two, (2) (4).

Stone: Hammers (broken): six, (2) (4).

Cutting 960/940

Flint: Roughouts: one, (-).

Stone: Hammers (broken): one, (-).

C Within the Deep Mine Field (fig. 2)

In support of the phosphate survey a series of small trenches was dug across the lips of six of the visible deep mines to try to establish the presence of a surviving pre-mine old land surface and the likely structure of the layers through which many of the sampling points would pass. These trenches were numbered T1–6.

Only in Trench 3 did an old land surface clearly survive other than as natural sand and was here associated with two hearths. Minor episodes of flint working were noted in Trenches 2, 4 and 5, apparently incorporated during redeposition of material dug from adjacent mines. Trench 1 shows a typical section through the ring of upcast material often seen surrounding a deep mine, layers of sand being backed by deposits of sand and chalk, then by heavier chalk blocks excavated from a greater depth as the mine progressed. By chance, Trench 3 also picked up the burial of a horse cranium (Clutton-Brock and Burleigh 1991) which had been placed diagonally and inverted above a small cutting dug through a layer of redeposited chalky sand. A direct association with the carved chalk blocks recovered (Varndell 1991, 118, C325–8) looks less certain. Three lay within the cutting at a lower level than the skull, while the fourth, which lay above the skull, protruded from the side of the trench. It is possible, therefore, that the association is fortuitous and that all the chalk blocks had once lain in the layer through which the cutting had been made, three being reincorporated in its backfilling. A new determination commissioned by Frances Healy for English Heritage on a reserved, untreated fragment of horse cranium points to a likely Late Iron Age date.

TRENCH 1 (fig. 66)
1154.8/981.9, 6 x 2 m. Orientation: 273 03'. E–W section through lip of deep mine.

Contexts
1 Topsoil
2 Small chalk rubble
3 Chalk rubble in orange sand

4 Large chalk rubble
5 Chalk rubble in yellow sand
6 Clean orange sand
7 Pale yellow chalky sand

TRENCH 2 (fig. 67)
1194.2/948, 5 x 2 m. Orientation: 322 47'. N–S section through lip of deep mine.
(Radiocarbon sample BM-1066 [3])

Contexts
1 Topsoil
2 Chalk rubble in hard orange sand
3 Flint chipping
4 Brown sand

TRENCH 3 (fig. 68)
1273/1019.5, 5 x 2 m. Orientation: 32 50'. N–S section through lip of deep mine showing redeposited material overlying old ground surface with hearth. Skull of horse in redeposited material, lying upside down aligned NE–SW above trench (Clutton-Brock and Burleigh 1991). (Radiocarbon samples BM-1065 [ogs] and 1546 [horse])

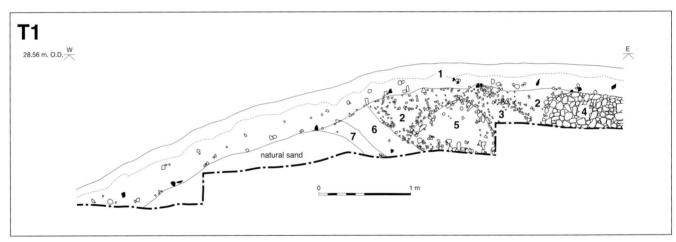

Fig. 66 Trench 1, 1154.8/981.9, section through lip of pit.

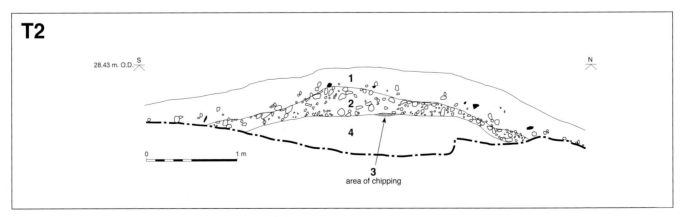

Fig. 67 Trench 2, 1194.2/948, section through lip of pit.

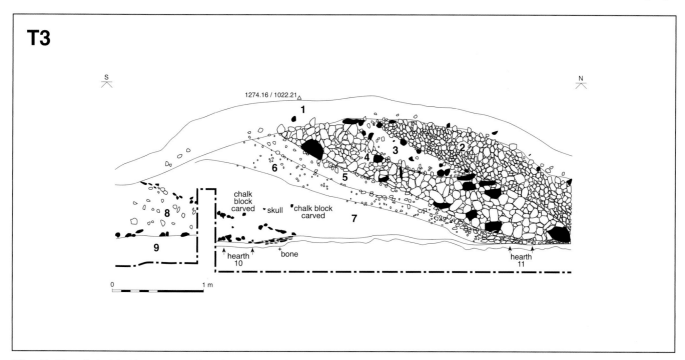

Fig. 68 Trench 3, 1273/1019.5, section through lip of pit.

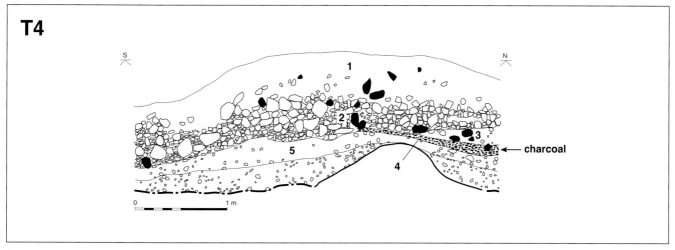

Fig. 69 Trench 4, 1240/1004.1, section through lip of pit.

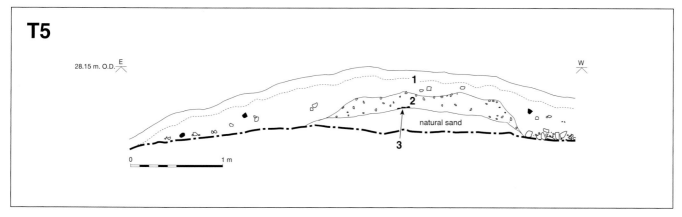

Fig. 70 Trench 5, 1120.5/928.5, section through lip of pit.

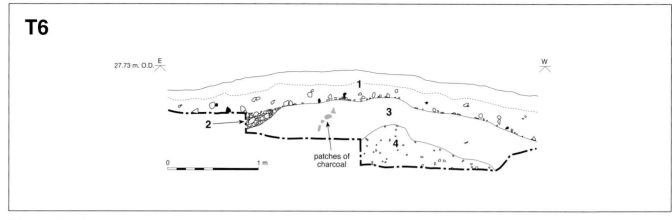

Fig. 71 Trench 6, 1117.8/1001.4, section through lip of pit.

Contexts
1 Topsoil
2 Small chalk rubble
3 Yellow sand and rubble
4 Large chalk rubble
5 Orange/brown sandy cryte with small chalk rubble
6 Chalk in yellow/brown cryte
7 Brown chalky sand
8 Brown chalky sand and flints
9 Brown sand
10 Hearth 1
11 Hearth 2

Finds
Chalk: Four carved chalk blocks (Varndell 1991, C325–8). C328 lay above the level of the horse skull and protruding from the side of the trench; the others lay within the trench and beneath the level of the skull.

TRENCH 4 (fig. 69)
1240/1004.1, 5 x 2 m. Orientation: 3 03'. N–S section through lip of deep mine, chipping floor incorporated in redeposited material.

Contexts
1 Topsoil
2 Chalk rubble
3 Orange sand and rubble
4 Chipping
5 Yellow sandy cryte

Finds
Flint: Discoidal knives: one, class 1 (4). Roughouts: two, (4).

TRENCH 5 (fig. 70)
1120.5/928.5, 5 x 2 m. Orientation: 267 40'. E–W section through lip of deep mine.

Contexts
1 Topsoil
2 Cryte
3 Chipping

TRENCH 6 (fig. 71)
1117.8/1001.4, 4 x 2 m. Orientation: 312 51'. E–W section through lip of deep mine. (2 pits open simultaneously?)

Contexts
1 Topsoil
2 Chalk rubble
3 Clean orange sand
4 Cryte

D Areas examined south of the Deep Mine Field (fig. 2)

Four cuttings, 990/765, 995/765, 1000/750 and 1000/755, 4 x 4 m, were opened in 1973 within and close to the Forestry Commission plantation to the south and west of the visible mine field. Additional cuttings were later opened at 990/755, 990/770, 995/755, 995/770, 995/775, 1000/745 (4 x 4 m) and 1005/745 (4 x 4 m). These proved featureless except for a modern v-cut ditch running through the last two cuttings.

E Reduction areas

1 The Neolithic chipping floor excavated in Area A, 1972–4, west of Shaft X
This chipping floor was first discovered during the 1972 season in cutting 1260.5/906.1, sealed beneath deposits clearly derived from the sinking of one or more mine shafts (fig. 72, and plates 5 and 6). During this season the flints lying on the surface of the floor were drawn

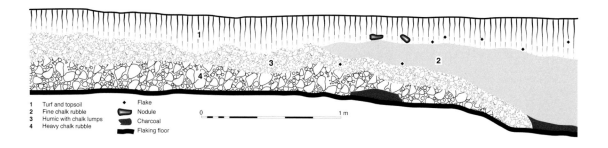

Fig. 72 Area A, cutting 1260/905.5, west face. Section showing chipping floor excavated in 1972–4 sealed beneath chalk rubble.

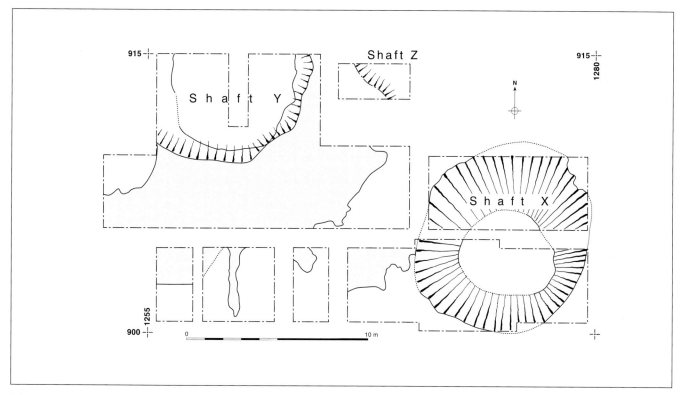

Fig. 73 Plan showing extent of chipping floor excavated in 1972–4 in Area A west of Shaft X.

and photographed. The extent of the floor, however, only became evident in subsequent seasons – the main bulk being lifted during 1973 and completed during 1974.

Since it quickly became apparent that the floor had a variable, but at times considerable, depth, the procedure of drawing the surface flints was abandoned in favour of lifting by ¼ sq m in arbitrary spits. All the material was passed through a ¼-in (6.35-mm) sieve. The material was then bagged with standard notation by cutting, metre square (capital letter), ¼ metre square (lower case a–d clockwise, beginning with the north-west) and by arbitrary spit level (I–VI, I being the uppermost). The floor was seen to extend over an area of 70 sq m, with edges well

defined in the south-east and partly in the west (fig. 73). The bulk lay well preserved beneath chalk rubble and redeposited till, but had been eroded to the south where this cover was not present. It was clear that this floor was already in existence when Shaft Y was sunk to the north and must therefore utilize flint taken from other mines, probably further to the north. Throughout, the floor lay directly on natural orange-coloured sand. As work progressed, it became evident that the floor was really an area of flint working, representing various episodes, during which more than one fire had been lit. One hearth lay on the east side of cutting 1255.5/905.5 in squares H and L, and was sectioned by the eastern baulk. Two

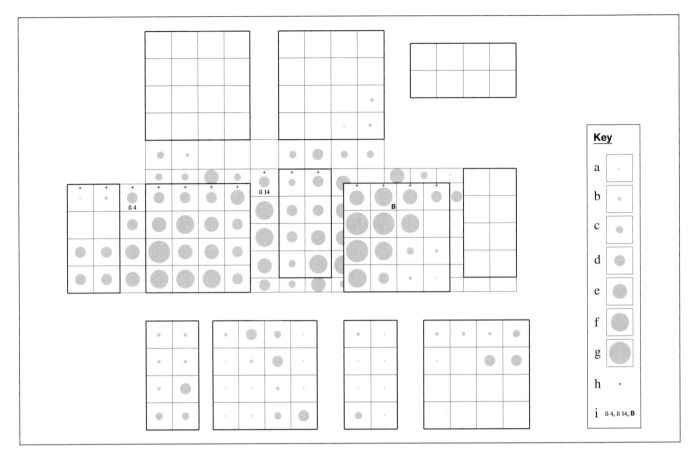

Fig. 74 Plan of 1972–4 chipping floor showing quantity of flint recovered per m sq.

a   < 100
b   101–500
c   501–1000
d   1001–2000
e   2001–4000
f   4001–8000
g   > 8000
h   metre squares from which flint was included in the current analysis (see fig. 77)
i   metre squares from which flint was analysed in fig. 93

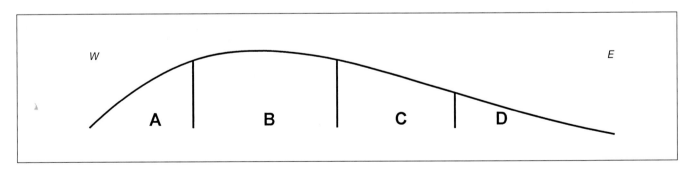

Fig. 75 Speculative reconstruction of original profile of Feature 112 chipping floor based on field sketch.

A   small flakes and waste
B   large and small pieces
C   large pieces with few small flakes and waste
D   large and medium-sized pieces

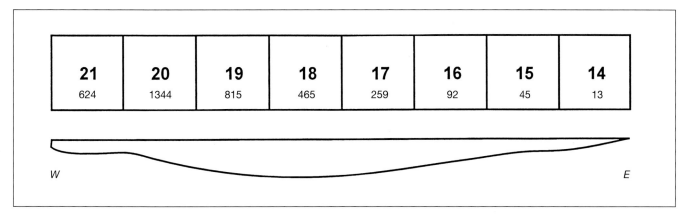

Fig. 76 Schematic section of Feature 112 chipping floor showing quantities of flint recovered per m sq.

further hearths lay on the chipping floor in 1260/905.5, extending into the western baulk. The density of the floor varied considerably, being at its greatest in squares E and I in cutting 1263/905.5, where up to 12,945 pieces of flint per sq m were recovered (fig. 74). In all, something in the order of 250,000 pieces of flint were recorded. Because upcast from the opening of one or more of the deep mines effectively sealed areas of the chipping floor and protected it from contamination by later events, the floor offers an ideal opportunity to assess how the raw mined flint was processed and what tools were being made from it. Pottery recovered from the floor is of the Grooved Ware style identical to that recovered from the deep mines, showing that the same segment of society was involved with both the extraction and the working of the flint. Few in the way of other non-flint artefacts were recovered from the floor. A single chalk ball (Varndell 1991, C140) and a small quantity of antler, mostly broken tines of red deer, were present, but these were insufficiently well preserved to say whether they had been used in pressure flaking. Sufficient charcoal was extracted from the hearths to provide determinations which appear not dissimilar to those recorded for the deep mines (BM-988, 995, 1013 and 1014).

2 The Neolithic chipping floor in the top of Feature 112 in the West Field

For comparison, a smaller chipping floor situated in the West Field was chosen for study by reason of its good preservation, and sampled in 1975 by Lech (figs 75 and 76). The floor lay in the top of a deeper feature, Feature 112, which was not fully explored. Feature 112 was located in an area of mainly shallow exploitation pits, approximately 300 m to the west and south-west of the 1972–4 chipping floor (fig. 55). It was clearly a much smaller workshop. The density of flint material was decidedly lower and the total number of flints present was probably only about 30,000–40,000. A sample of 7100 pieces forms the basis of the study presented here.

The sample comprised twenty-one squares measuring 25 x 25 cm; no sieving was done. A large number of early bifacial roughouts was recorded, providing the opportunity to examine the primary stages in the preparation of roughouts. A transect of the floor (squares 14–21) furnished the data used to study the distribution of flakes and waste (fig. 76). Field observations determined that the chipping floor had formed a low mound of flint (fig. 75), degrading to a flatter profile post-deposition. The chipping activity thinned out at the edges of squares 21, 15 and 14, the greatest thickness being recorded in squares 19–17. Vertically the material appeared to be homogeneous.

IV The Late Neolithic flint and stone industries

Any analysis of the Late Neolithic flint industries at Grimes Graves is faced with the problem of attempting to recognize the intended end product other than at a most advanced stage of manufacture. Since the vast majority of the flint mined at Grimes Graves was unlikely to have been for use solely on site, in what forms did it leave? If roughed-out implements were being made, at what stage were they considered to be ready for export? Did this stage differ between types of implement and was there a consensus view held by all those working the site – since we cannot assume that all belonged to the same segment of society? With datable contexts rare, did this view alter over time? Given that sharpening and polishing, with few exceptions, do not appear to have been practised on site, most 'implements' would only have been en route to their final form. If reduction had been efficient then relatively few implements would be found in the final stages of their shaping, being abandoned for whatever reason at an earlier phase, although we may expect that inevitably there would be accidents and that some breakages would occur at an advanced stage. If only part of the broken implement has been recovered this too can lead to problems and ambiguities as to the final intended form. Some broken discoidal knives and the broken cutting edges of flake adzes, for example, are difficult to set apart. Only in the lighter elements of the industry (or industries) do fully finished forms recur and with these we may assume perhaps that we are dealing with items which were principally for use on site, for example fabricators, borers and scrapers.

In two areas examined during the Museum's campaign – the chipping floor to the west of Shaft X and in the top of Feature 112 in the West Field – extensive areas of reduction were discovered *in situ*. These afford an opportunity to examine the reduction process in detail. The first part of this section is therefore devoted to a summary of the results so far achieved from the analysis of samples drawn from these two contexts, comparing their actual composition and drawing conclusions as to the likely products in the course of manufacture.

The second section offers a survey of finished implements and those in the course of manufacture recovered elsewhere during the Museum's campaign, including a comparison with other implements previously recovered from the site. Many of the pieces come from secondary contexts either redeposited in worked-out mine shafts or from superficial deposits, or stem from earlier explorations for which documentation is slight or non-existent. It is possible therefore that some earlier and later pieces may have become incorporated along with the bulk of the material which clearly belongs to the Late Neolithic mining phase. This differs little in content from other Late Neolithic industries recovered across much of southern England and sometimes found in direct association with Grooved Ware pottery. Where there seems to be genuine doubt as to the likely attribution, early forms of roughout and pieces showing provisional shaping have been excluded from the latter part of this survey.

The most striking fact to emerge from over a century of investigation is that, unlike on other extractive sites on the Continent, the flint pick appears to have played only a minor role in the actual mining process at Grimes Graves (cf. Saville 1981, 51). The antler pick was the mining tool par excellence. The reason lies in the type of deposit in which the flint lay (cf. Felder 1981, 57; Lech 1980, 40–45; Borkowski *et al.* 1991, 615). At Grimes Graves the chalk is seamed and fractured; in the case of the deeper mines this called for a tool which could exploit these weaknesses. Only in the shallower mines, where the flint lay in weathered and cryoturbated deposits, was the bone pick in evidence.

A Analysis of the chipping floors
J. Lech

Introduction
Although interest in flint mines in Western Europe developed early (Weisgerber *et al.* 1980; Smolla 1987; Lech 1991, 557–60; 1997, 611–13; Holgate 1995, 136–50; Collet *et al.* 2008, 44–8), for many years scholars could not surmount the conceptual and organizational barrier that led them to concentrate on finished tools or on tool roughouts at advanced stages of preparation (for example, Armstrong 1927). One reason for this was the apparent uniformity of the enormous mass of waste material rejected in the processing, containing as it did only a few tools and a small number of recognizable roughed-out implements. That is why for a long time now there has been a considerable discrepancy between what is known about shafts and galleries, mining techniques and tools, and what is known about flint working, the *chaîne opératoire* at prehistoric flint mines, chipping floors and the flint waste from mine fields (Lech 1983, 47–9; Borkowski

et al. 1991; Pelegrin and Richard 1995; de Grooth 1997, 71; Felder *et al.* 1998, 67; Millet-Richard 2006; Collet *et al.* 2008, 58–69). It should be noted, however, that of the largest and most interesting prehistoric flint mines in Europe (Cissbury, Grimes Graves, Krzemionki Opatowskie, Rijckholt-St Geertruid and Spiennes) our knowledge of how flint was worked is greatest at Grimes Graves, mainly due to the work of Saville (1981; see also Herne 1991; Lech and Longworth 2000, 40–59; 2006).

Until the 1970s there were no publications dealing with the structure of chipping floor (workshop) assemblages, or the characteristics of the waste material thus produced. These data therefore had never been used to reconstruct the actual process of flint working. Yet it is the analysis of mass-produced flint waste, which bears the attributes of an assemblage or its representative parts, based on comparison of the basic structure of the materials and observable changes in their fundamental characteristics, that is the most certain way to reconstruct the organization of work carried out on a mine field and provide the model, or models, for how the settlements were supplied with the raw material.

In the case of Grimes Graves, the first modern study of flint waste material was carried out by Alan Saville (1981). Saville studied the material associated with a shaft excavated in 1971–2 by Mercer (1981). From his research Saville concluded 'that many generalisations which have been made about Grimes Graves as an axe factory are unjustified, and they underscore the need for more objective data' (1981, 71).

One of the questions repeatedly asked of the material recovered from Grimes Graves has been what exactly was made from the flint extracted, and over what area was it dispersed? In particular, to what extent was the flint used for the manufacture of axes and adzes? All exploration on the site so far has failed to produce evidence for polishing and it may be concluded that whatever was produced left the site in an unpolished, roughed-out state. While Saville (ibid.) argued that the case for axe production on any scale was unproven, Healy (1991a) has stressed the likely importance of the production of prestige goods such as discoidal knives and elaborate arrowheads. She also wrote of 'our still lamentably poor understanding of flint mine sites' (1987, 27).

Yet the sheer quantity of *floorstone* being extracted argues against the continuing value of this material as a source for prestige items, suggesting that the prime aim was the satisfaction of a need for heavier implements that far exceeded needs for the production of the lighter component, be it for domestic or prestige use. Analysis of the extensive area of flint reduction in the neighbourhood of Shaft X, to the south of the Deep Mine Field – the 1972–4 chipping floor (figs 2, 72 and 73) excavated by Ian Longworth – has offered an opportunity to shed new light on this problem (Sieveking *et al.* 1973, 208–11; Lech and Longworth 1995; 2000, 40–59; 2006).

1 Aims and research methods

The approximately 250,000 flint specimens comprising the 1972–4 chipping floor immediately suggested that only a rudimentary study of this feature would be possible and the preliminary survey presented here was limited to a sample of the material. The definitive analysis of the material recovered from this chipping floor and a second in Feature 112 is being undertaken by the author and will appear in a future publication. The following provides a brief summary of the conclusions so far reached (see also Lech and Longworth 1995; 2000; 2006). A sample of 39,735 specimens (approximately 16 per cent of the total) was taken from the 1972–4 chipping floor. Results from the study of 27,946 pieces (representing 11 per cent of the total – see fig. 74h), together with a sample of 7100 pieces (approximately 25 per cent of the total) from the much smaller floor in the top of Feature 112 form the basis of this summary. The survey was limited to a morphological and statistical description of the flint specimens making up both assemblages recovered on these chipping floors, and to formulating conclusions about the final products. In the case of the 1972–4 chipping floor, sample material from chosen units (square metres) was analysed (fig. 74h). In the case of Feature 112 all the material recovered was included in the study.

The method was applied in seven stages:

1 Determine the type of material based on a preliminary analysis.
2 On the basis of this first stage, and using non-source-based knowledge (see Topolski 1976, 401–27), prepare a list of problems and questions to be answered.
3 Determine the scope of the analysis and construct an appropriate classification list, as well as determining the techniques to be applied.
4 Classify the flint material in accordance with stage 3.
5 Analyse the material in order to detect the essential features of the inventory and their interpretation.
6 On the basis of stages 4 and 5, attempt to determine the final product taken away from the chipping floors, to reconstruct the *chaîne opératoire*, the knapping process and the organization of the work as far as possible, to determine the extent of production and to describe elements of individual behaviour also using non-source-based knowledge.
7 If possible, arrive at a general interpretation of the assemblages studied.

The method devised for the assemblages from the Sąspów mine utilized an early study by Binford (1963; see Dzieduszycka-Machnikowa and Lech 1976). It was assumed that each flint specimen has an infinite number of features consisting of observed attributes, sometimes measured and weighed by the archaeologist. In other words, the features are defined in our classification list as attributes. The number of attributes is infinite but in practice only those which, from the point of view of the problem being studied, were considered diagnostic were chosen. Thus only a limited number were investigated. In the case of flakes from the 1972–4 chipping floor several possible variants were tested to determine the choice of features and attributes to be taken into consideration, from several hundred up to 1000 specimens being used in each test. The optimum variant, from the point of view of the objectives and of the economic use of the time available, was chosen. When analysing material en masse, the introduction of each additional feature or attribute extends the time necessary for the analysis. In the case of the 1972–4 chipping floor, it was decided that it would be more interesting to examine a greater number of units from that workshop and compare them with specimens from Feature 112, rather than conduct a more thorough study of fewer pieces. The method and classification structure have some features in common with questionnaires used in sociological research (cf. Kahn and Cannell 1957, 98–130), while mass material such as flint production waste from chipping floors has for many years now been described using statistical methods. In this study the simplest statistical tools have been employed (Guilford 1965).

Normally when creating a classification for flint material from chipping floors refits are of crucial importance (fig. 85f). They make it possible to recreate the order in which the technical procedures occurred and to determine the exact place of each specimen in the flint-working process (Schild 1980; Cahen 1987; Cziesla *et al.* 1990; Fiedorczuk 2006). With a huge amount of chipping floor material, refitting is extremely difficult. When analysing only samples of material – as in the case of the 1972–4 chipping floor and Feature 112 – the chances of successfully employing the refit method are even smaller. This approach was therefore abandoned. Instead, before beginning to create the classification, all the material which had been previously published was studied, as well as the rich collection of small finds from the Grimes Graves excavations carried out by the British Museum in the years 1972–6 as well as those from Armstrong's earlier excavations. Additionally, the results of the preliminary recording of flint material carried out in the field over the years 1974–6 was utilized. Saville's (1981) work was also very helpful. Already on the basis of this broad preliminary analysis using what was known about other flint material from Grimes Graves (the non-source-based knowledge mentioned earlier relating to the 1972–4 chipping floor and Feature 112), it was possible to determine the types of flint production of which these two assemblages are the remains. Without the clues given by the many roughouts in various stages of working that were left on the site it would not be possible to determine exactly what was being made. From the débitage alone one could only suppose that the main product was axes.

Before it could be examined, most of the flint material had to be soaked in a 10 per cent acetic acid solution to remove the calcareous deposit which impeded or even prevented the proper classification of specimens. Both flint assemblages, for functional and formal reasons, were divided into four separate morphological groups, each of these groups being classified according to a differently chosen set of features and attributes. In addition, the flint material was weighed according to these classificatory categories and in the case of the First Group also by individual specimen, but in the analysis presented here data gained from the weighing exercise have not been used.

Classification used in the flint assemblages from the Grimes Graves chipping floors

First Group: natural nodules, roughouts in different stages of preparation, cores

A Natural nodules and their larger fragments

B Specimens with primary working

   B.I. Nodules and their fragments with traces of initial working (fig. 78, and plates 7 and 8)
   B.II. Pre-cores or initial tool roughouts
   B.III. Broken pieces of categories B.I. and B.II.

C Roughouts of indeterminate tools

   C.I. Initial tool roughouts (fig. 79a)
   C.II. Early tool roughouts (fig. 79b)
   C.III. Fragments of initial and early tool roughouts
   C.IV. Advanced tool roughouts
   C.V. Fragments of advanced tool roughouts (fig. 79c)

D Cores

   D.I.   One-platform cores
            D.I.1. – for flakes (fig. 80a)
            D.I.2. – for flakes and blades
            D.I.3. – for blades
   D.II.   Two-platform cores
            D.II.1. – for flakes
            D.II.2. – for flakes and blades
            D.II.3. – for blades
   D.II.   Multi-platform cores
            D.II.1. – for flakes
            D.II.2. – for flakes and blades
            D.II.3. – for blades
   D.IV.   Other cores
   D.V.   Fragments of cores

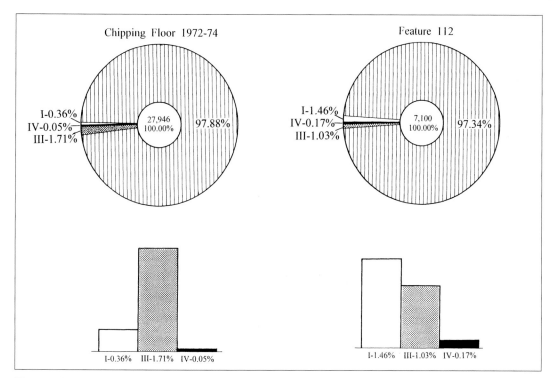

Note: the artefact drawings in this section (figs 78–92) were done to the specifications of J. Lech and use slightly different conventions (e.g. axes/adzes drawn blade upwards).
• striking platform and bulb of percussion
○ former position of striking platform and bulb of percussion where removed

Fig. 77 General structure of chipping floors of 1972–4 and Feature 112, in four morphological groups:
I   natural nodules, initial, early and advanced tool roughouts, pre-cores and cores
II   flakes and waste
III   blades and blade fragments
IV   retouched pieces and tools

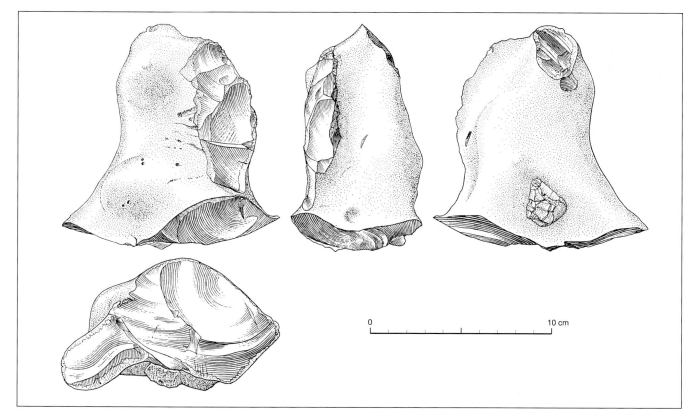

Fig. 78 The 1972–4 chipping floor. First Group.
B.I. Fragment of flint nodule with initial working. *Floorstone*, but similar to *wallstone* or *topstone*. Possibly beginnings of axe roughout. 119 x 119 x 63 mm, 836 g

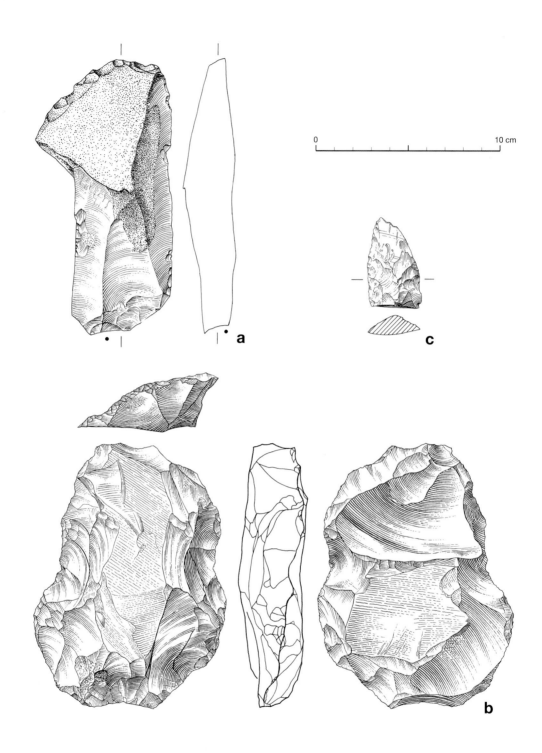

Fig. 79 The 1972–4 chipping floor. First Group.

a   C.I. Initial tool roughout. 143 x 78 x 27 mm, 252 g. Example of a flake blank (Flake category A.II.1.1.)

b   C.II. Early bifacial tool roughout. 140 x 103 x 31 mm, 538 g

c   C.V. Fragment of broken knife. Complete, it would have had the proportions of a blade. 49 x 28 x 9 mm, 13 g

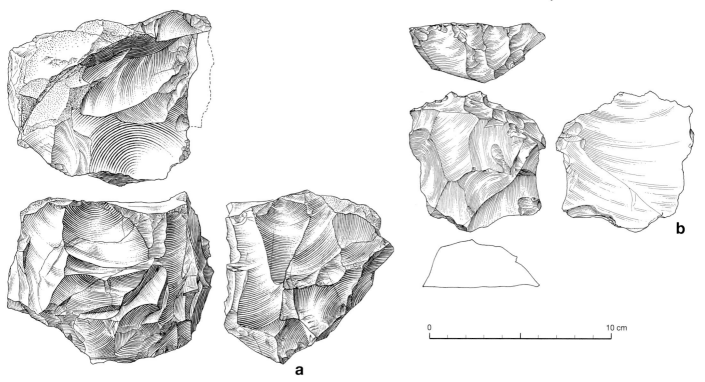

Fig. 80 The 1972–4 chipping floor. First Group.
a   D.I.1. Core for flakes with single platform. 89 x 123 x 95 mm, 963 g
b   E.I. Initial discoidal knife roughout. 89 x 76 x 29 mm, 154 g

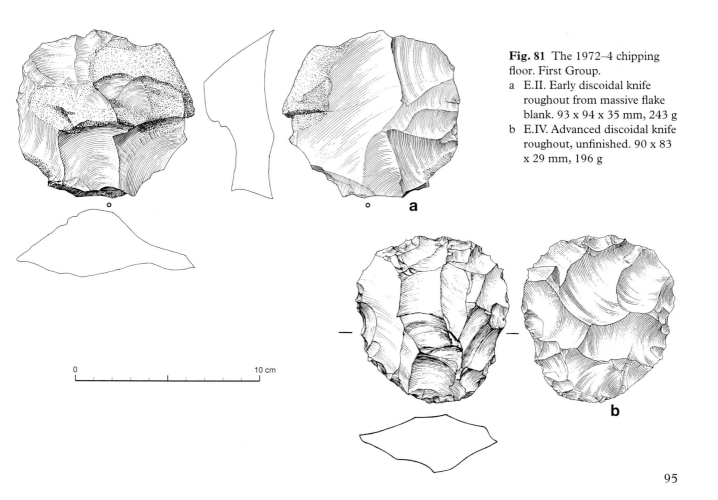

Fig. 81 The 1972–4 chipping floor. First Group.
a   E.II. Early discoidal knife roughout from massive flake blank. 93 x 94 x 35 mm, 243 g
b   E.IV. Advanced discoidal knife roughout, unfinished. 90 x 83 x 29 mm, 196 g

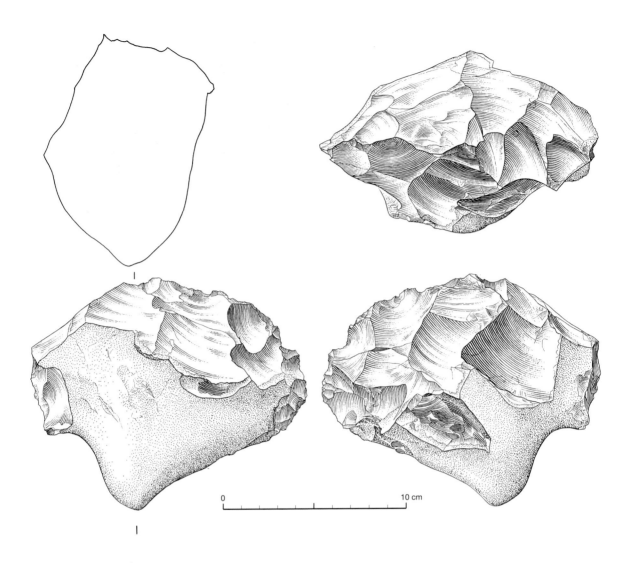

Fig. 82 The 1972–4 chipping floor. First Group.
F.I. Initial axe roughout. Example of an initial stage of axe preparation from a small *floorstone* nodule. 148 x 123 x 79 mm, 1352 g

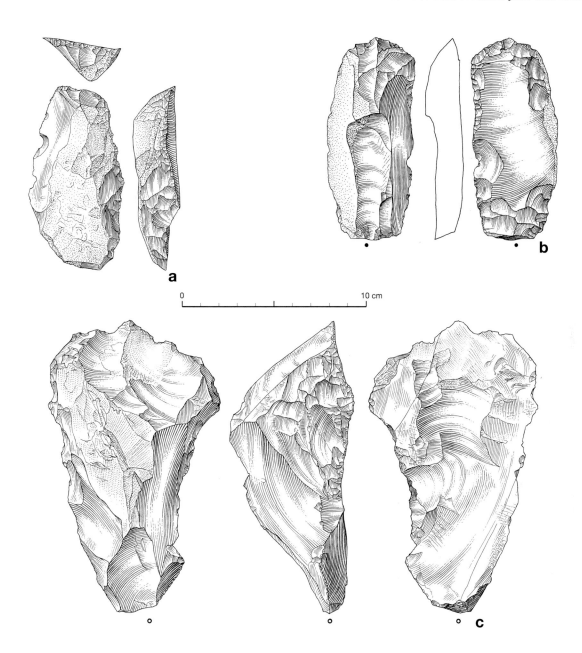

Fig. 83 The 1972–4 chipping floor. First Group.
a   F.I. Initial axe/adze roughout. 96 x 51 x 21 mm, 108 g
b   F.I. Initial axe/adze roughout. 108 x 47 x 19 mm, 113 g
c   F.II. Early axe/adze roughout on massive flake. 145 x 93 x 66 mm, 710 g

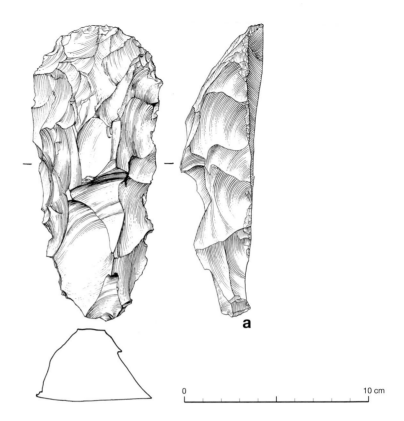

Fig. 84 The 1972–4 chipping floor. First Group.

a   F.IV. Advanced adze roughout on massive flake blank. 151 x 70 x 41 mm, 370 g

b   F.V. Fragment of advanced axe roughout. 50 x 51 x 18 mm, 65 g

c   F.V. Fragment of advanced axe/adze roughout from flake blank. 71 x 59 x 21 mm, 103 g

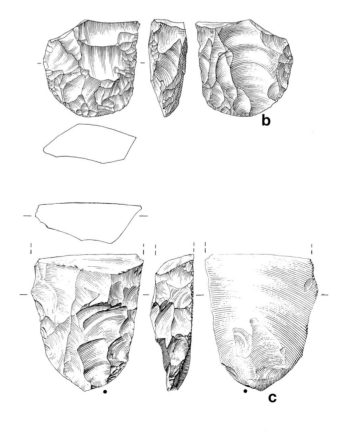

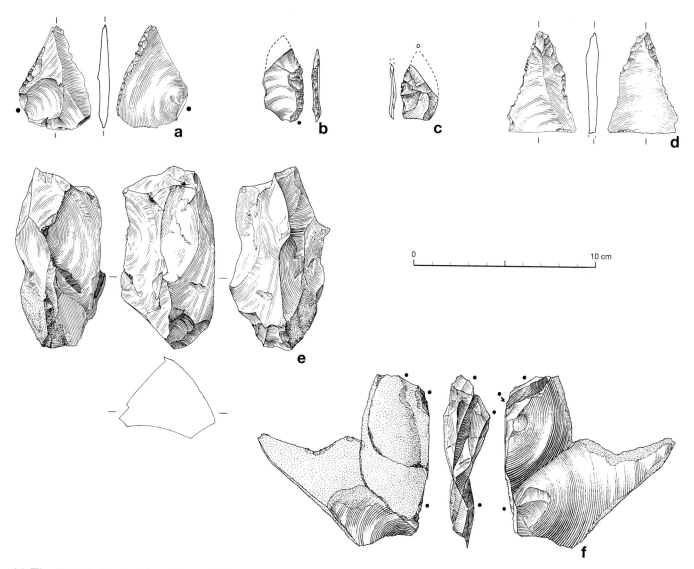

Fig. 85 The 1972–4 chipping floor. First and Second Groups.
a   First Group: G. Early roughout for projectile point (or retouched flake). 36 x 54 x 5 mm, 11 g
b   First Group: G. Early roughout for arrowhead (broken).
c   First Group: G. Early roughout for arrowhead (broken). 28 x 19 x 3 mm, 2 g
d   First Group: G. Early roughout for arrowhead. 53 x 37 x 6 mm, 9 g
e   First Group: H.II. Others. Early roughout for axe or pick (broken), with beginnings of further working. 96 x 47 x 46 mm, 210 g
f   Second Group: A.II.1.1. Large secondary flake with flat platform (three refitted flakes). Max. dim. 99 mm, 95 g

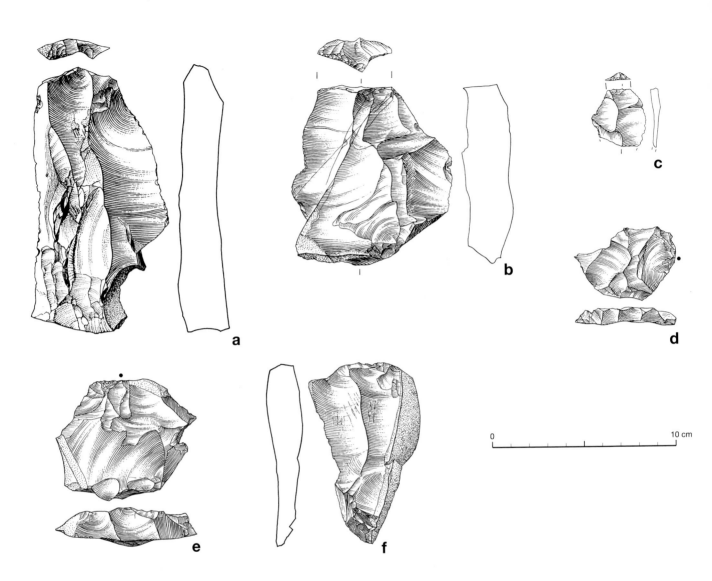

Fig. 86 The 1972–4 chipping floor. Second Group.

a   A.II.1.2. Large secondary flake with faceted platform (*floorstone*). 141 x 72 x 25 mm, 254 g

b   A.III.1.2. Large tertiary flake with faceted platform (blank for a discoidal knife roughout). 95 x 87 x 25 mm, max. dim. 103 mm, 235 g

c   A.III.3.2. Small tertiary flake with faceted platform. Max. dim. 33 mm, 3 g

d   B. Specific flake type (from core rejuvenation platform?). Max. dim. 55 mm, 15 g

e   B. Specific flake type (from core rejuvenation platform?). Max. dim. 80 mm, 84 g

f   B. Specific flake type (removal of flaking surface on a blade core). Max. dim. 93 mm, 83 g

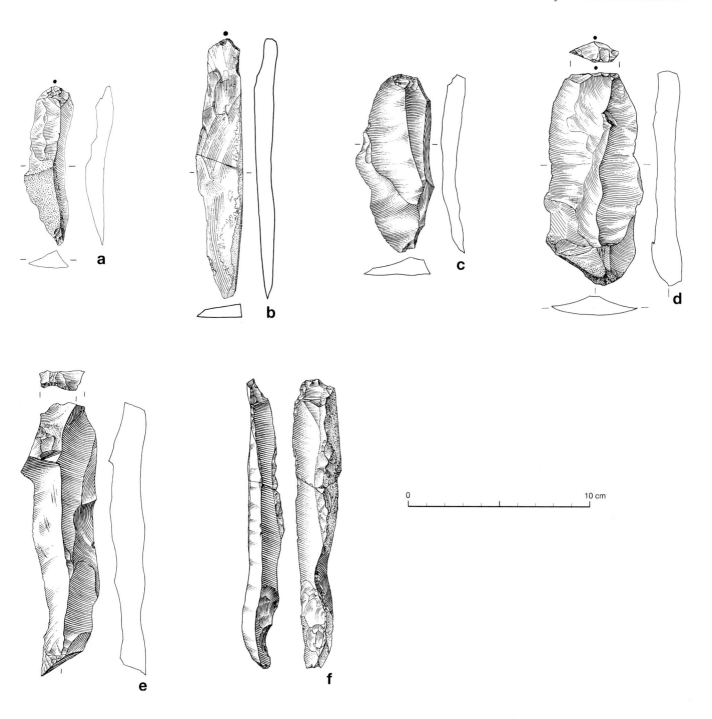

Fig. 87 The 1972–4 chipping floor. Third Group.
a   A.II.1. Secondary blade with flat platform. 84 x 22 x 9 mm, 14 g
b   A.II.1. Secondary blade with flat platform. 137 x 28 x 8 mm, 32 g
c   A.III.1. Tertiary blade with flat platform. 93 x 39 x 9 mm, 38 g
d   A.III.2. Tertiary blade with faceted platform. 112 x 53 x 13 mm, 78 g
e   A.IV.2. Tertiary blade from core with faceted platform. 147 x 41 x 18 mm, 95 g
f   D. Specific blade type. 147 x 26 x 14 mm, 57 g

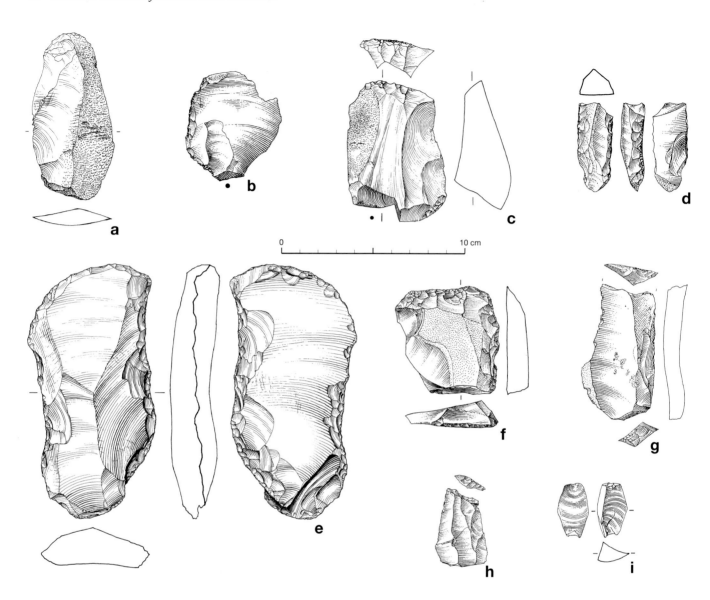

Fig. 88 The 1972–4 chipping floor. Fourth Group.

a   A. End-scraper on blade with faceted platform. 89 x 44 x 11 mm, 37 g

b   A. Side-scraper on flake. 58 x 52 x 11 mm, 28 g

c   A. End-scraper on massive flake. 76 x 53 x 31 mm, 122 g

d   G. Fabricator fragment. 48 x 19 x 12 mm, 14 g

e   I. Massive retouched blade. 136 x 66 x 23 mm, 230 g

f   I. '*Racloir*'.

g   I. Truncated blade A.IV.2. 73 x 39 x 10 mm, 30 g

h   I. Truncated blade. 42 x 27 x 5 mm, 5 g

i   I. Splinter (*pièce esquille*). 28 x 15 x 9 mm, 2 g

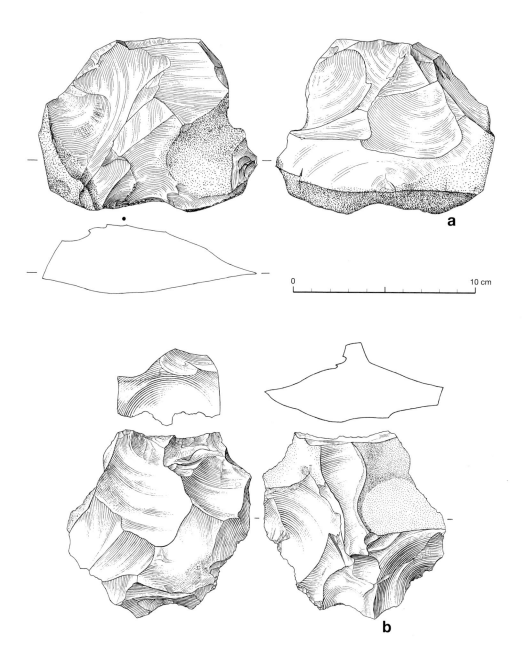

Fig. 89 Feature 112. First Group.

a   E.II. Early discoidal knife roughout. Good example of massive flake blank (A.II.1.3) of *floorstone*. 115 x 92 x 33 mm, 358 g

b   E.II. Early discoidal knife roughout with some attributes of a *levallois* core. *Topstone* or *wallstone*. 99 x 87 x 40 mm, diam. 108 mm, 343 g

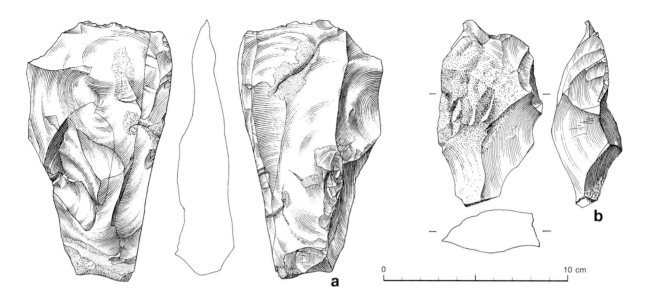

Fig. 90 Feature 112. First Group.
a   F.I. Initial axe roughout. 136 x 80 x 33 mm, 327 g
b   F.I. Initial adze roughout. 100 x 54 x 33 mm, 132 g

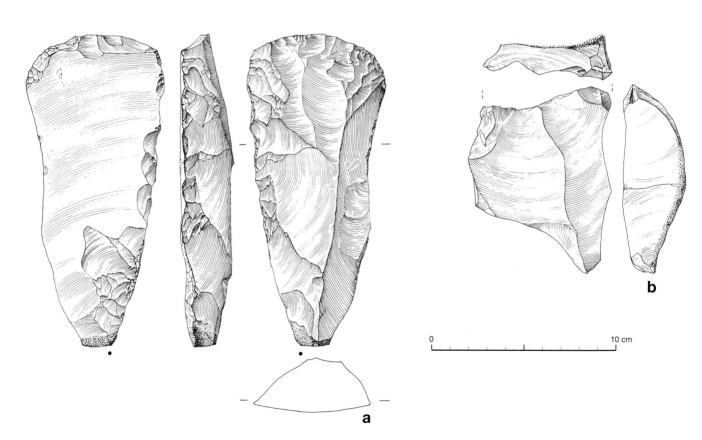

Fig. 91 Feature 112. First Group.
a   F.IV. Advanced axe roughout. Unique example of an unfinished axe roughout prepared on a massive flake from a *floorstone* nodule with cortex platform. A rare example of the use of *floorstone* in the Feature 112 assemblage. 164 x 75 x 29 mm, 356 g
b   H.I. Core or initial tool roughout on *wallstone*. 91 x 74 x 39 mm (measured as single platform core), max. dim. 105 mm, 193 g

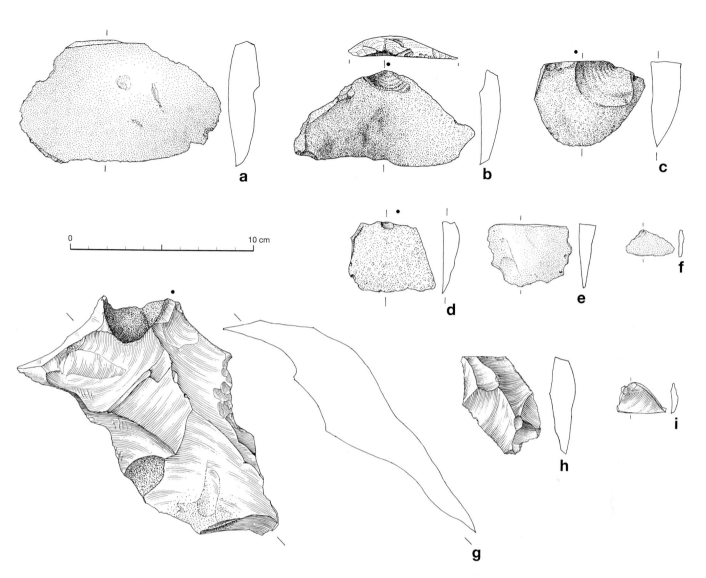

Fig. 92 Feature 112. Second Group.
a   A.I.1.1. Large primary flake with flat platform. 65 x 111 x 14 mm, 81 g
b   A.I.1.2. Large primary flake with faceted platform. 47 x 98 x 10 mm, 41 g
c   A.I.2.1. Medium primary flake with flat platform. Max. dim. 55 mm, 35 g
d   A.I.2.2. Medium flake with faceted platform. Max. dim. 52 mm, 15 g
e   A.I.2.3. Small primary flake with unprepared platform. Max. dim. 47 mm, 8 g
f   A.I.2.4. Small primary flake with punctiform platform. Max. dim. 26 mm, 1 g
g   A.II.1.1. Large secondary flake with flat platform. 161 x 87 x 40 mm, 374 g
h   A.III.2.1. Medium-sized tertiary flake with flat platform. Max. dim. 60 mm, 25 g
i   A.III.3.4. Small tertiary flake with punctiform platform. Max. dim. 26 mm, 1 g

E Early forms of discoidal knives

E.I. Initial discoidal knife roughouts (fig. 80b)

E.II. Early discoidal knife roughouts (figs 81a, 89a and 89b)

E.III. Fragments of initial and early discoidal knife roughouts

E.IV. Advanced discoidal knife roughouts (fig. 81b)

E.V. Fragments of advanced discoidal knife roughouts

F Early forms of axe and adze

F.I. Initial axe or adze roughouts (figs 82, 83a–b and 90a–b, and plates 9–11)

F.II. Early axe or adze roughouts (fig. 83c)

F.III. Fragments of initial and early axe or adze roughouts

F.IV. Advanced axe and adze roughouts (figs 84a and 91a)

F.V. Fragments of advanced axe and adze roughouts (fig. 84b–c)

G Projectile point roughouts in different stages of preparation (arrowheads etc.) (fig. 85a–d)

H Others

H.I. Pre-cores/cores or early tool roughouts and their fragments (fig. 91b)

H.II. Other: all other knapped but unfinished pieces (fig. 85e)

Second Group: Flakes and waste (plate 12)
Note: > 20 mm (e.g.) refers to length not breadth

A Complete flakes: > 20 mm

A.I. Primary flakes: > 90 per cent of cortex or other natural surface remaining

A.I.1. Large: > 80 mm
A.I.1.1. – with flat platform prepared by striking off a single flake (fig. 92a)
A.I.1.2. – with faceted platform (fig. 92b)
A.I.1.3. – with unprepared platform
A.I.1.4. – with punctiform platform

A.I.2. Medium: > 50 to ≤ 80 mm
A.I.2.1. – with flat platform prepared by striking off a single flake (fig. 92c)
A.I.2.2. – with faceted platform (fig. 92d)
A.I.2.3. – with unprepared platform (fig. 92e)
A.I.2.4. – with punctiform platform (fig. 92f)

A.I.3. Small: > 20 to ≤ 50 mm
A.I.3.1. – with flat platform prepared by striking off a single flake

A.I.3.2. – with faceted platform
A.I.3.3. – with unprepared platform
A.I.3.4. – with punctiform platform

A.II. Secondary flakes: > 10 to ≤ 90 per cent of cortex or other natural surface remaining

A.II.1. Large: > 80 mm
A.II.1.1. – with flat platform prepared by striking off a single flake (figs 79a, 85f and 92g)
A.II.1.2. – with faceted platform (fig. 86a)
A.II.1.3. – with unprepared platform (fig. 81a)
A.II.1.4. – with punctiform platform

A.II.2. Medium: > 50 to ≤ 80 mm
A.II.2.1. – with flat platform prepared by striking off a single flake
A.II.2.2. – with faceted platform
A.II.2.3. – with unprepared platform
A.II.2.4. – with punctiform platform

A.II.3. Small: > 20 to ≤ 50 mm
A.II.3.1. – with flat platform prepared by striking off a single flake
A.II.3.2. – with faceted platform
A.II.3.3. – with unprepared platform
A.II.3.4. – with punctiform platform

A.III. Tertiary flakes: < 10 per cent of cortex or other natural surface remaining

A.III.1. Large: > 80 mm
A.III.1.1. – with flat platform prepared by striking off a single flake
A.III.1.2. – with faceted platform (fig. 86b)
A.III.1.3. – with unprepared platform
A.III.1.4. – with punctiform platform

A.III.2. Medium: > 50 to ≤ 80 mm
A.III.2.1. – with flat platform prepared by striking off a single flake (fig. 92h)
A.III.2.2. – with faceted platform
A.III.2.3. – with unprepared platform
A.III.2.4. – with punctiform platform

A.III.3. Small: > 20 to ≤ 50 mm
A.III.3.1. – with flat platform prepared by striking off a single flake
A.III.3.2. – with faceted platform (fig. 86c)
A.III.3.3. – with unprepared platform
A.III.3.4. – with punctiform platform (fig. 92i)

B Specific flake types and their fragments
(fig. 86d–f)

C Microflakes and chips ≤ 20 mm (plate 13)

D Waste: fragments including of flakes showing even a very small amount of working

E Natural fragments of flint nodules and other natural flints smaller than roughouts and cores in the 1972–4 chipping floor

Third Group: Blades and their fragments

A Complete blades

A.I.   Primary blades: > 90 per cent of cortex or other natural surface remaining
    A.I.1. – with flat platform prepared by striking off a single flake
    A.I.2. – with faceted platform
    A.I.3. – with unprepared platform
    A.I.4. – with punctiform platform

A.II.   Secondary blades: 10 to ≤ 90 per cent of cortex or other natural surface remaining
    A.II.1. – with flat platform prepared by striking off a single flake (fig. 87a–b)
    A.II.2. – with faceted platform
    A.II.3. – with unprepared platform
    A.II.4. – with punctiform platform

A.III.   Tertiary blades: < 10 per cent of cortex or other natural surface remaining
    A.III.1. – with flat platform prepared by striking off a single flake (fig. 87c)
    A.III.2. – with faceted platform (fig. 87d)
    A.III.3. – with unprepared platform
    A.III.4. – with punctiform platform

A.IV.   Tertiary blades from core exploitation: < 10 per cent of cortex or other natural surface remaining
    A.IV.1. – with flat platform prepared by striking off a single flake
    A.IV.2. – with faceted platform (fig. 87e)
    A.IV.3. – with unprepared platform
    A.IV.4. – with punctiform platform

B Blades without distal section

B.I.   Primary blades without distal section: > 90 per cent of cortex or other natural surface remaining
    B.I.1. – with flat platform prepared by striking off a single flake
    B.I.2. – with faceted platform
    B.I.3. – with unprepared platform
    B.I.4. – with punctiform platform

B.II.   Secondary blades without distal section: 10 to ≤ 90 per cent of cortex or other natural surface remaining
    B.II.1. – with flat platform prepared by striking off a single flake
    B.II.2. – with faceted platform
    B.II.3. – with unprepared platform
    B.II.4. – with punctiform platform

B.III.   Tertiary blades without distal section: < 10 per cent of cortex or other natural surface remaining
    B.III.1. – with flat platform prepared by striking off a single flake
    B.III.2. – with faceted platform
    B.III.3. – with unprepared platform
    B.III.4. – with punctiform platform

B.IV.   Tertiary blades without distal section from core exploitation: < 10 per cent of cortex or other natural surface remaining
    B.IV.1. – with flat platform prepared by striking off a single flake
    B.IV.2. – with faceted platform
    B.IV.3. – with unprepared platform
    B.IV.4. – with punctiform platform

C Blades without proximal section or without proximal and distal sections

D Specific blade types (fig. 87f)

E Blade fragments

Fourth Group: Implements

A End-scrapers and other forms of scraper (fig. 88a–c)
B Borers and perforators
C Projectile points, arrowheads
D Axes and adzes
E Discoidal knives
F Picks
G Fabricators (fig. 88d)
H Hammerstones (plate 14)
I Other (fig. 88e–i)

The four groups taken together reflect the morphological structure of a flint assemblage, its parts and individual units. They provide the basis for further analysis and comparison. The categories listed above are in the main defined, but in some cases are partly arbitrary. As an addendum to the morphological classification a simple system of measurements, different for each group, was also used.

1.1 Classification of specimens in the First Morphological Group

In this group were classified natural nodules and their larger fragments, and all specimens displaying evidence of knapping but unfinished, i.e. all stages of roughouts and cores, and their fragments.

The basis for attributing specimens to categories A and B was our knowledge of early tool roughouts and roughouts (preforms) already distinguished as small finds recovered from the 1972–4 chipping floor and from other features at Grimes Graves during the excavations carried out by Armstrong, Mercer and the British Museum. Examples that could potentially have been initial forms for preparing early roughouts of discoidal knives (category E), axes or adzes (category F) were attributed to categories A, B.I. and B.II. (fig. 78, and plates 7 and 8). The basic criterion for distinguishing category B.III. in the First Group from category D in the Second Group was the weight of the specimen. With just a few exceptions, specimens weighing more than 200 g were attributed to category B.III.

The basis for distinguishing between initial (figs 80b, 82, 83a–b and 90a–b, and plates 9–11), early roughouts (figs 81a, 83c and 89a–b) and tool roughouts (figs 81b, 84a–c and 91a) was the amount of preparatory work that had been carried out. The division depended on the number of surfaces that had been worked and whether in one or two directions:

a   Specimens that were worked on not more than two sides in one or both directions were attributed to the category 'initial tool roughout'.

b   Specimens that were worked on more than two sides in one or both directions, but whose shaping had not been finished, were classified as 'early tool roughouts'.

c   Specimens categorized as 'tool roughouts' had a finished form but needed further work, usually the removal of a series of small flakes and chips before they were ready for polishing.

Early roughouts and roughouts of indeterminate tools were attributed to group C (fig. 79). Usually these were specimens that when worked further could have been made into a roughout for a discoidal knife, axe or adze. The categories C.IV. and C.V. apply to roughouts for different types of indeterminate tool (fig. 79c).

Among the additional criteria used for classifying specimens of the First Group were measurements. On the basis of an analysis of the small finds it was assumed that the grounds for distinguishing cores (category D) was the intention to obtain blades or flakes more than 50 mm as blanks for further use. A minimum length or maximum dimension of 50 mm was taken as the limiting size as analysis of small flake tools, especially arrowheads, indicated this to be appropriate. Length and width of early roughouts and roughouts were also important criteria which, together with morphological criteria, served to

distinguish potential axes or adzes from discoidal knives. It was assumed that early roughouts and roughouts of axes or adzes have a length at least 50 per cent greater than their width. Exceptions to this rule were rare. In contrast, initial and early discoidal knives should not have a length more than 25 per cent greater than their width. The above measurements were used in addition to morphological criteria. Specimens that, on the basis of measurement or unambiguous morphological criteria, did not fit into category E or F were attributed to category C (fig. 79). When classifying and analysing the material it was found that these ratios were very useful criteria but unfortunately insufficient for a specimen to be attributed solely on their basis to the axe/adze or discoidal knife group. There had to be other indications of how the specimen was going to be worked, as from large early specimens having the proportions of a discoidal knife an axe could have been made, and vice versa. Therefore the basic criterion for classification was the form of the specimen and analysis of the direction in which the work was being taken.

Category E was termed 'early forms of discoidal knives' because these were not always bifacial forms. The term 'discoidal' is also understood in a wider sense (figs 80b, 81a–b and 89a–b). This category includes not only round or nearly round specimens (see Saville 1981, 108, F129 and F130), but also bifacial subdiscoidal knives (see Saville 1981, 109, F131) and similar shapes, for instance sub-rectangular. Nevertheless, some specimens close to this group were attributed to the C.V. category (for example, fig. 79c). Probably during the early phase of knapping it was difficult to determine what final shape the bifacial knife being worked would assume. Category E could also include individual early roughouts of other tools, for instance leaf-shaped points, as in the initial or early phases of preparation they may differ only slightly from discoidal bifacial knife roughouts.

During the formation of roughouts for bifacial discoidal knives pseudo-levalloisian cores could sometimes occur (according to the old view, presented also by Grahame Clark [1952, 172], 'The striking of flakes from elaborately prepared cores in the Levallois technique, which survived, even if in somewhat specialized form, in the manufactories of Grimes Graves till the end of neolithic times ...'). They were similar in shape to levalloisian cores and when worked produced flakes that matched the criteria for flake blanks, but in the mass of material from the 1972–4 chipping floor and Feature 112 such examples were rare (fig. 89b). Discoidal knives are discussed further by Varndell (this volume, p. 176–7).

1.2 Classification of specimens in the Second Morphological Group

Category A flakes comprise the basic group of production waste from both assemblages (figs 85f, 86 and 92, and plate 12). Moreover, large massive flakes removed from large fragments of *floorstone* were the basic blanks for preparing axes/adzes and discoidal knives (figs 81a, 83c, 84a, 84c, 89a and 91a).

All complete specimens and flakes with small defects of more than 20 mm were categorized as flakes. Defective specimens were classified as flakes as long as their bulb was intact, and the size and features of the dorsal surface could be determined (or the size of the cortical surface). Microflakes and chips, as well as worked flint fragments of 20 mm or less, were included in category C (plate 13).

Category B in the group of flakes and waste included core trimming flakes and other examples of typical flakes, for instance those resulting from a change in the orientation of preparation of early roughouts and roughouts (fig. 86d–f).

Additional features used to classify complete flakes in category A were the attributes of their dorsal surface, their size and the type of striking platform. These were all defined in the classification. Several different size categories were considered. All were tested on samples of several hundred up to about a thousand flakes. The set of flake sizes given in the classification turned out to best match the material from the 1972–4 chipping floor. The two size categories greater than 50 mm included mostly specimens selected as blanks for the production of flake tools, for instance end-scrapers or arrowheads. From among specimens of 50 mm or less potential flake blanks for making retouched tools were very rarely chosen.

Category D included all flake fragments and other specimens displaying even a very small area of worked surface, while category E comprised natural fragments of flint nodules and other natural pieces of flint smaller than tool roughouts and cores from the chipping floors under investigation.

1.3 Classification of specimens in the Third Morphological Group
A blade is a flake with a width to length ratio of less than 1:2, with more or less parallel sides, its striking platform perpendicular to the longest axis and therefore consistent with the direction of blade removal (category A). The surviving proportion of the specimen allows us to distinguish a blade from a blade fragment. Pieces with a width to length ratio of less than 1:2 were attributed to one of the categories of blades (A, B, C, D) if they fulfilled the remaining criteria mentioned earlier (fig. 87). Each specimen that was a part of a blade, but did not at the time of classification possess the proportions of a blade, was treated as a blade fragment (E).

Classification of specimens belonging to the Third Morphological Group – blades and blade fragments – takes into consideration four attributes: state of preservation, proportions, character of the dorsal surface of the artefact, and type of butt.

In the assemblages from Grimes Graves blades are rare; regular blades which could be supposed to have been removed from blade cores occur only exceptionally,

but are found (fig. 87e). It is known that blades were an important end product of chipping floors in some of the other large flint mines with deep shafts such as Spiennes and Rijckholt-St Geertruid (Lech 1983, 77–8; de Grooth 1991, 180; Collet *et al.* 2008, 59). For this reason, when studying the material from the Grimes Graves chipping floors it was worth trying to describe all the blades recovered. The classification applied to complete blades was based on the principles established for flakes from Grimes Graves, utilizing the classification devised for assemblages from the Sąspów flint mine, Cracow district (Poland), where blades were one of the main products (Lech 1975; 1983, 52–62; Dzieduszycka-Machnikowa and Lech 1976, 25–31 and 43–4). Since the initial analysis and non-source-based knowledge showed that most of the specimens from this small group were produced accidentally, during the removal of flakes, the category A.IV. was introduced, comprising only specimens which could have been removed from blade cores (fig. 87e). Three measurements were noted for each specimen of categories A and B: maximum length, width and thickness. At Grimes Graves, blades and blade fragments could be considered as a subgroup of the Second Morphological Group: flakes and waste.

1.4 Classification of specimens in the Fourth Morphological Group
This group comprises only recognizable implement types, including hammerstones (plate 14) and fabricators (fig. 88d), leaving out roughouts and utilized flakes, blades and their fragments. Amongst the flint material from Grimes Graves implements are extremely rare. Therefore the Fourth Morphological Group was divided into basic categories only (see classification). In the case of implements three measurements were also noted for each specimen: maximum length, width and thickness, with the exception of hammerstones, whole or fragmentary, in which case only the diameter was measured.

2 A comparison of the two chipping floor assemblages

2.1 Raw material
In the 1972–4 chipping floor knappers worked mainly *floorstone*, extracted from the base of the shafts and galleries of the deep mines (fig. 82 and plate 2), probably in the immediate vicinity (Mercer 1981, 1–2; Mortimore and Wood 1986, 7–9; Longworth and Varndell 1996, 84–9, plates 3, 8 and 14; see also Craddock *et al.*, this volume pp. 156–7). In some cases *top-* or *wallstone* from the upper layers of deposits cut by a shaft was also utilized, but instances of this seem to be rare; no early roughout made from *topstone* could be found (plates 7 and 14a). However, it should be noted that in some instances distinguishing between the three types of flint is impossible in the case of an actual tool. Taking as a test the flint nodule from

the 1972–4 chipping floor, cutting 1255.5/905.5: P b: attributed to category B.I., it weighs 2242 g and measures about 220 x 136 x 77 mm (fig. 78, and plate 8). On the one hand, its shape and thin cortex in some areas (less than 1 mm) might suggest that this nodule was *topstone*. On the other, the 18-mm-thick cortex elsewhere and the black colour of the flint are like those of *floorstone*. This conclusion seems even more certain when we compare the raw material from both assemblages. In Feature 112 knappers worked mostly *top-* or *wallstone* (figs 89b and 91b), and a few large flakes of what is clearly *floorstone* (figs 89a and 91a), which were probably collected from abandoned chipping floors associated with the deep mines.

Looking at the material we may conclude that on the 1972–4 chipping floor initial and early roughouts were formed from large massive flakes removed from large nodules of *floorstone*, at times perhaps also *wallstone* (figs 79a, 83c, 84c and 86a). This confirms the observation once made by J.G.D. Clark (1928, 44) that the 'discoidal knife is essentially a flake implement' (figs 81a, 86b and 89a). It should be added that axes and adzes made at Grimes Graves from *floorstone* were also in the most part flake tools. Analysis of both assemblages and of the small finds leads to this conclusion.

The breaking up of large *floorstone* nodules into appropriate pieces (fig. 78) and massive flakes (figs 87a

and 94a–b) must have taken place at the bottom of the shaft or directly next to it. In the material from the 1972–4 chipping floor there is no indication that flint nodules were broken up there. There are examples of some small nodules of *floorstone* being worked into axe/adze roughouts (fig. 82, and plates 9–11), but there is a lack of the fragments of nodules of various sizes which occurred in large amounts at the bottom of shafts and in the galleries, for instance in Greenwell's shaft or in Shaft 15.

2.2 The general structure of the assemblages

On analysis both chipping floors could be seen to have a very similar structure, with 97–8 per cent of the material falling into the Second Morphological Group, i.e. flakes and waste (fig. 77). The remaining three morphological groups are only marginal on both chipping floors and make up, altogether, between 2 and 3 per cent of the assemblages. Differences between adjoining metre squares of both chipping floors are not great. In the case of the 1972–4 chipping floor this breakdown seems to be remarkably consistent. The three metre squares crossing the floor from west to east, i.e. β4, β14 and square B in 1963/905.5, showed very similar values for waste and flakes, in spite of the variation in total number of specimens examined (1027, 1611 and 5212 respectively). The most notable variation was a greater presence of

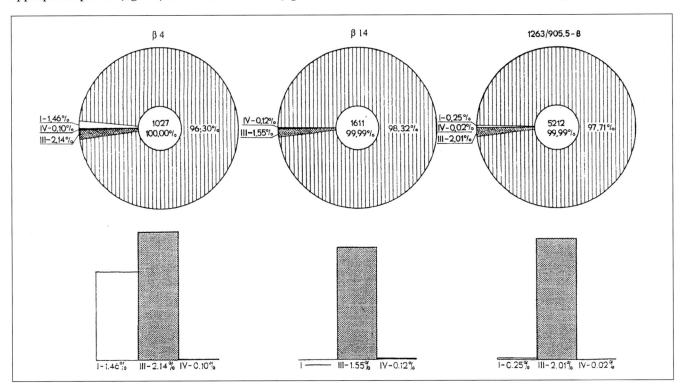

Fig. 93 Comparison of general structure of material from 3 metre squares of the 1972–4 chipping floor: β4, β14 and 1263/905.5 B, according to four morphological groups (see fig. 74).

I   natural nodules, initial, early and advanced tool roughouts, pre-cores and cores
II   flakes and waste
III blades and blade fragments
IV   retouched pieces and tools

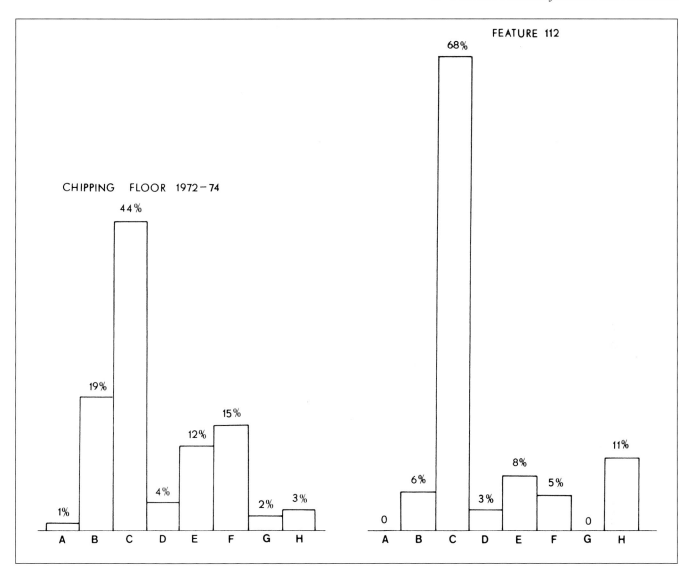

CHIPPING FLOOR 1972–74

FEATURE 112

Fig. 94 Comparison of structure of First Group between the 1972–4 chipping floor and Feature 112.

A   nodules and their large fragments
B   specimens with primary working
C   roughouts of indeterminate tools
D   cores
E   early forms of discoidal knives
F   early forms of adzes and axes
G   projectile point roughouts at various stages of working
H   others

Group I material in β4, although even here the total amounts to less than 2 per cent (fig. 93). This difference in the composition of β4 may perhaps indicate that this was where early roughouts were collected before further reduction (figs 74i and 93). It is interesting that tool roughouts in the early stages of preparation occur four times as frequently in Feature 112.

2.3 The structure of the First Morphological Group
Both chipping floors represent debris from the production of axe and adze heads, as well as from the preparation of discoidal bifacial knives – a flint tool type of unknown use found only in the British Isles (Clark 1928). The roughouts of these tools were manufactured mainly from large massive flakes, both cortical and non-cortical. In such cases they were flake tools (figs 81a and 89a). Axe and adze heads were also made from small flint nodules or smaller blocks of flint (fig. 82 and plates 9–11). In both cases they were prepared in the same way as classic core implements. However, the material from the First Morphological Group from both chipping floors indicates that the initial and early forms for preparing tool roughouts of axes/adzes and discoidal knives were mainly large flakes (figs 83a, 84a, 84c and 91a) and not small nodules or blocks which, it seems, were rare. Small flint tools were also produced, although in what quantity it is difficult to say. A difference between the chipping floors is at once visible in the better quality of raw material (*floorstone*) and in the much greater scale of production evident in the 1972–4 chipping floor.

On both chipping floors there is a complete lack of large

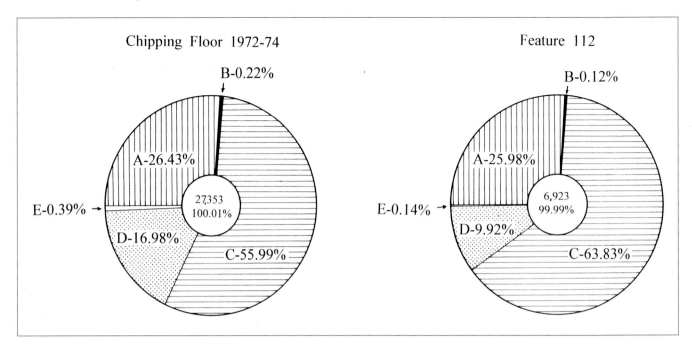

Fig. 95 Comparison of structure of Second Group between the 1972–4 chipping floor and Feature 112.

A   whole flakes
B   specific flake types (e.g. core rejuvenation)
C   microflakes and chips < 20 mm
D   waste
E   small natural fragments of nodules and other natural flints of small size

cores which could have been the source of the large flakes used to produce axes/adzes and discoidal knives (see Mercer 1981, 23). This confirms the initial conclusion, reached on the basis of preliminary analysis, that there must also have existed places (chipping floors) where, from large nodules of *floorstone*, smaller blocks of flint and very large flakes were removed to obtain preforms for the above-mentioned tool categories. Such work must have been done very near to where the flint was extracted – probably in part at the bottom of the shaft (see Mercer 1981, 23–4) or nearby.

Interesting results were obtained when comparing the structure of the First Morphological Group taken from each chipping floor, comprising roughouts in various stages of preparation and cores (fig. 94). The 1972–4 chipping floor had a much higher frequency of early roughouts of discoidal knives (fig. 81), axes or adzes (figs 82–4, and plates 9–11) and arrowheads (fig. 85a–d) – 29 per cent altogether – while Feature 112 contained only 13 per cent of the First Morphological Group (figs 89–91a), without a single example of an arrowhead. Feature 112 is much more clearly dominated by specimens of indeterminate purpose that were rejected during the initial and early stages of working. The reasons for this were twofold: the poorer quality of the raw material and probably the more

limited manual abilities of the flint knapper or knappers who worked there. Neither assemblage contains many cores (figs 80a and 91b). However, their occurrence is important as it confirms that smaller flakes and, to some degree, also blades were used as blanks for the manufacture of certain categories of tool.

The variety of early roughouts and tool roughouts in both assemblages rather suggests that they served to produce a variety of tools of different sizes. There is no indication of a marked standardization of final products on the 1972–4 chipping floor.

2.4 The structure of the Second Morphological Group
Whereas a comparison of the First Morphological Group from both chipping floors shows definite similarities but also important differences, the structure of the Second Group – flakes and waste – is, with one exception, basically identical (fig. 95, and plate 12). It seems, therefore, that both workshops had a similar place in the organization of the work cycle carried out on the mine field. Over half of the specimens are microflakes and chips – category C – small flakes, less than 20 mm in size (plate 13), created in large amounts during the final stages in the preparation of axes, adzes and discoidal bifacial knives. Whole flakes – category A – comprise one quarter of both assemblages (figs 85f, 86 and 92). The greater number of category D specimens (fragments of flakes and other specimens with evidence of working) in the material from the 1972–4 chipping floor may result from the fact that other tools such as arrowheads (fig. 85a–d) were manufactured from the smaller flakes, and some were intentionally broken. Another reason for the greater number of pieces assigned to category D could have been the greater time span over which knapping took place, during which previously worked material could have been trampled. There is

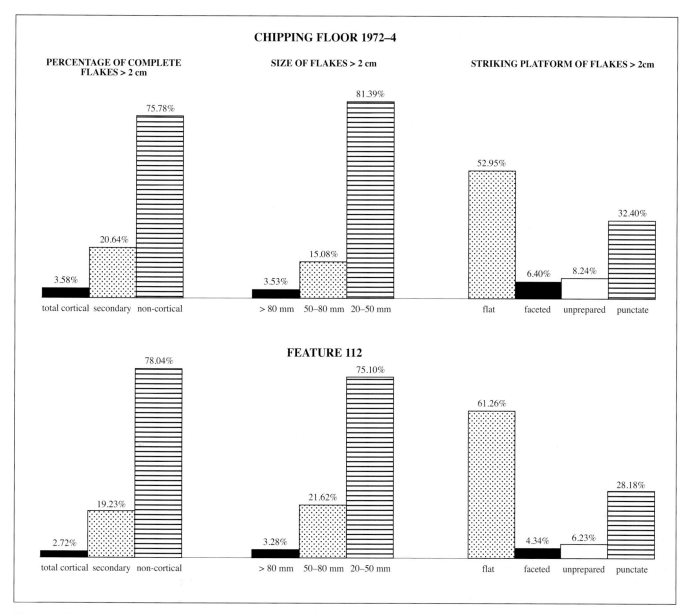

Fig. 96 Comparison of the basic attributes of flakes > 20 mm from the 1972–4 chipping floor and Feature 112.

also a characteristic sparsity of natural flint fragments – category E. This, together with other supporting factors, leads to the conclusion that the selection and initial working of the flint extracted from the shafts was carried out elsewhere and both workshops received this selected raw material.

The group of flakes that underwent further examination showed far-reaching similarities as to the frequency of occurrence of the various attributes taken into consideration (figs 96–8). The proportion of three of the categories – cortical flakes, secondary flakes and non-cortical flakes – is practically the same in both workshops (fig. 96). The small proportion of cortical flakes confirms the supposition that the raw material went through a process of initial selection and preparation elsewhere.

In both of the assemblages analysed specimens

greater than or equal to 5 cm were waste; exceptions, if present, were very rare. The 1972–4 chipping floor is primarily composed of waste. Very few of the remaining specimens were suitable for further use in the production of the type of tools which were characteristic of both assemblages. For this reason, the size of the desired flake blank produced outside the 1972–4 chipping floor is better demonstrated by the remaining initial and early tool roughouts from categories C, E and F of the First Morphological Group than by the surviving flakes. Large flakes that served to make preforms (tool roughouts) of axes/adzes and discoidal knives were obtained from appropriately prepared nodules. Such flakes and blade-flakes from categories A.I.–A.III., and sometimes D, had a considerable weight – about 150 to about 300 g, at times even more; a length of about 13–15 cm, or even

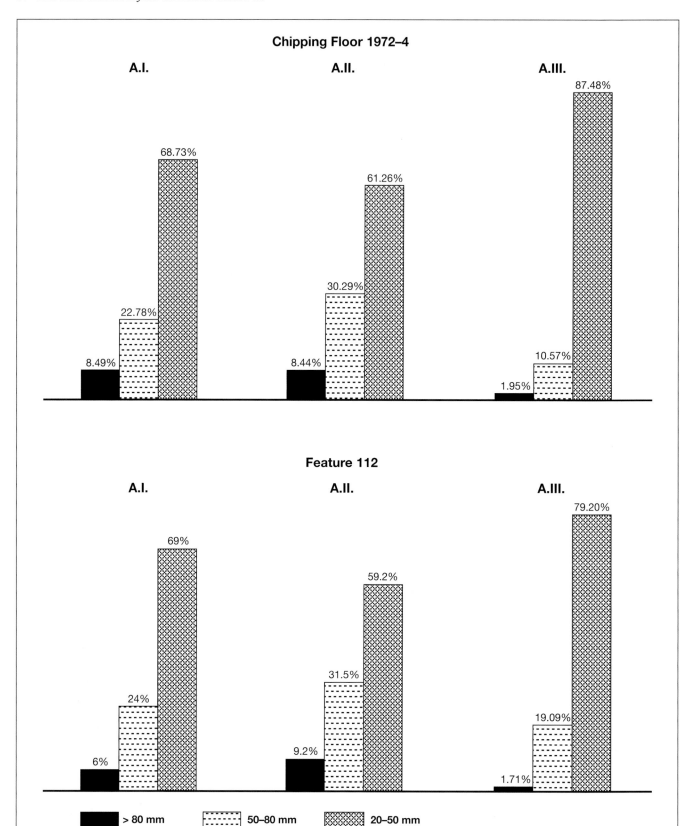

Fig. 97 Comparison of flakes by sub-categories between the 1972–4 chipping floor and Feature 112.

A.I.   cortical flakes
A.II.   secondary flakes
A.III. non-cortical tertiary flakes

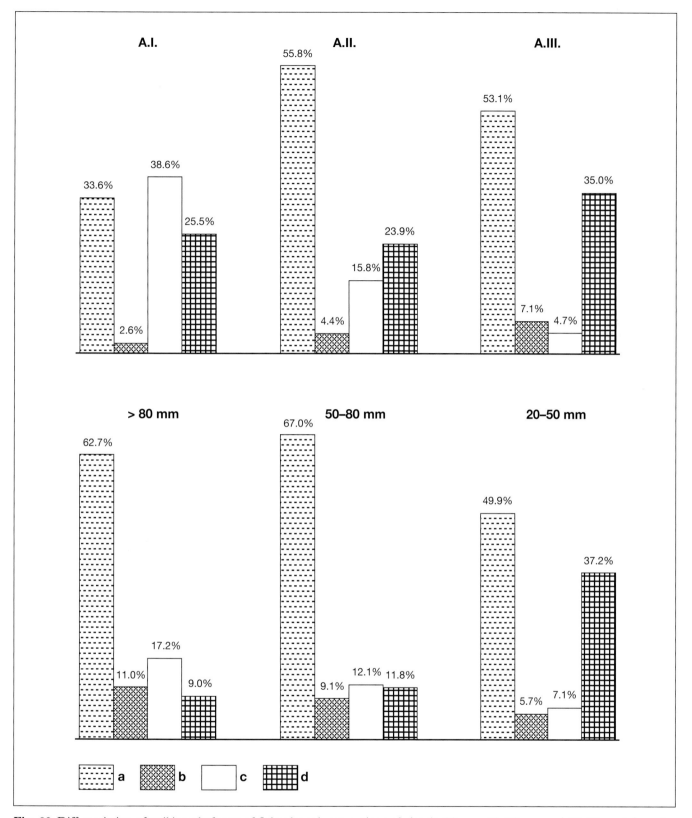

Fig. 98 Differentiation of striking platforms of flakes by sub-categories and size (> 80 mm; 50–80 mm and 20–50 mm) from the 1972–4 chipping floor.

A.I.   cortical
A.II.   secondary
A.III. non-cortical tertiary
a: flat; b: faceted; c: unprepared; d: punctiform

greater, and a width of not less than several centimetres (figs 79a and 86a; see also fig. 92g). In the material from the 1972–4 chipping floor they occur rarely, as they were either made into roughouts (figs 81a, 83c and 84a) or removed by later flint knappers looking for valuable *floorstone*. Such abandoned chipping floors that had worked *floorstone* probably acted as a secondary source for those chipping floors that otherwise utilized mainly *topstone* and *wallstone*, such as Feature 112 (figs 89a, 91a and 92g). The greater frequency of flakes with faceted (fig. 86a–c) and punctiform striking platforms from the 1972–4 chipping floor may be connected with the more advanced preparation of roughouts in this assemblage, as confirmed by the composition of the First Morphological Group (figs 96 and 98).

The greater number of medium-sized flakes in Feature 112 (fig. 92c–d) suggests that in the 1972–4 chipping floor they served more often as blanks for the manufacture of small tools, such as arrowheads (figs 96 and 97). Other data also support this view. The size of the flakes, according to the basic sub-categories of specimens more than 20 mm – cortical flakes, secondary flakes and tertiary (non-cortical) flakes – supports the hypothesis that some of the non-cortical flakes from the 1972–4 chipping floor were used as blanks to produce small flint implements (fig. 97). The knappers from Feature 112 probably proceeded in the same way, but the practice is more evident in the 1972–4 chipping floor assemblage.

In category C, microflakes and chips, there are decidedly more microflakes, i.e. pieces 10–20 mm in diameter, and fragments of larger specimens of the same size (plate 13). Chips, unbroken pieces and fragments of 10 mm or less are rare. Practically no pieces of 5 mm or less were recovered; in the case of the 1972–4 chipping floor this was, of course, an artefact of the sieving process.

If we assume that preparing an axe/adze or discoidal knife involved the removal of something in the order of 1000 flakes and chips, then the number of tool roughouts (preforms) produced on the 1972–4 chipping floor was about 250; however, if 250 flakes and chips were removed to make one preform then the number increases to 1000 (see Newcomer 1971; Hansen and Madsen 1983). This simple and completely theoretical calculation is intended to show that even a very large chipping floor does not produce a great number of final products, as has previously been suggested (Sieveking 1979, 39). According to P.V. Hansen and B. Madsen (1983, 48–55), the number of chipped flakes greater than 20 mm in the manufacture of large thin-butted flint axes was between 462 and 557 specimens for one replica axe (Experiments IIIA and IVA–E), but it seems that the average weight of flint blanks and size of finished preforms of axe blades was much higher in the case of the described experiments than in the case of both chipping floors from Grimes Graves (see also Saville 1981, 69; Burton 1984, 244; Holgate 1995, 155–7). Tool roughouts from

both chipping floors showed a lack of uniformity and the degree of standardization was not especially high.

2.5 Brief comments on the Third and Fourth Morphological Groups

Most blades were made by chance, during the preparation of tool roughouts or in the exploitation of rare flake cores (fig. 87). Blade blanks were also produced intentionally, though in small quantities. The problem needs further study. Present in the 1972–4 chipping floor was a long tertiary blade with faceted platform struck from a core (fig. 87e). From the sample studied other long blades are also known: A.II.1. (fig. 87b) and a category D blade form (fig. 87f).

Small tools such as end-scrapers (fig. 88a and c), side-scrapers (fig. 88b) and 'racloirs' (fig. 96f) were probably intended for immediate use (the term 'racloir' is used here in inverted commas to describe larger, massive side-scrapers). Also from the 1972–4 chipping floor came two truncated blades (fig. 88g and h), a massive retouched blade (157 x 63 x 14 mm and weighing 147 g), a fragment of fabricator (fig. 88d), a flint hammerstone (weighing 356 g) and a small splinter (*pièce esquille*) (fig. 88i). A macrolithic burin (maximum dimension 97 mm and weighing 256 g) is probably an 'accidental tool' produced as a by-product of retouching flakes. In the sample from Feature 112 were side-scrapers, retouched flakes, a 'racloir' and another burin (accidental?). It would be useful to try functional (microwear) analysis in order to assess the present suppositions as they apply to the entire group of 'retouched tools' from chipping floor 1972–4 (see Cook and Dumont 1987; Gijn 1990, 3–57); the names customarily given to the artefacts may not reflect their use correctly. It is entirely possible that this very modest group of artefacts is all that remains of a much greater number of which most were taken away from the site by the flint knappers.

3 Discussion and conclusions from the study of the flint assemblages

Study of the material from the chipping floors has shown that roughouts were being made for various tools as well as flake and blade blanks (fig. 99). The range of products from the 1972–4 chipping floor includes axe/adzes (fig. 84) and roughouts for all the most frequent forms: discoidal and other knives (fig. 81), less frequently arrowheads (fig. 85a–d), side-, end- and plane scrapers, rare 'racloirs', truncated blades (fig. 88) and very rare picks (fig. 85e?). The greater number of medium-sized flakes present in Feature 112 suggests that comparable flakes on the larger floor were probably being more frequently utilized as blanks for the manufacture of smaller tools (figs 97–8).

The comparative analysis of the contents of the samples drawn from the two floors therefore leads to the conclusion that, while the approach to the utilization of the flint was very similar (see figs 89–91), choice or availability of raw

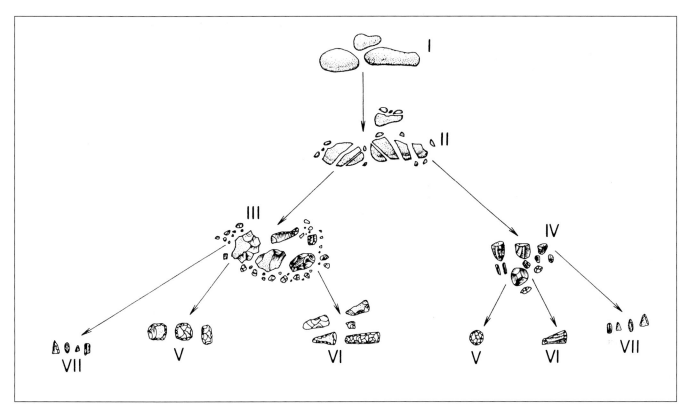

Fig. 99 A model of the reduction sequence seen in the 1972–4 chipping floor.

I   natural nodules and fragments

II   natural nodules/fragments with traces of initial working

III   initial, early and advanced tool roughouts and waste including some blanks for flake tools and arrowheads

IV   cores, flake and blade blanks

V   discoidal knives

VI   axes and adzes

VII   arrowheads and other small tools

material and the latent skill of the knappers as well as the actual scale of the operations underline a significant difference in the two contexts. These reflect procedures geared towards the processing on the one hand of high-quality material procured from the deep mines in contrast to the more limited opportunities for extraction in the West Field (Sieveking 1979, 12–16; see also Olausson 1983, 18). If the two operations were being undertaken simultaneously then this seems to support clear evidence for more than one segment of society (more than one community or big kinship group) being at work at the site. If the West Field operations continued later, as some of the ^{14}C dates suggest, then the hitherto prevailing desire primarily to procure and work the top-quality *floorstone* was now no longer current, or social structure and organization (for example, ceremonial exchange system) necessary for the further exploitation of the raw material from the deep mines had collapsed (Firth 1956, 41–79; Rappaport 1968, 105–9, 190–91, 211 and

220–31; Strathern 1969; 1971, 1–14, 101–14 and 214–22; McBryde 1984, 278–9; 1997; Burton 1987, 189–90; see also Mercer 1981, 32–3; Olausson 1983, 9–30; Lech 1991, 568–9; 1997, 632–4; de Grooth 1997, 73–4).

Saville (1981, 70–72) showed that the chipping floors found at Grimes Graves cannot be considered simply as the remains of axe factories, as had been assumed earlier following Clark (1952, 180) and Piggott (1954, 37). The 1972–4 chipping floor is the largest of the hitherto excavated floors. The assemblage consists of an imposing number of 250,000 flint pieces. However, as has been mentioned earlier, there is a possibility that this represents a conflation of several assemblages, closely related in time but not necessarily connected with the exploitation of one mine by one group of miners and flint knappers.

The survey of the 1972–4 chipping floor enables us to attempt a reconstruction of the stages and directions in which the flint processing was being taken (fig. 99). The flint was extracted and initially worked at the bottom of the shaft or nearby. Selected fragments of flint nodules and large flakes were brought to the chipping floor workshop. An analysis of the chipping floor material showed that knappers made roughouts of various tools – axes, adzes and discoidal bifacial knives (see Smith 1931), as well as flakes and blade blanks. Flakes and blades, in small numbers, were also obtained from cores (fig. 80a).

The analysis also showed that, even if the whole assemblage was the output of one group of miners and knappers from one period, the final product was less imposing than it had first seemed, although the need for new axe/adze blades would have been high (see

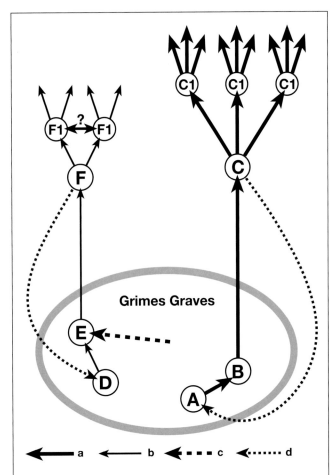

Fig. 100 A hypothetical model for the organization of labour within the area of the mine field.

A deep mine: primary fragmentation and selection of *floorstone* nodules and blocks in galleries and shaft base, with further early-stage preparation on surface close to shaft

B 1972–4 chipping floor: large-scale production of various tool roughouts from smaller blocks and large flake blanks brought from elsewhere (A)

C miners' and knappers' settlement (several households) at a greater (unknown) distance from the mine field; polishing of discoidal knives, polishing and hafting of axe/adze heads, preparation of arrowheads

C1 stage 1 of long-distance distribution of mined flint; settlements of end-users of axes and other chipping floor products; probably polishing and hafting of some flint blades and projectile points

D shallow West Field pit: primary fragmentation and selection of *wallstone* and *topstone* nodules, production and selection of smaller blocks and large flake blanks being carried out at the surface close to the pit

E Feature 112: small-scale production of various tool roughouts from smaller blocks and large flake blanks brought from elsewhere (D); production for miners'/knappers' own needs and for limited local exchange

F settlement of miners/users of small chipping floor products at a greater (unknown) distance from the mine field; polishing of discoidal knives, polishing and hafting of axe/adze heads, preparation of arrowheads

F1 local distribution of mined flint, mainly *wallstone* and *topstone*; settlements of end-users of axes and other products of Feature 112 near the miners'/knappers' household cluster, probably polishing and hafting of some flint blades

a direction of transport of *floorstone* products from deep mine

b direction of transport of *top-* and *wallstone* products from shallow pit

c transport by West Field knappers of selected flakes and blocks of *floorstone* from area of Deep Mine Field and large chipping floors to West Field (Feature 112)

d hypothetical route taken by mining/knapping teams from settlements to mine field

Olausson 1983, 67–9). Over half of the flint specimens were microflakes and chips of 20 mm or less (plate 13). The 250,000 flint pieces from the 1972–4 chipping floor weighed 1220 kg. Comparing these two figures underlines the high proportion of small pieces. An average specimen weighed just under 5 g (4.9 g). Depending on the number of flakes, microflakes and chips assumed to be the waste from the preparation of one axe, adze or discoidal bifacial knife, the total number of roughouts of such tools could be anywhere from several hundred to one thousand, although the lower figure is more probable. To this we must add an indeterminate number of flakes selected and removed from the chipping floor. In considering the quantity of final products likely to have been made we should remember that the 1972–4 chipping floor probably represented various episodes of flint-knapping over a

short duration of time (see Newcomer and Sieveking 1980). Therefore it seems probable that the total number of roughouts produced would have been taken away in batches.

4 A hypothetical model for the organization of labour

From the analysis of both chipping floors in the context of the extraction of flint from both deep shafts and shallow pits, it is possible to present two variants of a hypothetical model for the organization of labour within the area of the mine field (fig. 100), while accepting Mercer's reservation that the data 'can be subject to more than one interpretation ...' (Mercer 1981, 28).

A group of Grooved Ware miners would arrive at the mine field area from a settlement lying at an unknown distance from Grimes Graves. For the extraction of the *floorstone* from the deep mines the group probably consisted of over ten to about twenty people (Felder 1981, 60–61; Mercer 1981, 30–32). After clearing the workplace of trees and shrubs a shaft was dug (Sieveking 1979; 1980, 530–39; Holgate 1995, 153–5). On reaching the level of the *floorstone*, the miners would begin extraction of the raw material and its transportation to the surface (fig. 100A). The work was time-consuming. According to Mercer's rough calculations it would have taken a group of ten men about fifty days (compare de Grooth 1991, 181). However, it seems that the group of miners/knappers would have been larger – probably twelve to sixteen men or more. Felder (1981, 62) argued that 'At Grimes Graves the miners preferred a working method which favoured the exploitation of a large amount of flint in a short time'. In his view the relationship between shaft depth and the number of workers employed was as follows (Table 3):

Shaft depth (m)	Number of workers	Number of working days	Daily output pp (kg)
2–4	2–9	7–19	140–62
4–6	9–12	19–30	62–50
6–8	12–15	30–47	50–39
8–10	15–18	47–80	39–30
10–12	18–21	80–115	30–24

Table 3 Relationship between shaft depth and number of workers (after S. Felder).

According to Mercer (1981, 32), a group of this size could be part of an extended-family type unit, although, if we follow the suggestions of de Grooth (1995, 169; 1997, 74; see also 1991, 174–5), it could also have been made up of members of a larger group belonging to the same lineage – 'a lineage mode of production' or a big kinship unit – for example, the totemic subclan (Malinowski 1922, 118 and 125; Burton 1984, 239–41; see Topping 1997, 130; Sillitoe 1998, fig. 9.1).

The manufacture of axes/adzes and discoidal knives was subdivided into three separate activities – preparation of blanks, production of advanced roughouts (preforms) – both carried out on the Grimes Graves mine field – and the finishing of tools at settlement sites (see also Holmes 1919, 280–81; Dzieduszycka-Machnikowa and Lech 1976, 124–5; Lech 1983, 52–64; de Grooth 1991, 166–72). Initial selection and breaking up of flint nodules was carried out at the bottom of the shaft and finished on the surface, in the vicinity of the shaft. Flint blanks were also produced here, mainly in the form of large flakes and small flint blocks, and then transferred to workshops – chipping floors located further away (fig. 100B), where axes/adzes of various sizes, bifacial knives and arrowheads were made; here, too, small flakes to be used as implements in the settlements and blanks for arrowheads were selected. The final products of the chipping floors were taken to settlements, perhaps (but not necessarily) those from which the miners/knappers had come (fig. 100C). Here the most labour-consuming work was done – work which only slightly decreased the weight of the preforms and flake blanks. This included grinding, polishing and hafting (see Olausson 1983, 22, 43–4 and 60–63; Madsen 1984; Harding 1987). Most of

the laborious work involved in making arrows together with their flint heads would have been done in the settlements, probably in the winter season. Long-distance distribution of the final product made from *floorstone* (fig. 100C1) began in the settlements of the miners/knappers. Bradley and Edmonds (1993, 194–5) draw attention to the siting of Grimes Graves in the marginal zone between two major exchange systems, those of Group VI and Cornish axes, and suggest that 'artefact production may have been directed towards the north, as well as the southern network characterised by Group I axes'. They surmise that exchange may have been longer distance rather than local, referring to Healy's view (1991a) that the lithic industries of nearby settlement sites made but little use of mined flint. The scale of activity at Grimes Graves, considering particularly the deep mines and the extent of the 1972–4 chipping floor, belies the seeming absence of evidence for the distribution of the product (see also Craddock *et. al.* 1983 and this volume). This conundrum is not restricted to Britain. According to Whittle (1996, 280), 'there are frustrating contrasts between our knowledge of flint mine extractions, as at Rijckholt, Spiennes, Jablines, Cissbury or Grimes Graves, and our ignorance of the subsequent distribution of their products ...'. However, it seems highly probable that the extraction of *floorstone* from deep mines and the large-scale production of various preforms was at least in part stimulated by mechanisms activated by an unknown ceremonial exchange system with social and symbolic meaning created by the Grooved Ware communities, and some special symbolic significance attached to the Grimes Graves mine field (see Malinowski 1922, 172–5 and 358; Mauss 1990; Strathern 1971; compare Zeitlin 1987, 173–5; Douglas 1990, vii–xi; Thomas 1991, 22–3; Bradley and Edmonds 1993, 181–7 and 189–97; Sherratt 1994, 195; Tilley 1994, 7–34; Topping 1997; Felder *et. al.* 1998, 70; Sillitoe 1998, 69–98).

The Grimes Graves mine field also revealed evidence for the simple exploitation of *topstone* and *wallstone* from shallow extraction pits (West Field). In this case also, the flint was initially worked next to where the flint had been procured (fig. 100D) and flint blanks were transported to the site where the axe/adze blades and discoidal knives were manufactured (fig. 100E). The shallow pits can be associated with small chipping floors such as Feature 112 (fig. 100E). Axe/adze blades and discoidal bifacial knives were also prepared here but in much smaller numbers than at the chipping floors connected with the deep mines (for example, the 1972–4 chipping floor). According to rough calculations carried out for the flint mine at Sąspów near Cracow, the work would not take a group of three to five people more than one to two weeks, depending on the size of the group and the size of the shallow open pit (Lech 1975; Dzieduszycka-Machnikowa and Lech 1976, 124–5); in Sieveking's opinion (1979, 13 and 38), still less. On the West Field chipping floors, apart from *topstone* and *wallstone*, exceptional flakes and blocks of *floorstone* were collected from chipping floors connected with the deep mines. The size of production on the West Field chipping floors was much smaller but the organization of work was in three stages, as in the case of the extraction and processing of the *floorstone* (fig. 100A–C). The size of Feature 112, the volume of its final product and the organization of work that it entailed can be compared to the Danish flint axe manufacturing site of the Funnel Beaker culture at Hastrup Vænnget, East Zeland (Hansen and Madsen 1983).

In the case of the West Field, it can be assumed that the exploitation of flint (fig. 100D–E) served primarily to meet the needs of the community from which the miners/knappers came (fig. 100F), whether group of households, members belonging to the same lineage, 'sub-sub-clan' or other kinship group (Burton 1984, 237–9; de Grooth 1995, 169; Sillitoe 1998, 140–44). It probably also provided a certain surplus of axe/adze blades and discoidal knives for limited local exchange (fig. 100F1). In both cases (fig. 100A–C1 and D–F1) manufacturing of final products was subdivided into three separate activities: production of flint blanks (fig. 100A and D), production of advanced roughouts (preforms) (fig. 100B and E) and the final production of tools (fig. 100C and F). This supports the results of the earlier research and theoretical reflections of de Grooth (1991; 1995, 163–4; 1997; see also Felder 1981, 62 and Whittle 1996, 278–82).

Following de Grooth's studies of European flint mining (1995, 170; see also 1991; 1997), it would seem that the deep mines and the 1972–4 chipping floor were connected at least in part with the manufacture of artefacts '... as prestige objects in long-distance exchange networks' (see fig. 100A–C1), perhaps still connected with a 'lineage mode of production' (see also Bradley and Edmonds 1993, 195), while the shallow pits and chipping floors on the West Field were connected with a domestic mode of production, perhaps also as part of a lineage mode of production and local, limited exchange. It can only be surmised that the Grooved Ware communities 'hunting for *floorstone*' probably attributed to it some unknown symbolic and mythical significance connected with its origin (Healy 1991a; Taçon 1991; Tilley 1994, 53–4; Whittle 1995, 252–6; Thomas 1996, 148–64; Topping 1997, 130–31). As de Grooth writes: 'If one tries to understand Neolithic flint mining and distribution in purely economic terms, the combination of data from mines and other sites leads to a rather confusing picture' (1997, 73).

In this context of seeking reasons for the extraction of *floorstone* one is reminded of Malinowski's observation: 'Value is not the result of utility and rarity, intellectually compounded, but is the result of a sentiment grown round things, which, through satisfying human needs, are capable of evoking emotions. The value of manufactured objects of use must also be explained through man's emotional

nature, and not by reference to his logical construction of utilitarian views' (1922, 172).

If we accept that the Grimes Graves flint mine site was located in a marginal area 'outside the main settled landscape' (Bradley and Edmonds 1993, 41 and 196; Whittle 1996, 238–9), there is nevertheless in eastern England a concentration of sites with Grooved Ware in the neighbourhood of Grimes Graves (Cleal 1984, 142; 1999, 5; Ashwin 1996, 47–53; Longworth and Cleal 1999; Garrow 2006). This concentration may be associated with the exploitation and distribution of flint from the mine field. In the case of Grooved Ware settlements in eastern England, the work of Bakels (1978, 5–9, 140–42) on relations between Early Neolithic site assemblages and their environment may be brought to bear (de Grooth 1997, 73). This would mean that the nearest settlements occur perhaps within a radius of two hours' walking distance from Grimes Graves, i.e. at a distance of about 10 km. Within a radius of 30 km (six hours' walking distance) several Grooved Ware settlements have been discovered, as well as some stray finds (Bakels 1978, 7; Cleal 1984, 142; Bradley and Edmonds 1993, 185 and 187; see also de Grooth 1991, 176; Felder *et al.* 1998, 69).

In the light of the analysis of the 1972–4 chipping floor and Feature 112, the earlier view that '... miners were professionals' (Clark 1952, 179) must be modified. It seems that in the case of the deep mines and the 1972–4 chipping floor, observations allow us to define the Grooved Ware miner/knappers as specialists, who were highly skilled in the mining and knapping of flint (Firth 1965, 113; Lévi-Strauss 1973, 225; Sillitoe 1998, 123; see also Malinowski 1922, 113–16 and 125; Olausson 1983, 20–21; de Grooth 1991, 154–5, 177 and 179; 1997, 71 and 73; Topping 1997, 131; Felder *et al.* 1998, 66 and 68), while in the case of the shallow pits and chipping floors in the West Field, there is no evidence of anything exceeding the average skills of any Late Neolithic person. To summarize, specialized flint extraction and processing were taking place on the site but with no need to invoke full-time craftsmanship (Felder 1981, 62; Lech 1981, 45; de Grooth 1991, 182; Felder *et al.* 1998, 68).

This interpretation seems acceptable, taking into account the extensive exchange networks which existed among Grooved Ware communities and their other activities, evidenced, for instance, in their great ceremonial monuments. Apart from antler picks, axes and adzes as woodworking tools would have been essential for the construction of such monuments by Late Neolithic communities in the British Isles (Sieveking 1979, 39–40; Thomas 1991, 169–75). This need was answered by the production of quantities of preforms of various sizes on chipping floors working flint from deep mines such as Greenwell's and Mercer's shafts. It served primarily economic objectives but the fragments of very large axes and subdiscoidal knives from the 1972–4 chipping floor may be evidence that on this chipping floor preforms were produced which, after careful polishing, could have possessed symbolic meaning and/or conferred prestige. For example, one large fragment of an axe broken in an advanced stage of preparation (not illustrated) indicates a size of around 20 cm in length. The fact that they were made from *floorstone* probably also contributed to their significance (see Whittle 1995, 252–6; Lech 1997, 632–5; Felder *et al.* 1998, 66; Rudebeck 1998, 322–6).

Closing remarks

Analysis of samples from both assemblages enabled certain fresh observations to be made on differences in production trends on chipping floors associated with Grooved Ware communities. Flint picks were rare. They occurred in chipping floors from excavations carried out by Mercer in 1970–71 and published by Saville (1981, 50–51, 67–8, F78, F79 and others; see also Sieveking 1980, 539, Abb. 549c). Picks were also found in material excavated by Armstrong during his exploration of Shaft 15 in 1938. There were just two possible examples in the 1972–4 chipping floor (fig. 85e?).

Not much is yet known about the settlement and economic systems employed by Grooved Ware communities (Thomas 1991, 9–10 and 93–102; Bradley and Edmonds 1993, 189–97; Cleal 1999), but the scale of the exploitation of the shafts excavated by Greenwell and Mercer suggests a high degree of collaboration and organization among these groups.

It seems likely that the deep mines and extensive chipping floors such as the 1972–4 chipping floor catered for the needs of more than one Grooved Ware community, and that the mining and processing of flint was in this case more highly specialized. Smaller chipping floors such as Feature 112 and shallow pits perhaps served the needs of small local groups, whose participation in exchange networks may have been limited (fig. 100). The survey of these two chipping floors, as well as the evidence gained from earlier excavations, demonstrates that most categories of flint tool known from the domestic and ceremonial sites of Grooved Ware communities were being manufactured on the Grimes Graves site.

B Implements recovered from Areas A–C and the West Field

1 Axes

The problems associated with categorizing axes have been well rehearsed, most recently by Pitts (1996). Many attempts, even where successful, have been found to have only localized application. Clearly replication of specific forms was not uppermost in the minds of those fashioning these implements, although individual knappers may have been more successful in reproducing their own specific 'platonic' template. On the whole it was a range of forms no doubt in turn satisfying a range of woodworking needs that seems to have been acceptable. Quality was not always of paramount concern, and from what evidence we have from elsewhere in East Anglia we know that axes were produced from whatever, usually local, source made this possible. At Hunstanton, for example, the main flint source was beach pebbles, although it is not clear that axeheads were made from them (Healy 1993, 28 and 35).

At Grimes Graves, where the process towards achieving, rather than the actual completion of the product, provides the source of information, problems of definition become acute. For this reason it seems entirely acceptable to follow the type of broad definition employed by Saville (1981). In what follows, axes therefore embrace adze and mattock forms (plate 15) and are categorized as '"Heavy" tools with transverse cutting edges' (ibid., 8). In this analysis, however, chisel forms have also been included under form 3 (see below).

Given the caveat that we are dealing here largely with implements in the process of being chipped to a 'roughed-out' final shape, a number of forms appear to be recurrent. Work during the Museum's research programme has underlined the fact that final polishing was not part of the implement manufacturing process carried out on the site, only one butt end from a partially polished flint axe being recovered from Shaft X (plate 16; see below).

Since we are dealing here with a mixed assemblage, including both partially prepared and broken pieces, no attempt has been made to define types. Nor does this type of assemblage lend itself to the form of detailed analysis undertaken by Pitts (1996). Rather, it seems more useful simply to indicate general characteristics which recur and appear to indicate that axes of a certain form or profile were in the process of being manufactured.

Forms

1 The butt is pointed. The sides are either straight, with only modest convex curvature, or are occasionally more markedly convex expanding towards the cutting edge, which can be hemispherical, shallow rounded or flattened. The length is usually twice but less than three times the width. The section is more often asymmetric than symmetric, often retaining some of the original flake surface.

The largest, most finished and most exceptional axe recovered from the site is of this form and was found by Armstrong in Floor 85B (plate 17; Armstrong 1927, 135, fig. 34). While in fifteen cases only the butt end with its characteristic pointed form can be recognized (for example, fig. 101c–e), sixteen complete axes come from the site (example, fig. 101a and b).

The form is widely distributed across the site, being found redeposited in Pits 1 (Clarke 1915, 154, fig. 26), 2 (ibid., fig. 36), 4 (Peake 1919, 85, fig. 17k), 5, 9, 14 and 15, as well as Mercer's 71 shaft (Saville 1981, F113 and F115). It occurs in Floors 3C (Clarke 1915, 178, figs 54 and 55), 12A (ibid., 194, fig. 70), 16 (Peake 1916, 282, fig. 47), 23 (Peake 1917, 427, fig. 86G), 46

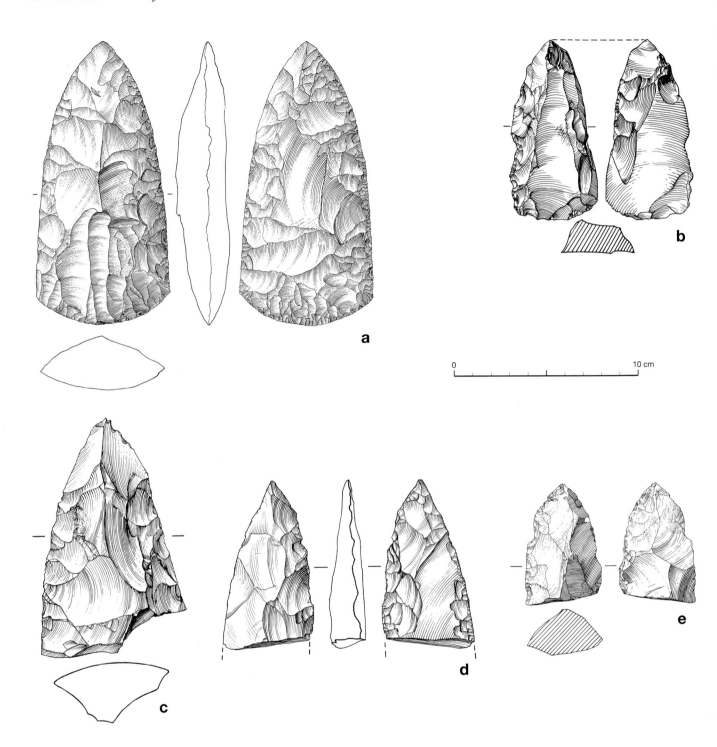

Fig. 101 a, b: Flint axes of form 1; c–e: broken flint axes of form 1 with pointed butt.

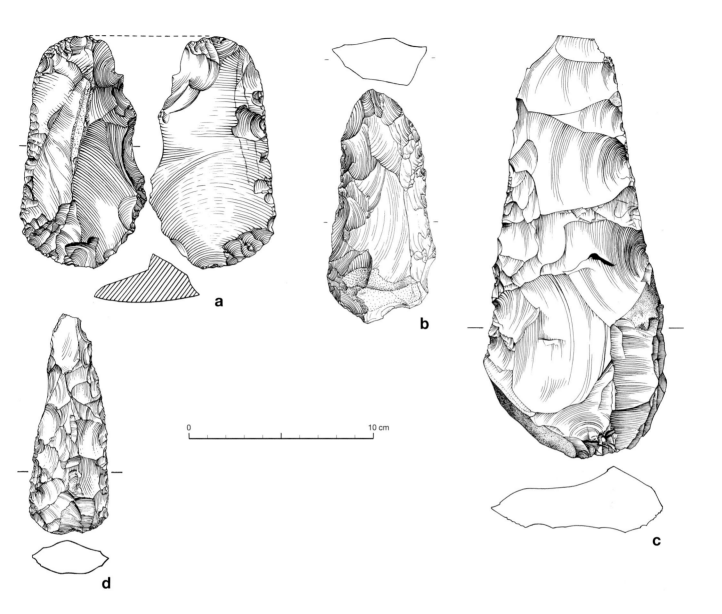

0   10 cm

Fig. 102 a–d: Flint axes of form 2.

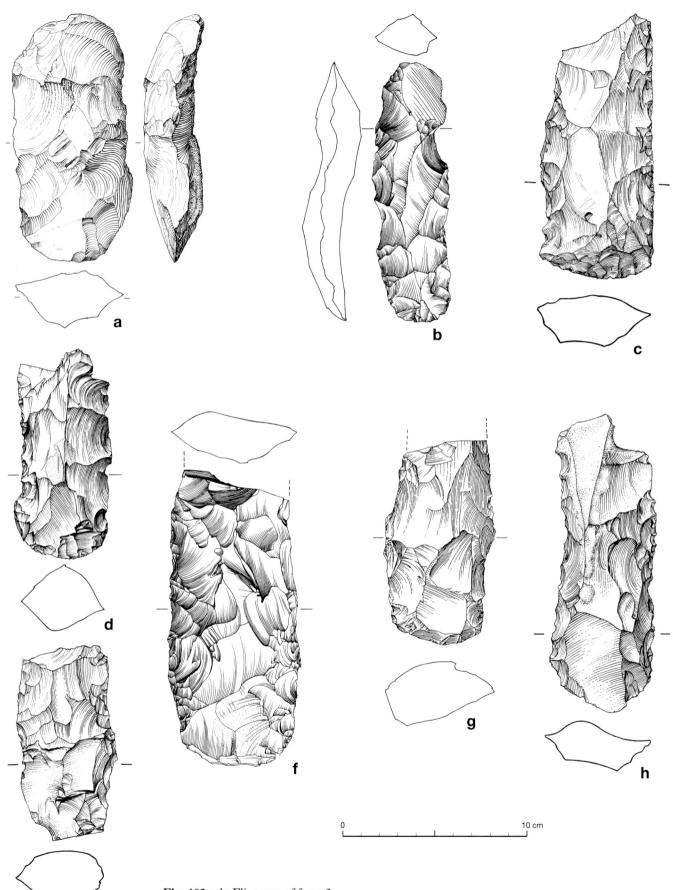

Fig. 103 a–h: Flint axes of form 3.

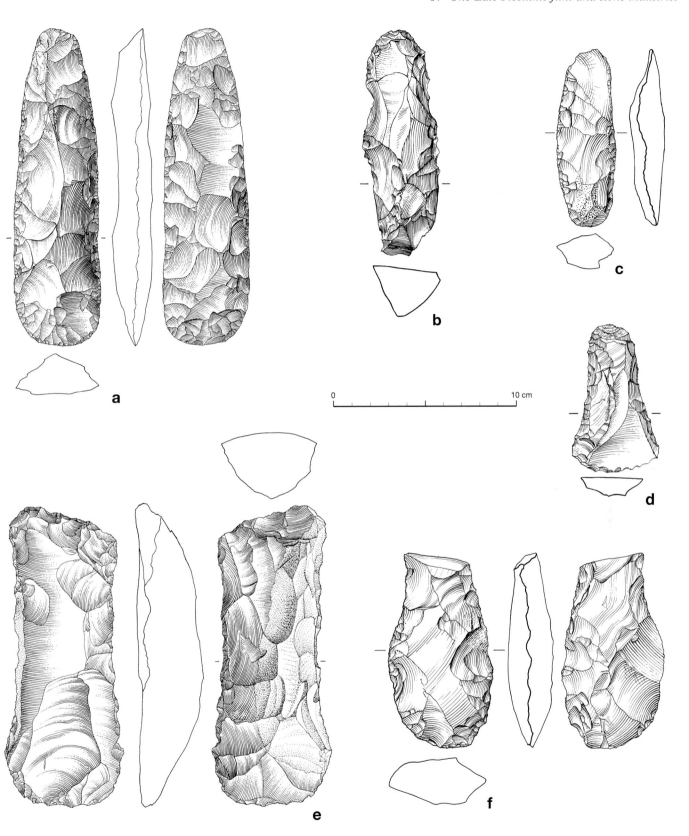

Fig. 104 a–c: Flint axes of form 4; d: flint axe of form 5; e: flint axe of form 6; f: flint axe of form 7.

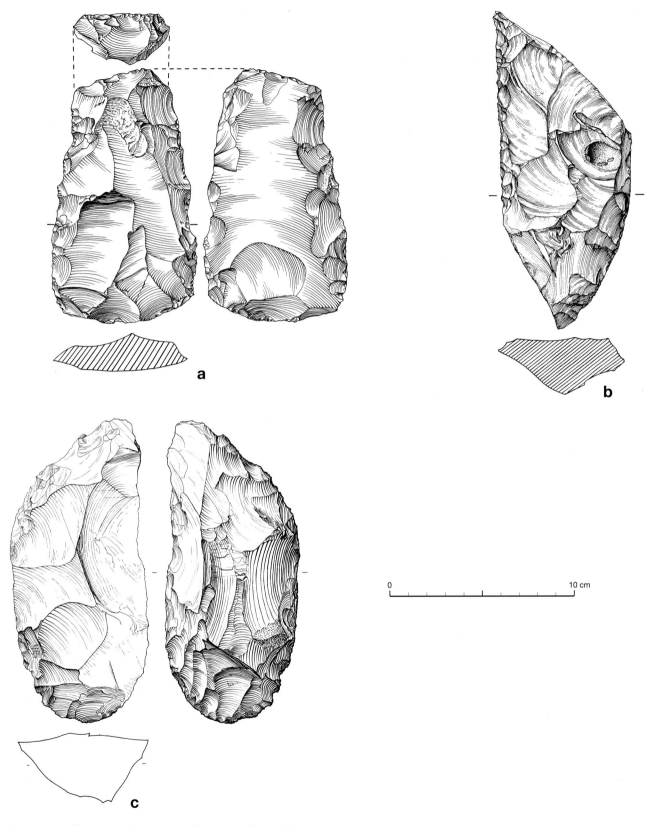

Fig. 105 a: Flint axe of form 8; b, c: flint axes of form 10.

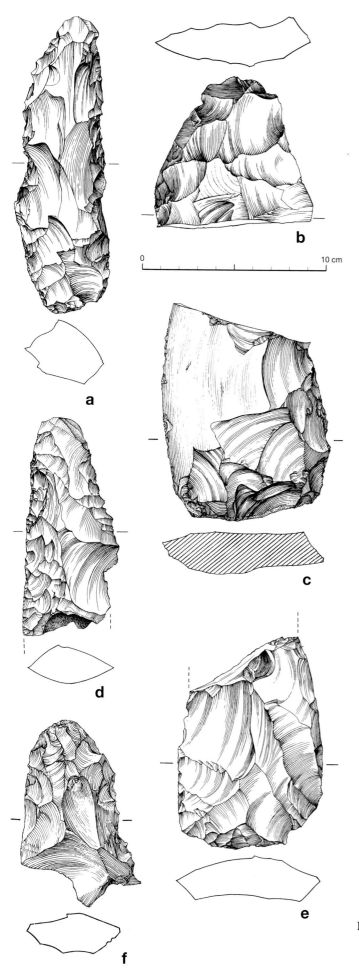

Fig. 106 a-f: Flint axes of indefinite form.

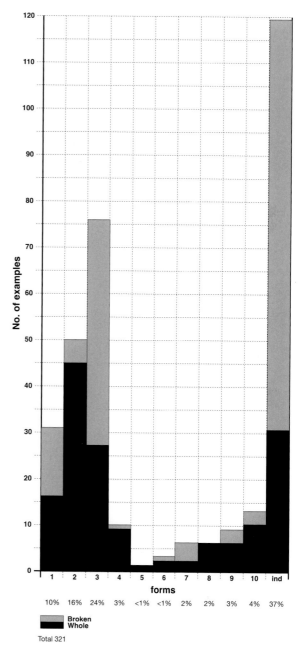

Fig. 107 Histogram showing frequency of axe forms recovered.

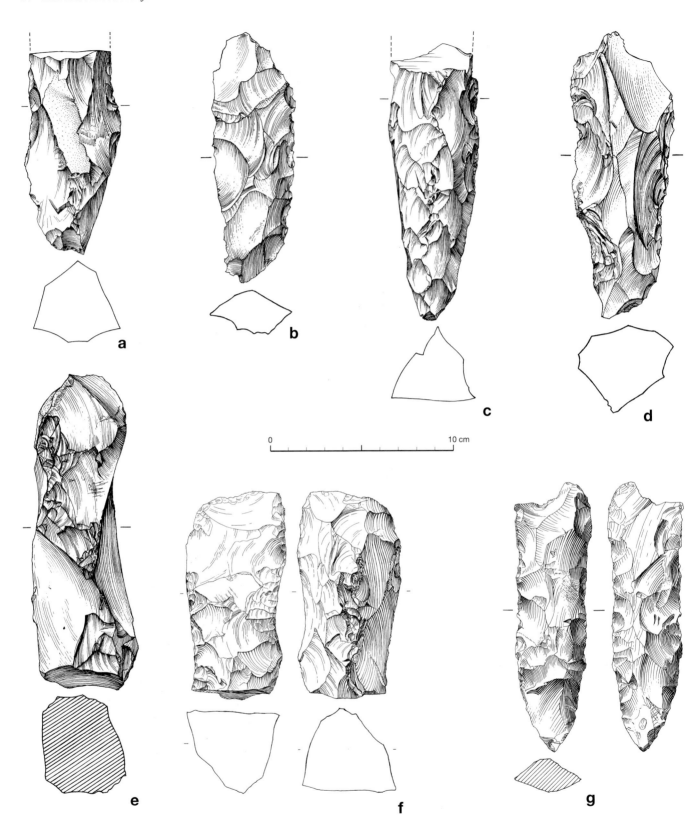

Fig. 108 a–f: Flint picks; g: flint rod.

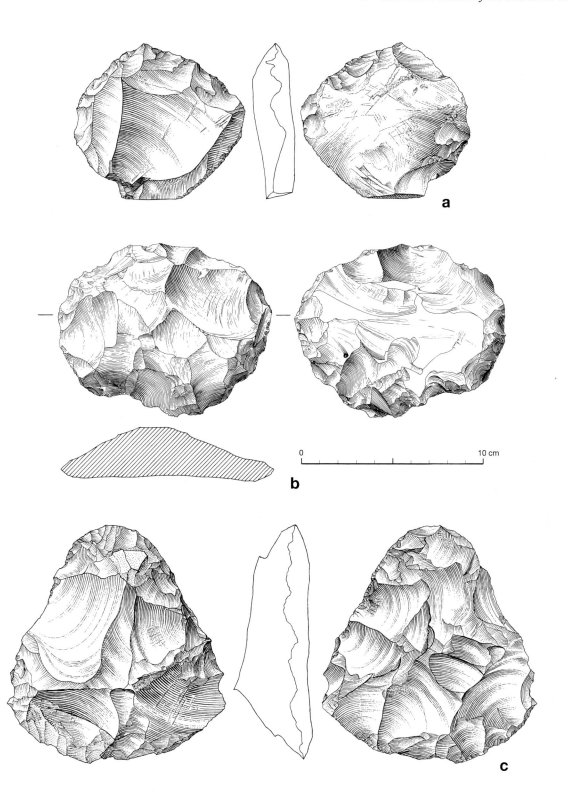

Fig. 109 Flint discoidal knives. a: I Early roughout; b, c: II Roughouts.

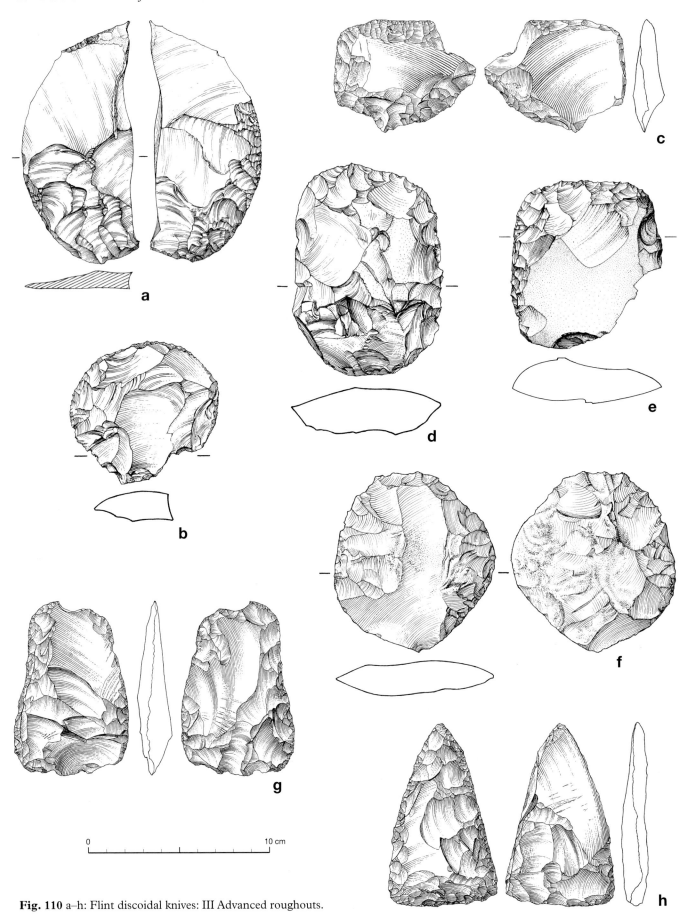

Fig. 110 a–h: Flint discoidal knives: III Advanced roughouts.

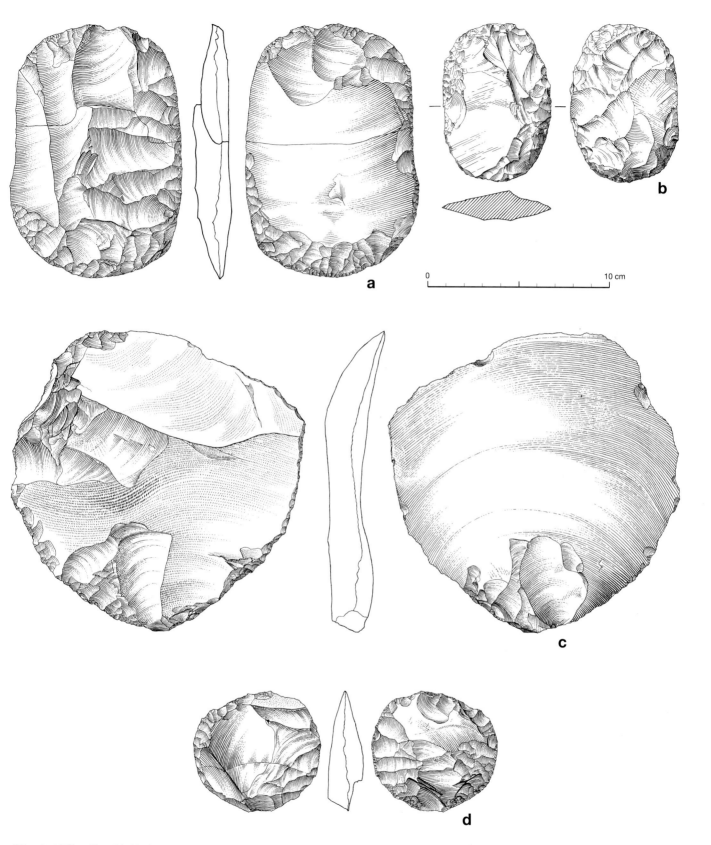

Fig. 111 Flint discoidal knives: a, b: IV Near finished; c: large roughout; d: small advanced roughout.

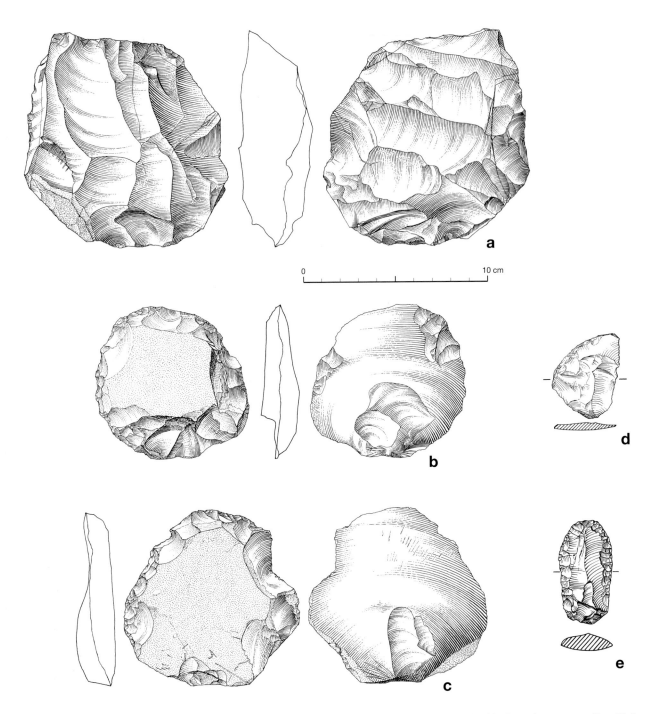

Fig. 112 a: Flint core or discoidal knife roughout; b: discoidal knife roughout showing removal of bulb and cortex; c: discoidal knife roughout showing removal of cortex; d, e: flint knives, other.

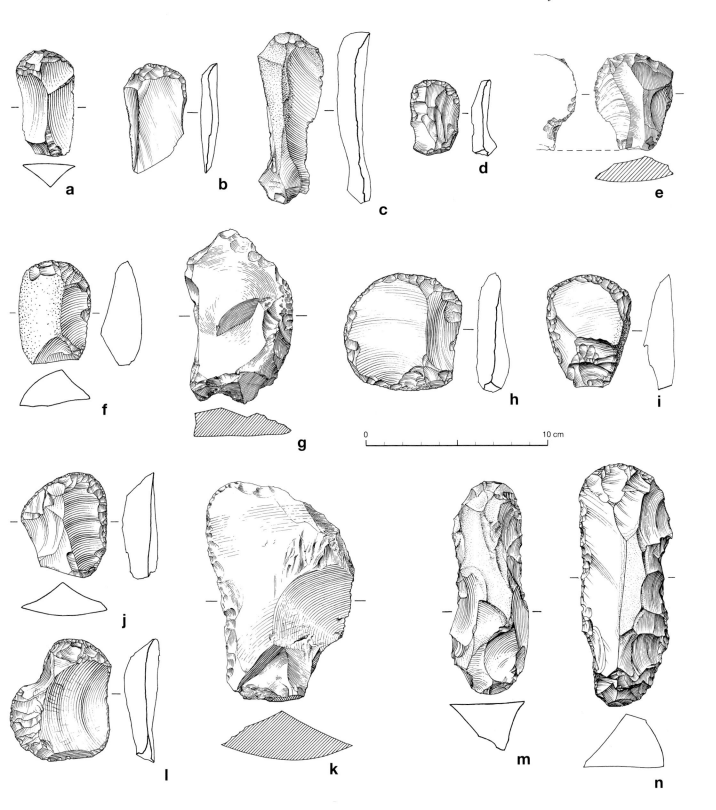

Fig. 113 Flint scrapers. a–c: End, long; d–f: End, short; g: Side; h–k: End and side; l: Double-ended; m, n: Plane.

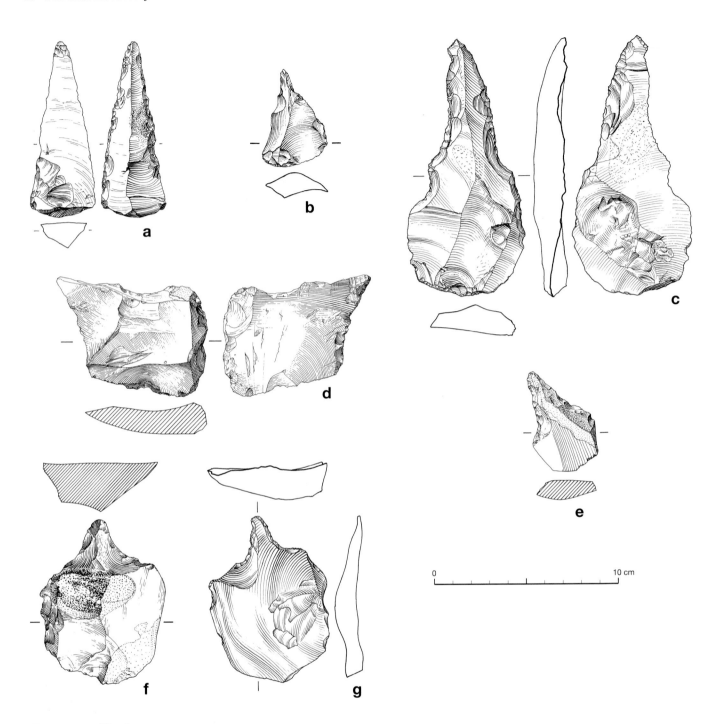

Fig. 114 a–g: Flint borers.

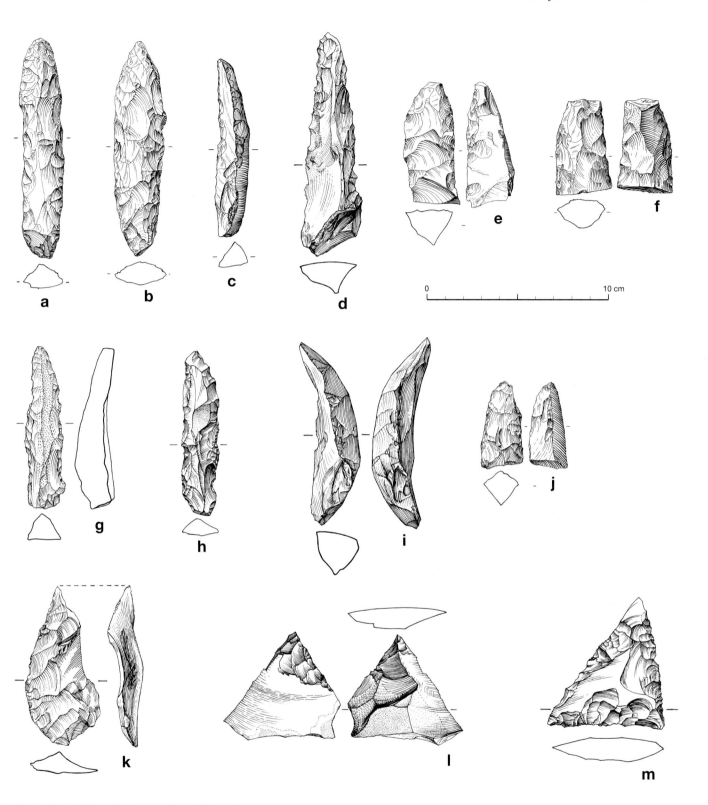

Fig. 115 a–j: Flint fabricators; k–m: flint points.

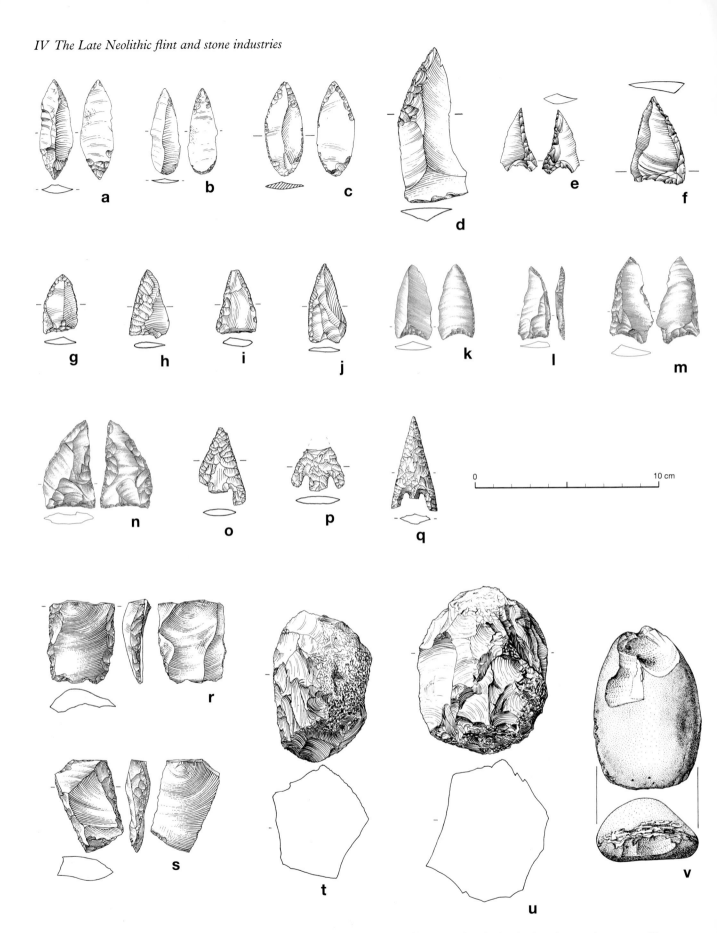

Fig. 116 a-c: Flint arrowheads, leaf; d–n: flint arrowheads, oblique; o–q: flint arrowheads, barbed and tanged; r, s: gunflints; t, u: hammerstones, flint; v: hammerstone, stone.

(Richardson 1920, 246, figs 57.1 and 2 and 58.7), 85B (Armstrong 1927, 135, fig. 34) and 85C (Armstrong 1921b, 437, figs 1 and 2; 1924b, 199, fig. 7). From the Museum's excavations examples were recovered from the 1972–4 chipping floor to the west of Shaft X, in features and superficial deposits in the West Field and again in superficial deposits in Area C.

(CF = Chipping Floor)

Area A	Area B	Area C	Shaft X	West Field
1255.5/ 900.5 H d I CF broken		1327/1040 2		940/940 F108 1 broken; F114 broken
				940/950 2 broken
				950/820 F32 2 broken
				955/820 2 (x 2) broken

2 Similar but the butt is rounded or of indefinite form and the sides can sometimes be concave as well as convex. Some at least of these axes may be in the process of being worked into those of Form 1. The length is usually more than one and a half times but less than three times the width. Some forty-five whole examples (for example, fig. 102a–d and five fragmentary examples) can be recognized. These again are widely distributed across the site, being redeposited in Pits 1 (Clarke 1915, 157, fig. 29), 9, 10, 12, 14 and 15, and in Mercer's 71 shaft (Saville 1981, F75, F111, F120, F121 and F123). One example was found by Peake displaced but probably from one of the galleries in Pit 1, but this was made on a flint pebble and is likely to have been brought to the site (Smith 1915, 157 and fig. 29; this volume, plate 25, extreme left). A similar axe was found in the entrance to Gallery 5 in Pit 2 (Clarke 1917, 465, fig. 98). This form occurs also in Floors 3B, 3C, 4 (Clarke 1915, 190, fig. 66), 46 (Richardson 1920, 246, figs 57.3, 58.4, 59.10 and 59.11), 85B, 85C and elsewhere (for example, Peake 1916, 292, fig. 53c, 294, fig. 54b and 296, fig. 55; 1919, 89, fig. 18A).

Three examples were found in the 1972–4 chipping floor, in features and superficial deposits in the West Field and in superficial deposits in Areas A and C.

3 The butt is rounded, the sides roughly parallel, leading to a rounded or flattened cutting edge. The section is either symmetric or asymmetric with the length varying usually from more than one and a half times to more than three times the width (fig. 103a–h). At its narrowest this form subsumes 'chisel' forms, many of which are found broken, for example, in Pit 12, Floor 85B and the Black Hole. This is the most frequent axe form to come from

Area A	Area B	Area C	Shaft X	West Field
1255.5/ 905.5 1		1313/927 2		940/940 F105 53 broken; F112 CF II sq. 3 (fig. 91a)
1258/900.5 M c I CF				950/820 F21 3
β25 6 b II CF				
β25 6 a II CF				950/820 1 (x 2)
				955/820 1

the site, being represented by twenty-seven whole and forty-nine broken examples. They are widely distributed, being found redeposited in Pits 1 (Clarke 1915, 151, fig. 21), 2 (ibid., fig. 33), 5, 9, 14 and 15, the Black Hole and Mercer's 71 shaft (Saville 1981, F80–82, F94, F105, F110, F114, F117 and F122), but a noticeable concentration comes from Pit 12 (thirteen examples). The form has also been found on Floors 1, 3C, 4, 11 (Peake 1919, 76, fig. 13H), 15, 16 (Peake 1916, 284, fig. 48B), 52 (Kendall 1920a, 291, fig. 70F), 85B and 85C. In the Museum's excavations the form was also recovered from the 1972–4 chipping floor, from a number of features in the West Field, as well as superficial deposits both there and in Areas A and C.

Area A	Area B	Area C	Shaft X	West Field
1252.5/905.5 G c I CF broken		1327/ 1040 2	β43 6	900/870 1 broken
1255.5/905.5 H a I CF broken				910/870 2 (x 2)
1260.5/911.1 J3 broken				940/940 F105 6, 8, 14; F108 1 broken; F114 3
				940/940 1 broken
				950/820 F1 broken; F5; F7 (+ 1 broken); F10 3; F11; F21 2 broken; F28 broken; F33 2 broken
				950/820 broken; 950/820 1 (1 + 3 broken)
				952.5/964 broken

4 The butt is narrow, rounded or indeterminate. The sides are convex, narrowing to a rounded cutting edge. The maximum width occurs well down the body (fig. 104a–c). The length varies from slightly less than twice to almost three times the width. The form is relatively rare, only nine whole examples and one broken being represented. One each was recovered from Pits 12 and 15, one from P5 (see also Peake 1916, 294, fig. 54C). The remaining six came from features and surface deposits in the West Field and from Pit W.

West Field	Pit W
940/940 F104 3	1240/940.3
950/820 F6 4; F18 2	
955/820 1	
995/860 3	

5 The butt is narrow and rounded, the sides concave expanding to a broad, shallow, rounded cutting edge. The length is almost one and a half times the maximum width (fig. 104d). Only a single axe of this form has been recovered from 950/820 Feature 6 1 in the West Field. Evans (1872, fig. 22), illustrating a similar example, a surface find from Thetford Warren, Suffolk, suggested the possibility that this was a deliberate attempt to copy an early metal form. This remains highly likely.

6 The rounded butt and cutting edge are of similar width, the sides concave. The length is approximately two and a half times the width (fig. 104e). The form is absolutely rare, only two whole examples being recovered from Pit 12 and Floor 3B (Clarke 1915, 184, fig. 59) and a broken example from the West Field 950/820 Feature 32 2.

7 The butt is rounded, the sides ogival, expanding giving a 'spatulate' profile. The length is slightly over twice the maximum width. The form is rare, only two whole and four broken examples being noted (fig. 104f). The broken examples come from Pits 1 (Clarke 1915, 153, fig. 25) and 2, Floor 15 (Peake 1919, 78, fig. 14D) and one unlocated. The complete examples are from Mercer's 71 shaft (Saville 1981, F103) and from West Field 950/820 Feature 6 4. A similar example from Undley Common, near Lakenheath, Suffolk, is illustrated in Evans (1872, fig. 38).

8 Of squat, trapezoidal shape with flattened butt, straight sides, expanding to a flattened cutting edge. The length is approximately one and a half times the maximum width (fig. 105a). A rare form, only six examples have been noted redeposited in Pit 15, two from Floor 3B, one from Floor 16 (Peake 1916, 281, fig. 46B), one from Floor 28 (Peake 1919, 78, fig. 14H) and one from Floor 46 (Richardson 1920, 250, fig. 59.12).

9 Similar to form 8 but more elongated. The length is slightly less than twice to two and a half times the maximum width (plate 18). A rare form, six whole and three fragmentary examples have been recovered, redeposited in Pits 10 and 12, two from Mercer's 71 shaft (Saville 1981, F104 and F116), from Floor 85 and two

from superficial deposits in the West Field 900/870 1 and 950/820 1 (broken).

10 A number of axes, perhaps broken during shaping, have sides of markedly different lengths, giving the implement an asymmetric profile. The fact that these axes show shaping along the length of the asymmetry suggests that they were still being taken as acceptable axe forms (fig. 105b and c). The length varies from slightly less than twice to three and a half times the maximum width. Some thirteen examples have been noted: four from Floors 4, 16 (Peake 1917, 417, fig. 83B), 21 (ibid., fig. 83C) and 85 (Armstrong 1927, 135, fig. 33), a single example from the Black Hole, six from the West Field features and superficial deposits, and one from Area C.

Area C	West Field
1325/973.1	950/820 F3 (1 + 1 broken); F15 2; F37 1
	950/820 2 broken
	1005/945 1

Indefinite (fig. 106) The remaining 119 roughouts, or 37 per cent of the collection, are too irregular or insufficiently processed to fall into any formal category. Examples discovered during the Museum's excavations come from Areas A and C, and Shaft X, but were mainly recovered from features in the West Field.

Area A	Area B	Area C	Shaft X	West Field
β30 6 b I CF broken		1313/927 3 broken	1270/905 2 broken	940/940 F105 9, 46 broken
β1 6 c III CF broken		1400/1065 1 broken	1270/900 15	950/820 F1 3 broken; F3 broken; F5 22 broken; F6 4 broken, unstrat.; F7 broken; F10 2 broken; F14 5 broken; F17 3 broken; F18 2; F21 2; F24 4; F28 2, 5 broken; F33 2 broken; F36 5 broken; F37 1 broken
1260.5/911.1 P b II CF broken				
1263/905.5 I c II CF				
1267.5/ 906.1 5				950/820 1 1 + 3 broken
				950/820 2 broken
				995/765 1 broken
				995/860 2 broken; PA 12 3 broken

Two further possible initial axe roughouts come from 940/940 F112 I squares 6 and 9.

A metrical examination was made of 287 axes and axe roughouts in the Museum's collections from Grimes Graves. Taking only the complete examples, the weight ranged from 42 to 859 g, with over 80 per cent lying in the range 100–549 g. The heaviest roughout recovered weighed 1784 g.

Figure 107 summarizes the frequency with which these forms occur on site. Given the type of material studied, it seems wise to draw only broad conclusions, but clearly the main discernible output is of axes which are either parallel-sided (form 3) or with a broad cutting edge tapering to a narrow, sometimes pointed, butt (forms 1 and 2).

Whether the remaining forms, representing in each case less than 5 per cent of the total, represent specific forms in preparation or chance products is impossible to say, but the recurrence of asymmetric forms (form 10) may indicate a willingness to utilize forms which fit uncomfortably with the prehistorian's quest for specific types. While Healy (1991a) was correct in seeing axes of Form 1 as a recurrent Grimes Graves product, it is only one of the axe forms being produced; parallel-sided forms are numerically more prevalent.

Stone

No new discoveries of stone axes have been made during the Museum's research programme. The only examples recorded therefore remain those recovered from two earlier contexts:

1 Greenwell's Pit: Clough and Green 1972, N 47
   Cornish greenstone. Group IIIa: Longworth and Varndell 1996, pl. 11. Plate 19.
2 Floor 15: Clough and Green 1972, N 48
   Cornish picrite. Group IV: Peake 1917, 431, fig. 84. Plate 20.

2 Picks

As noted above, picks here defined as 'heavy' implements of triangular or polygonal section, with a more or less pointed working end (when present), are a relatively rare component of the assemblage. Two possible examples came from the 1972–4 chipping floor, and eleven whole and six fragmentary examples come from features in the West Field (fig. 108a–f).

Area A	West Field
β20 6 CF c I β20 6 CF a II	940/940 F105 15, 19, 25; F108 1 broken
	950/820 F3 –; F5 –; F6 1, 2, – (inc. 4 broken); F16 7 broken; F36 4
	950/820 1, 2

A pick was also recovered from Floor 21 (Peake 1917, 411, fig. 81E).

3 Rods

Roughly parallel-sided in profile, with triangular or polygonal section but of indeterminate form. Less massive than the pick but, being more than 13 cm, larger than the fabricator. Some may be early fabricator roughouts (fig. 108g).

Two whole and five broken examples were recovered from features in the West Field.

West Field

900/870   F5 broken

940/940   F108 1 broken

950/820   F5 broken; F16 3 broken; F20 5 broken; F36 4; F38 –
          including 1 broken

950/820   1, 2

4 Discoidal knives (see also Appendix 2)

As with flint axes, there are difficulties with the recognition of early manufacturing stages where intent cannot be discerned. Indeed, decisions about the final form of a piece could have been made some way down the *chaîne opératoire*, and there is a grey area where some core forms are concerned. Even allowing for these doubts, discoidal knife roughouts were present in significant numbers. A relatively small number was approaching a finished state and none was polished.

In terms of manufacturing stages, discoidal knives are divided into:

I   Early roughouts (fig. 109a)
II   Roughouts (fig. 109b and c)
III Advanced roughouts (fig. 110)
IV   Near-finished (fig. 111a and b)

Typologically they may be classified by shape as:

a Mitriform
b Trapezoid
c Rectangular
d Triangular
e Discoid
f Ovoid
I Indeterminate. Even quite advanced roughouts may
   be indeterminate in shape.

Discoidal knives are widely distributed over the site, but with no discernible patterning according to shape. When reduced to basic geometric descriptors (three-sided, four-sided and rounded), recognizably four-sided and rounded examples are approximately equal in number, with three-sided accounting for about a fifth of the total. The Museum's excavations recovered examples from Areas A, B and C; Shaft X; the West Field features and superficial deposits; small cuttings south of the main mine field (990/765 and 995/860) and Trench 4 (1240/1004.1).

Catalogue numbers refer to the catalogue of discoidal knives from Grimes Graves that is archived at the British Museum. Roman numerals in italics refer to manufacturing stages.

Two discoidal roughouts, one broken, were retrieved from the same Late Neolithic context at the edge of Mercer's 1971 shaft (Saville 1981, F129 and F130). F131 is a sub-rectangular example from the Middle Bronze Age midden deposits in the upper fill of the 1972 shaft, which Saville accepts as of Bronze Age manufacture. However, typologically there seems no reason to attribute a date other than Late Neolithic, especially given the problems of residuality on the site.

From Armstrong's excavations, early roughouts of indeterminate form (stage I) were recovered from Pits 9, 10, 11, 12 and 15, Floors 3B, 3C, 11, 13, 21, 85B, 85C, 85/42 and 88, and the Black Hole.

Roughouts (stage II) of indeterminate form: Pits 1, 2, 9, 10, 11, 12, 14 and 15, Floors 2, 3B, 3C, 12, 15, 85C and 85C/42, and the Black Hole. Advanced roughouts (stage III): Pit 12.

Form a (mitriform) examples were recovered from Pits 14 (stage II) and 11 (stage III).

Form b (trapezoid): Pit 9 and Floors 13, 15, 16, 85C and 88 (stage II); Pits 10 and 15 (stage III).

Form b/c (trapezoid/rectangular): Floor 85/42 (stage II).

Form b/d (trapezoid/triangular): Floor 87 (stage III).

Form c (rectangular): Pits 12, 14 and 15, and Floors 3B, B and 85C (stage II); Pits 2, 11, 12 and 15, and Floors 3C and 12 (stage III).

Form d (triangular): Pits 1 and 12, and Floor 85C (stage II); Floor 16 (stage III).

Form e (discoid): Pits 1, 10 and 12, and Floors 5 and 85C (stage II); Pit 15 and Floor 15 (stage III).

Form f (ovoid): Pit 10 and Floors 15, 85C and 'near Black Hole' (stage II); Pits 14 and 15 (stage III).

	a Mitriform (fig. 110h)	b Trapezoid (fig. 110g)	b/c Trapezoid/ rectangular	c Rectangular (figs 109d–e; 111a)	b/d Trapezoid/ triangular	d Triangular (fig. 109c)	e Discoid (fig. 109b)	f Ovoid (fig. 111b)	I Indeterminate (no. of examples)
Area A				β25 6 CF d *III* *IV* cat. 86					15
Area B									2
Area C	1325/970 1 *III* cat. 1			1327/1040 2 *IV* cat. 85				1327/1040 2 *IV* cat. 85	5
Shaft X						1275/905 N 6 *II* cat. 44			2
West Field		940/940 F105 6 *III* cat. 81	950/820 F16 3 *II* cat. 51	950/820 F5 2 *III*, broken cat. 76 950/820 F6 1 *III* cat. 78 950/820 F14 5 *III* cat. 80	950/820 F24 4 *II*, broken cat. 54	950/820 F28 2 *II* cat. 56 950/820 F28 5 *II* cat. 57 940/940 F113 4 *II*, broken cat. 61	950/820 F36 4 *II* cat. 58 950/820 F43 2 *II* cat. 59 990/765 2 *II* cat. 72 990/765 1 *II* cat. 73 900/870 F4 *III* cat. 82	950/820 F17 2 *II* cat. 52 940/940 F114 II *II* cat. 62 950/820 1 (ploughsoil) *II* cat. 65 950/820 F5 *III* cat. 77 950/820 F13 4 *III* cat. 79	42
Trench 4						1240/1004.1 *IV*			
Pit U									1
? Context						*III* cat. 84			

Indeterminate: contexts

Area A	Area B	Area C	Shaft X
D 4 *I* cat. 1	1285/910 G 3 *I* cat. 8	1400/1065 I *I* cat. 6	1275/905 F6 a *I* cat. 11
O (sand beneath till) *I* cat. 2	1280/910 D 3 *II* cat. 43	1313/927 (topsoil) *I* cat. 10	1275/900 2 (topsoil) *II* cat. 41
unstrat. *I* cat. 3		1313/927 III *I* cat. 14	
1255.5/905.5 CF M a I *I* cat. 4		1313/927 (topsoil) *II* cat. 37	
β40 6 CF d I *I* cat. 5		1325/973 (topsoil) *II* broken cat. 42	
1258/900.5 A 2 *I* cat.7			
1265.5/912.5 C and D F1 6 *I* cat. 9			
M 5 *I* cat. 12			
β15 4 (flake scatter) *I* cat. 15			
1255.5/905.5 CF E c I *I* cat. 16			
β28 6 CF *I* cat. 17			
1258/900.5 topsoil 2 *II* cat. 36			
1255.5/905.5 CF F c I *II* broken cat. 38			
1263/905.5 CF I a I *II* cat. 39			
1263/905.5 CF M d I *II* cat. 40			

Pit U	West Field	West Field	West Field
1070.1/844.8 *I* cat. 13	995/860 sq. V3 *I* cat. 18	950/820 F37 1 *I* broken cat. 32	950/820 F9 *II* cat. 50
	952.5/964 4 *I* cat. 19	940/940 F106 1 *I* cat. 33	950/820 F17 3 *II* cat. 53
	950/820 1 *I* cat. 20	940/940 F112 I sq. 8 *I* cat. 221	950/820 F27 3 *II* broken cat. 55
	950/820 1 *I* cat. 21	940/940 F112 I sq. 8 *I* cat. 222	940/940 F105 44 *II* cat. 60
	950/820 2 *I* cat. 22	940/940 F112 I sq. 19 *I* cat. 223	940/940 2 *II* broken cat. 63
	950/820 1 *I* cat. 23	940/940 F112 II sq. 5 *I* cat. 224	950/820 2 *II* cat. 64
	940/940 (ploughsoil) *I* cat. 24	940/940 F112 II sq. 6 *I* cat. 225	940/940 (ploughsoil) *II* broken cat. 66
	950/820 F6 4 *I* cat. 25	940/940 F117 26 *I* cat. 34	950/820 2 *II* cat. 67
	950/820 F7 8 *I* broken cat. 26	940/940 F118 1 *I* cat. 35	950/820 1 *II* broken cat. 68
	950/820 F9 2 *I* cat. 27	950/820 F5 2 *II* cats 45 and 46	950/820 1 *II* cat. 69
	950/820 F10 1 *I* cat. 28	950/820 F5 2 *II* broken cat. 47	950/820 1 *II* broken cat. 70
	950/820 F24 5 *I* broken cat. 29	950/820 F6 *II* broken cat. 48	900/870 F1 2 *II* cat. 71
	950/820 F32 3 *I* cat. 30	950/820 F7 *II* cat. 49	950/820 F3 *III* broken cat. 75
	950/820 F32 2 *I* cat. 31		no context *II* cat. 74

5 Knives, other

These were fashioned usually on thin flakes, but display no regularity in type or form (fig. 112d, e); fig. 112e is, however, a common form elsewhere in Beaker and Early Bronze Age contexts, grading into plano-convex knives, and is frequent for example in settlements on the fen edge to the west (for example, Bamford 1982, fig. 32a and c).

Area A	Area B	Area C	West Field
1255.5/905.5 CF O a I	1285/910 G 3 (x 2)	1313/927 (topsoil) (x 2)	940/940 F101 3; F105 4; F106 2; F114 1.I; F118 –
β1 6 CF bII		1325/967	
		1327/1040 2	940/950 2
			950/820 F10 8; F14 8; F28 3; F32 2, 2a

A further example comes from Pit 15.

6 Scrapers

Formal scrapers comprise only a limited component of the tool types recovered, reflecting perhaps the essentially industrial rather than domestic nature of many of the activities examined. They are almost invariably the commonest retouched form in settlement assemblages throughout the Neolithic and Early Bronze Age (Healy pers. comm.).

End-scrapers made on a variety of flake forms, both long – i.e. more than 1.5 times their width (figs 113a–c and 88a) – and short (fig. 113d–f), are the most recurrent form, being more than twice as frequent as either side or end and side varieties.

	Side	End	End and side	Double	Thumb	Plane
Area A Chipping floor	1	2	–	–	–	1
Other	–	4	–	–	1	–
Shaft X Pre-MBA	–	1	–	–	–	–
MBA	–	3	1	1	–	–
Area C	4	4	2	–	–	–
West Field	7	20	8	1	1	5

Table 4 Occurrence of scrapers recovered during British Museum excavations.

Side (figs 113g and 88b)

Area A	Shaft X	Area C	West Field
β21 6 CF C I (rough) (fig. 88b)		1313/927 (topsoil)	940/940 F105 2; F113 4 (broken); F114 Unit II
		1325/970 2 (rough)	
		1325/973	950/820 F13 4; F14 5; F32 2
		1327/1040 (topsoil)	

End (figs 113a–f and 88a)

Area A	Shaft X	Area C	West Field
1260.5/911.1 C 3 (rough)	1270.5/900.5 2	1325/967 2	900/970 2
1255.5/911.1 D 4 (rough)	1270.5/900.5 26 D	1325/970 1 (rough)	940/940 F105 2, 6; F106 2; F108 1; F114 Unit II; F117 31
1255.5/911.1 F 4 (rough)	1270.5/905 (topsoil)	1325/970 2	
1255.5/905.5 I CF I d		1400/1065 2	950/820 F3; F4 3; F16 7; F18 2; F29 2; F32 2
1266/900.5 7			950/820 1 950/820 2
1266/900.5 D c I			1000/755 1

End and side (fig. 113h–j, k?)

Area A	Shaft X	Area C	West Field
	1275/900 (topsoil)	1327/1040 (topsoil)	940/940 F105 2, 3, 6; F106 2
		1392/1040 (topsoil)	950/820 F7; F18 1
			950/820 2

Double-ended (fig. 113l)

Shaft X 1270.5/900.5 2
West Field 910/870 2

Thumb

Area A 1255.5/911.1 J 4
West Field 940/940 F101 3

Plane scrapers (fig. 113m, n, and plate 21)

Parallel-sided – steeply keeled, end (sometimes double-ended)

Area A 1263/905.5 CF B b 1
West Field 910/870 2; 940/940 F105 8; 940/940 – , 2; 950/820 F 5 – ; 950/820 F 6 4; 950/820 F7 –

7 Borers (aka piercers, points) (fig. 114)

Most were fashioned on thick flakes, more rarely on core fragments. Size varies from those capable of being held between finger and thumb (fig. 114b, d and e), for example from Area C 1313/927 and Shaft X, and those intended to be gripped in the hand (fig. 114c), for example from Area C 1313/927, 1325/970 and 1325/973.

During the Museum's excavations borers were recovered from:

Area A	Shaft X	Area C	West Field
1255.5/911.1 D 3	1270/905 (topsoil)	1313/927 (topsoil)	940/940 F101 3; F113 4; F114 1.I, 1.II; F117 26
1260.5/906.1 Aa II (broken)		1313/970 2	
		1313/927 3	940/940 –
1260.5/911.1 I 3		1325/970 (topsoil) (x 3)	940/950 2
β4 –		1325/970 2 (x 2)	950/820 F28 2
β1 4			950/820 2
		1325/973 (topsoil)	
		1325/973 2	

In addition, a borer fashioned on a notched blade was recovered from 950/820 Feature 18 2.

These implements appear to be those employed, for example, to perforate the pieces of chalk illustrated in Varndell (1991), for example figs 61 and 63. It is for this apparent functional use that the term 'borer' has been employed in preference to other descriptors.

8 Fabricators (aka punches, strike-a-lights)
(figs 115a–j and 88d)

These are made on rods of triangular or lozenge section. On the more finished specimens working usually extends to three sides. Within this category (*pace* Saville 1981) are included forms showing no signs of actual use. The distinction between these and other forms of rod is based therefore on length, the cut-off being taken here as 13 cm.

Examples from the Museum's excavations come from:

Area A	Shaft X	Area C	West Field
1955.5/911.1	1270.5/900.5 12	1325/973 (topsoil)	940/940 F105 36; F108 1; F114 1.I
1260.5/906.1 Aa II (broken)	1275/905 3	1325/973 2	940/950 2 (broken)
1260.5/906.1 Ad II (broken)		1325/973 2 F2	950/820 1, 2 (1 unfinished)
			950/820 F1 7; F7, 8; F9 2, – (broken); F16 2, 7 (broken); F17 6; F32 2
			950/950 2

Other examples have come from Pit 15 (x 3), Floor 16 (Peake 1917, 419, fig. 84D; Richardson 1920, 257, fig. 63, nos 33 and 34 [broken]). Two asymmetric forms were recovered from Pit 12 (Armstrong 1934, 387, fig. 8) and Floor 88 (Armstrong 1927, 131, fig. 23). Similar examples were recovered during Mercer's excavations, for example Saville 1981, F497–8, F591 (broken), F516–18 (broken and unfinished) and perhaps some of the smaller rods, for example F375, F377, F384, F392 and F400.

9 Burins

No convincing examples of deliberately fashioned burins have been noted.

10 Points (fig. 115k–m)

A triangular point was recovered from 950/820 F5 24 in the West Field (fig. 115m). This shows bifacial thinning and is made on a thick flake. A possible broken roughout for a comparable piece was recovered from 950/820 F43 2 (fig. 115l). Another example in the course of manufacture had been recovered by Armstrong from Floor 85C (1936 5-8 17).

These pieces are too large and thick to be satisfactory as arrowheads, but could have been used as points for a thrown or thrusting spear. A broken laurel leaf roughout was recovered from the top of another of the West Field features, 950/820 F6 1. This can be compared with the roughout for a probable laurel leaf recovered by Mercer (Saville 1981, F495).

Three further points were recovered from 940/940 F105 6 (fig. 115k), 940/940 F114 1.II and 950/820 F28 17.

11 Arrowheads

At least thirty-four arrowheads have been recovered from the site. As might be expected on a site with known Grooved Ware presence, the majority – twenty-five – are of oblique forms (following Green 1980). The recovery during excavation of a more 'hollow-based' form of oblique arrowhead from the 1972–4 chipping floor (Lech and Longworth 2000, fig. 37b) suggests that comparable pieces recovered by Armstrong from Floors 16 and 87 also belong to a Late Neolithic horizon. Two of the three leaf forms were found in a feature (880/910 F2) in direct association with Middle Neolithic plain bowl pottery. The remaining example comes from the base of the 1972–4 chipping floor (β20) – where it may be residual. In view of the minimal retouch on these pieces, it seems probable that a further possible example reported by Saville (1981, F283) should be accepted as well as two broken pieces from the 1972–4 chipping floor: β40 b II 6 and d II 6 (fig. 85b, c).

During the Museum's excavations twenty examples were recovered:

Leaf (fig. 116a–c)

Area A	Area B	Shaft X	Area C	West Field
β20 6 bIII CF (Green type 2B)				880/910 F2 – (Green type 2C)
				880/910 F2 – (Green type 2C)

Oblique (fig. 116d–n)

Area A	Area B	Shaft X	Area C	West Field
1252.5/ 905.5 D aI CF	1280/910 H bII CF (ripple flaked)	1270/900 2	1392/980 1	950/820 F3 2; F20, 2; F33 1
1255.5/ 911.1 (topsoil) (roughout)	1280/910 B dIII CF	1275.5/ 900.5 F9 5 1270/ 900 23a		950/820 2 (unfinished)

+ 1 Unstratified.

Barbed and tanged (fig. 116o–q)

None of the barbed-and-tanged arrowheads recovered lay in helpful contexts, one being redeposited in Shaft X, the others lying in superficial deposits.

Area A	Area B	Shaft X	Area C	West Field
	1285/910 N 8 (broken)	1270/900/23a (broken)		1000/755 1 (broken)

To the five arrowheads listed by Green in 1980 (nos 370–74) as coming from the site from previous exploration can be added:

370 Floor 16	? Crude Oblique	Peake 1916, 280, fig. 45C
371 Floor 75	Oblique	Kendall 1925, 65, fig. 1
372 Floor 85c	? Oblique	Armstrong 1924b, 201, fig. 10
373 Humus above Pit 10	Barbed and tanged	Armstrong 1932, 59
374 Pit 12, Chipping Floor F	Oblique	Armstrong 1934, 387, fig. 9

A further oblique example comes from Floor 87, and oblique forms from Pit 15 and Floor 4.

In 1981 Saville added a further five recovered during Mercer's excavations of the 1971 and 1972 shafts; one tranchet (F72), three oblique (F70–71 and 74), and one broken barbed and tanged from the surface (F73). One possible leaf form, a surface find, was also noted (F283).

12 Gunflints (fig. 116r, s)

Evidence for the probably *ad hoc* knapping of gunflints is represented by at least sixty-three examples from the West Field, almost without exception from superficial layers. Early excavations at the site also produced these, notably in the upper levels of Pit 12 (see Appendix 3).

All appear to belong to a variety of wedge gunflints, which were easy to produce at need. All examples from the Museum's excavations are from the West Field:

West Field

940/940 F101 3: four
940/940 F105 2: thirty
940/940 F106 1: two. 2: eleven
940/940 F107 3: two
940/940 F112 2: three
940/940 F114 1.II: four

940/940 F115 5: one
940/940 F117 31: one
940/940 F120 1: four
940/940 F121 2: one

Even allowing for differences in patterns of exploration and recovery, there seems to be a concentration in this part of the West Field, and Pit 12 is not far to the east.

13 Hammerstones (fig. 116t–v)

Hammerstones made of flint outnumber those of stone (quartzite and sandstone) roughly in the ratio of 5:3. Since broken examples are included and since flint shatters far more readily than stone, these figures almost certainly overstate the use of flint, although Herne noted that in the Middle Bronze Age deposits in Shaft X flint appeared to be the only hard hammer employed (Herne 1991, 32–3). It must be assumed, however, that over the site as a whole hammerstones were employed to serve a variety of different functions in addition to the reduction of flint in tool manufacture.

The following table shows the general spatial distribution of hammerstones across the site, most lying in superficial or redeposited contexts:

	Stone	Flint
Area A	28%	72%
Area C	4%	96%
West Field	71%	29%

Table 5 Percentage occurrence of hammerstones made from stone or flint recovered during British Museum excavations.

While the emphasis on the use of flint in Area C may again reflect Middle Bronze Age activity in this area, the contrast between Area A and the West Field is striking and is perhaps further evidence of the cultural or temporal separation of those working the West Field and the rest of the mine field.

14 Rubbing stones

West Field

940/940 F105 2, 53 (plate 22)

15 Polishing

Traces of deliberate polishing on flint implements are all but absent and it is clear that this form of finishing was not normally practised on the site. The only examples so far recorded are from Armstrong's excavation of Floor 16, on which a single flake showed polishing (Peake 1916, 303, fig. 58D) and the broken axe butt from the pre-Middle Bronze Age phase of Shaft X (plate 16).

No other examples of polished stone implements have been recovered other than the two already known from Greenwell's Pit (Smith 1912, 117, fig. 16) and from Floor 15 (Peake 1917, 419, fig. 84G).

V The provenancing of flint axes by chemical analysis and the products of the Grimes Graves mines: a reassessment

P.T. Craddock, M.R. Cowell and M.J. Hughes

This section addresses two related themes: a reassessment of the programme to provenance Neolithic flint axes by their composition published in 1983; and, arising from the general failure to find axes that were chemically assignable to the mines at Grimes Graves, a more recent programme of chemical analysis on a range of flint artefacts from East Anglia.

Prior to the 1983 programme, it was usual to make two assumptions with regard to the flint artefacts of the British Neolithic: that most of the polished flint axes were of mined flint and that the main products of the flint mines were axes. An attempt was made to test these assumptions by trace element analysis (Sieveking *et al.* 1970; 1972; Craddock *et al.* 1983). The results of the project were generally inconclusive, but did show that the majority of the axes tested were likely to have come from sources in the South Downs. Very few of the axes could be assigned to East Anglian sources, and in particular Grimes Graves, suggesting that a reappraisal of the products of that mine was necessary.

The recent programme of analyses of an enlarged selection of material now suggests that Grimes Graves mined flint was used to make a wide range of artefacts in the Late Neolithic of East Anglia.

The original programme

A major research project was initiated at the British Museum in the 1960s to attempt to locate the sources of the flint used for the polished flint axes found in large numbers in southern Britain dating from the Neolithic period (Sieveking *et al.* 1970; 1972; Craddock *et al.* 1983). This was to be achieved by analysing flint from the major mine sites and comparing the trace element composition with that of flint axes found as stray finds over the countryside as well as on Neolithic sites throughout southern Britain and beyond.

Flint is micro-crystalline silica, and is classified as a type of chert, specifically that which formed in the chalk during the Cretaceous period. The flint exploited in the English mines was still *in situ* in the discrete horizons within the chalk where it had originally formed.

Thus the project sought to establish an analytical fingerprint for each of the mines and then to compare them with the composition of a selection of flint axes chosen in the main from the general vicinity of the selected mines in three regions: East Anglia, Wessex and the South Downs. The *a priori* assumption was that the axes should assign primarily to their local mines and this would provide a test of the overall ability of the project to assign flint axes from all over Britain to source.

The elements selected for analysis were in the main those associated with clay minerals and should reflect to some degree the composition of the seabed muds and incipient chalk beds in which the flint had originally formed. They were aluminium, iron, magnesium, potassium, sodium, lithium, phosphorus and calcium. For a discussion of the formation of flint relevant to its composition, see Cowell (1981a and 1981b) and Clayton (1986). The calcium content was not used in the statistical treatment of the data, even though the overall low calcium content was highly diagnostic for Grimes Graves. This was because the calcium content fluctuated wildly in the flint from some of the other mine sites. After dissolution the sample solutions were analysed, initially by emission spectrography. This technique was subsequently replaced by a combination of atomic absorption spectrometry (AAS) and flame photometry; the phosphorous content was determined colorimetrically (see Sieveking *et al.* 1972 and Hughes *et al.* 1976 for details of the analytical methods). The most recent analyses were performed using inductively coupled plasma spectroscopy (ICP) (see below, p. 153). Discriminant analysis was selected as the most appropriate statistical treatment, with assigned probabilities given between 0 and 1; where the probability was below 0.02 it was considered unassignable (Craddock *et al.* 1983).

The aims of the project were as follows:

1 To establish that the flint used for the axes was not from field flints in the immediate vicinity of where the axes had been found.

2 To establish a distinct composition for each of the mines.

3 To test the validity of the compositional assignment of axes generally to mines by comparing the composition of the flint at the mines with that of a selection of axes found in their vicinity.
4 To look for evidence of unrecognized sources in compositional or geographical clusters among the unassigned axes.

The project met with mixed success.

It had long been noted that in assemblages of flint artefacts the axes seemed to be of different flint from the rest, and the first aim of the project was to establish that field flints from the immediate vicinity were not being used. To test this assumption a group of unworked field flints was selected from the causewayed enclosures at Maiden Castle, Dorset, and Windmill Hill, Wiltshire, and treated as a mine source along with other mines. Only one axe out of the thirty-four from these two sites was assigned to the field sample groups, the others remained with the mine sites to which they had been previously assigned before the field samples were included. This suggested that flint in the immediate vicinity was not used for the axes.

Having demonstrated this, the project assumption was that the non-local sources of the flint for the axes were the flint mines. A further assumption made was that sufficient of the more important mine sites had been identified to make the project viable. The first assumption has been challenged (see below), but the most recent comprehensive survey (Barber *et al.* 1999) would suggest that no presently known major mine sources were omitted. On the contrary, several sites that we included in our survey are now regarded as worked surficial clay-with-flint deposits, or as not having been worked in antiquity at all (see below, p. 148).

The material from the mines formed into compositional groups that were generally differentiable, although usually not sufficiently well enough to permit the unambiguous assignation of individual flint axes to specific mines (see below). The degree to which any one mine could be separated from the rest clearly depends on the composition of its flint, and some mines were more distinct than others. In this respect Grimes Graves has by far the most distinctive composition of the recognized English flint mines, with a relatively high aluminium content and, generally, a low calcium content being especially noticeable. Thus when each of the flints that formed the Grimes Graves sample was individually treated as an unknown and compared with the remainder, over 90 per cent were correctly assigned to the mine. This should be borne in mind when considering the lack of success in assigning the axes from East Anglia, or indeed from anywhere else, to the Grimes Graves mine.

Analysis of samples of flint taken from the different horizons or bands of flint in the chalk from a quarry exposure at Taplin's Pit, Thetford, a few kilometres from Grimes Graves, showed that there was little variation between the *floorstone* (the primary mined material) and the horizons immediately above, through which the miners had to dig (Cowell *et al.* 1980). Thus, where some of the *wallstone* flint had been used on occasion at Grimes Graves and some of the other flint mines this should not cause problems. The flint in the horizons below the *floorstone* in the Thetford quarry showed progressively higher trace element levels with depth, especially for aluminium and calcium.

Because of the spread in composition of the flints from the majority of the mine sites, with the exception of Grimes Graves, they could not be unambiguously separated from each other, which meant that it was not possible confidently to assign individual axes to specific mine sites. In addition, there were several more practical indications that the individual assignments made by the statistical analysis were unreliable. In particular, in hoards where the colour, texture and typology of the axes clearly indicated that they belonged together, the axes were almost invariably assigned individually to different mines. Also there was often little difference in the probability between the first and second choice of mine as determined by discriminant analysis. It was, however, suggested that when the material was considered collectively indications of regional sources of mined flint used for the axes could be made with more confidence. On this basis the majority of the axes overall seem to have come from the South Downs mines. Support for this came from the regional studies where over 70 per cent of the axes from the south-east, mainly from the South Downs or the Sussex coastal strip, were assigned to the South Downs mines. This compared with only 15 per cent of the Wessex axes and 12 per cent of the East Anglian axes being assigned to their local mines. When the sources that are now not thought to have been exploited in antiquity are removed, the discrepancy between the regions becomes even more marked (see below, p. 149 and fig. 117).

Just two axes out of about one hundred and twenty analysed from the East Anglian region, one from Mildenhall, Suffolk, and the other from Burwell Fen in Cambridgeshire, were positively assigned to Grimes Graves, and three of the unassigned axes from nearby Santon Downham, Stanford and Fleggburgh, all in Norfolk, had Grimes Graves as their first choice of origin, but with low probability. None of the axes from the other two regions were assigned to Grimes Graves, lending some credence to the assignments. Also, both of the assigned axes and two of the three unassigned axes had the low calcium contents typical of Grimes Graves flint. As explained above, calcium was not included in the statistical treatment and so this further strengthens the case that the axes do belong to Grimes Graves.

The search for indications that other sources of flint were used also met with some success. Overall approximately 25 per cent of the axes were unassignable, showing that

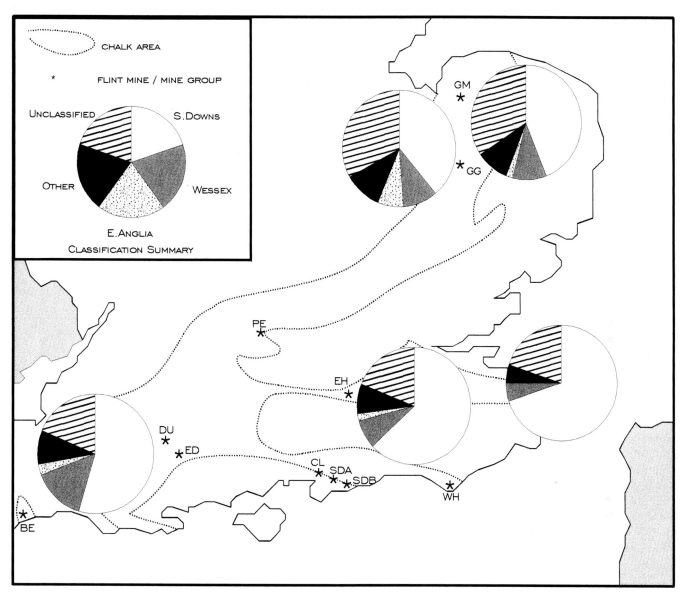

Fig. 117 Classification summary of flint sources based on fig. 2 in Craddock *et al.* (1983).
In addition to the two original pie-charts based on the complete set of analysed sites, new charts for the South Downs and East Anglia omit sites now known not to be ancient. **DU** = Durrington Walls; **ED** = Easton Down (Wessex); **CL** = Clanfield; **SDA** = South Downs A group (Long Down and Stoke Down); **SDB** = South Downs B group (Blackpatch, Findon and Cissbury); **WH** = Windover Hill (South Downs); **GM** = Great Massingham; **GG** = Grimes Graves (East Anglia); **BE** = Beer Head; **PE** = Peppard; **EH** = East Horsley (Other).

almost certainly other sources of flint were being used. This broke down to 19 per cent each in both the Wessex and south-east groups, but rose to 33 per cent for the East Anglian material, suggesting that there are other sources in the latter region from which a substantial proportion of the flint axes were made. This is perhaps not unexpected, given that of the two East Anglian mine sites we included, Great Massingham was unlikely ever to have been a flint mine, although artefacts may well have been made there using surface flint; and at Grimes Graves the mining did not commence until the third millennium BC and cannot

have been a source of flint for axes, or anything else, in the Early and Middle Neolithic periods. Also, there are a number of potential but uninvestigated flint mine sites in Norfolk. These sites include Buckenham Tofts, Stanford; Swell Pit, Lynford; Great Melton; Markshall, Caistor St Edmund; Westwick St, Norwich; and Whitlingham, Kirby Bedon. In fact, half of the total 'possible' mines for England noted by Barber and his colleagues (1999, 74–80) are in Norfolk. Coupled with this, it now seems likely that surface flint in various forms was also used extensively in East Anglia (see below, p. 148).

Fieldwork since 1983

Through the intervening years since 1983 there has been a great deal of fieldwork, excavation and discussion in Britain, based in part, at least, on the sources of flint used for artefacts in general and axes in particular, and their distribution. More specifically, detailed field survey around the fen edge and elsewhere in East Anglia has brought into focus the problems first raised by us of the apparent absence of axes assignable to Grimes Graves (Healy 1991a and 1998; Edmonds *et al.* 1999), and several of the papers on these field surveys discuss our project directly. Perhaps it was inevitable that there is some degree of confusion and contradiction between the various papers on a subject that is still so problematic.

Flint sources

Pitts (1996) suggested that there are up to thirty mine or quarry sites in England, and that we had therefore missed a significant number of potential sources in our analytical survey. Holgate (1991, 8–10) uncritically listed fifteen flint mines and a further five quarries. The more comprehensive survey of the Royal Commission of Ancient and Historical Monuments (Barber *et al.* 1999, 74–80) of some forty or so sites that have been claimed at some time as being ancient flint mines accepted only ten as certain. Russell (2000a, 12–13) basically followed Barber *et al.*, but listed fourteen. The additional four included two, Nore Down in Sussex and Buckenham Tofts in Norfolk, regarded by Barber *et al.* as only possible pits, as well as two mine sites from Scotland that were bell pits sunk into gravel deposits for large flint cobbles (Russell 2000a, 34). The rejected mines are now regarded as being later, including one, the Lavant Caves on the South Downs above Chichester in West Sussex, that was probably the subject of a hoax. Recent re-examination (Russell 2000a, 51–3 and 2000b) has shown that they are very likely to have been medieval or later chalk mines. However, they were excavated in 1893 by none other than Charles Dawson of Piltdown fame, and the heterogeneous collection of prehistoric, Roman and medieval material that was supposed to have been found therein was very possibly largely introduced by Dawson himself.

The ten certain sites had all been sampled as part of our project, suggesting that we had in fact covered the main certain sites of ancient mining activity (although with the caveat of the uninvestigated possible Norfolk sites mentioned above). The sites we analysed that Barber *et al.* considered as certain were: Cissbury, Church Hill Findon, Blackpatch and Harrow Hill (our South Downs B group); Long Down and Stoke Down (our South Downs Group A); Grimes Graves in Norfolk; and Durrington and Easton Down in Wiltshire. The adjacent site of Martins Clump, just over the county border in Hampshire, was not sampled by us, but was assumed to be geochemically similar to Easton Down. Peppard in Oxfordshire is not accepted by Barber *et al.* as a true flint mine, but they suggest that it may have been a Neolithic flint quarry, which would amount to the same thing as far as our project was concerned. We also analysed material from the then recently discovered potential flint mine at Clanfield in Hampshire (Cunliffe 1973), which is now believed to have come from the exploitation of a clay-with-flint surficial source rather than a mine, but still a potential source of flint for axes. It is interesting to note that the spread of composition of the knapped material from Clanfield was not noticeably larger than for the true mine sites where the flint usually came predominantly from one horizon. This suggests a degree of selectivity of the material, obviously not based on composition, but possibly on size, the larger, more usable nodules originally emanating from a limited number of horizons.

Of the other British sites analysed by us, East Horsley in Surrey was always regarded as unlikely to be prehistoric, and it has now been joined by the site of Windover Hill in Sussex as being predominantly medieval or post-medieval workings. There is no evidence that flint mining ever took place at Great Massingham in Norfolk, although it is possible that surface concentrations of nodules of flint were exploited in the Neolithic period.

Perhaps the main change in the perception of the sources of flint used for the manufacture of axes has been the recognition of the use of flint from sources other than the flint mines, notably the clay-with-flint beds lying on the chalk (Catt 1986) and the glacial tills in East Anglia. Care (1979) was perhaps the first to recognize the importance of the clay-with-flint sources for the production of axes, suggesting that their use commenced in the Mesolithic. The work of Gardiner (1984, 1987 and 1990) and others has shown that there was extensive flint-knapping activity on these beds, although mainly confined to the Late Neolithic. This activity was described in Wessex by Gardiner (1990) and in Barrett *et al.* (1991), in Hampshire by Gardiner (1990), and in the South Downs by Gardiner (1990) and Holgate (1988). In East Anglia it seems that flint from the glacial tills was also extensively exploited (Healy 1984 and 1991a) and in the Brecklands around Grimes Graves there was abundant good-quality flint at the surface (Healy 1996 and 1998).

Mercer (1987) suggested that very local sources might have been opened specifically to serve the needs of major sites on the chalk, citing the so-called trial mines at Durrington Walls in Wiltshire (Booth and Stone 1952) as an example.

However, it still seems to be accepted in Britain and in Europe generally that the majority of the mined flint was intended for axe production (Weisgerber *et al.* 1980), as exemplified by the recent work at the major flint mines at Jablines Le Haut Château (Bostyn and Lanchon 1998). Gardiner (1990) suggested that the South Downs deep-mined flint was exploited for axes in the Early Neolithic, quoting our 1983 paper, but was largely replaced in the Late Neolithic by the clay-with-flint sources, although the latter had been used to some extent earlier. Barber *et al.* (1999, 26) noted that several areas, notably Hampshire and the North Downs, have dense clay-with-flint beds but little evidence of flint mining. They suggested that the two sources might be complementary, deep mining only having been undertaken where suitable surface deposits of flint were not to be found. The same is probably true of East Anglia and, in the absence of any proven Early Neolithic flint mines, clay-with-flints together with glacial and river gravel material become the obvious source for many of the disproportionately high percentage of unassigned axes from that region in our original analytical survey. The marine transgression in the Late Neolithic and subsequent peat growth (Waller 1994, 118–55) could have covered many of these sources, prompting an increased reliance on flint from the adjacent chalk (Healy 1991b, 125, fig. 65). At the height of the transgression (which locally occupied the earlier part of the third millennium BC – that is, the Late Neolithic), there is less evidence for settlement on the south-eastern fen edge than in earlier or later periods (Silvester 1991, 85). A shift of the local focus of activity, rather than of flint procurement alone, towards the 'upland' to the east could have been the context in which mining at Grimes Graves developed. Neolithic quarry pits, dug for flint, have now been reported from Cambridgeshire, but with no information as yet on whether any of the material was intended for axe production (Begg and Lucas 1997).

Russell (2000a, 119–20) accepted our figure of approximately two thirds of Neolithic flint axes originating from the mines of the South Downs, but noted that other artefacts were likely to have been made as well, especially at Grimes Graves. Pitts (1996, 328), when examining the potential sources for both the stone and flint axes, discussed our programme of analyses. He suggested a more careful and focused selection of axe material, and that more flint axes could probably be related to source by analysing material from a larger number of potential sources. As noted above, more detailed surveys of the putative mines sites (Barber *et al.* 1999, 74–80) now suggest that we had in fact covered the most important mines, with the possible exception of the rather large number of unproven sites in Norfolk. Pitts also very properly drew attention (1996, 342) to the problem raised by axe hoards where the members were alike in colour, texture and type and almost certainly belonged together, but were nevertheless assigned analytically to different mines. He specifically mentioned the hoards of Lound Run, Suffolk, Trowse Newton, Norfolk and Great Baddow, Essex, the latter at least being definitely Late Neolithic (Varndell 2004). All are in the East Anglia region, but none of the axes was assigned to Grimes Graves, just one to Great Massingham, and the majority assigned to the South Downs.

Reassessing the flint analytical programme

Sources

The effect of removing the discredited ancient production sites of Windover Hill in Sussex, Great Massingham in Norfolk and East Horsley in Surrey is to accentuate the pattern already established, with the majority of assignable axes going to the South Downs mines and by far the highest percentage of unassignable axes coming from the East Anglian region (fig. 1).

As noted above, no axes were assigned to Windover Hill, and so its removal had no effect. Of the eight South Downs axes that had previously been assigned to the site at East Horsley, three went to the South Downs mines and five became unassignable. Of the five East Anglian axes formerly ascribed to East Horsley, four became unassignable and the fifth was assigned to the South Downs (fig. 117).

Removing Great Massingham had quite a pronounced effect. In Norfolk, where there is a high proportion of unassignables with little coming from the main site of Grimes Graves, no less than fourteen of the axes were previously assigned to Great Massingham. After that site's removal, none of the fourteen axes was reassigned to Grimes Graves; instead four went to South Downs A or B, three to other mines and seven became unassignable. By contrast, the three axes found in the South Downs area that had previously been assigned to Great Massingham were all reassigned to the South Downs mines. This is not too surprising as the near-surface flint beds exposed in the chalk at Great Massingham are from the same geological horizon as those exploited in the South Downs flint mines 200 km to the south, and do show that, although there is regional variation within beds, it is the differences between different geological zones that are all-important. It should be noted that, although it is now believed very unlikely that there was ever any flint mining as such at Great Massingham, the prehistoric flint artefacts sampled could have resulted from working of local surface concentrations of flints. Their analysis underlines the significant differences in the minor element concentrations between the Grimes Graves mined flint and flint from the East Anglian surficial deposits generally.

The East Anglian axes would seem to have a small but real component from Grimes Graves (approximately 4 per cent), with a much larger component (approximately 40 per cent) attributable to the South Downs mines, and approximately the same percentage of unassignable axes. There are two possible explanations for this: either there are as yet undiscovered primary sources, mines or quarries, in East Anglia, or there was a much greater reliance than elsewhere on other, secondary, sources, derived from the clay-with-flints, river gravel, the glacial tills or the surface of the Breckland. As the unknowns from East Anglia do not form into obvious compositional groups, it is more likely that there were no major deep mines in East Anglia producing axes on a significant scale during the Early and Middle Neolithic. The results leave open the whole question of the production of axes from Grimes Graves flint.

The Problem of Grimes Graves

Research in the field and laboratory over the last thirty years has resulted in an apparent contradiction. The very low percentage of flint axes attributable to Grimes Graves in our analytical survey and in the East Anglian field surveys is at variance with the large number of axes recovered from the site itself and, until recently, the prevalent perception of Grimes Graves as primarily a producer of axes.

All of the axes that we analysed from well-dated archaeological contexts were Early or Middle Neolithic, and the majority of stray finds that make up the bulk of the material analysed were typologically indistinguishable. Thus it could be argued that the analysed axes are earlier than the mines at Grimes Graves. However, some hoards, such as that from Great Baddow, near Chelmsford in Essex (which is included in the East Anglian region), found with a discoidal knife, were of Late Neolithic/Early Bronze Age date (Varndell 2004). Here, although they could not be convincingly assigned to a source, it could be said with some confidence that they did not come from Grimes Graves. Similarly, it seems unlikely that the 120 or so axes from the East Anglian region did not include some of the Late Neolithic/Early Bronze Age period, yet few assigned to Grimes Graves.

Another suggested explanation is that the superior quality of the Grimes Graves flint was recognized and that when axes of that material broke they were not discarded but served as raw material for other tools, thereby becoming unrecognizable, and thus would not have been included in our programme. By contrast, other tools, such as discoidal knives, not being involved in percussive activity, could be expected to have a higher survival rate in a recognizable form. This is possible, but does not explain why Grimes Graves flint was not found in the complete axes which had been deposited, lost or discarded before becoming broken, and which formed the majority of our sample, such as those in the Great Baddow hoard.

It is also possible that a number of the axes made at Grimes Graves were intended for use on site in connection with activities, supporting the actual mining of the flint, as seems to have been the case at Jablines (Bostyn and Lanchon 1998). This has also been suggested by Weiner (2003) for the triangular flint axes found at the mines at Veaux-Malaucène, dépt Vaucluse, Provence, France (Schmid 1980). Cut marks made by polished axes in the chalk have been observed on rare occasions in the galleries of Grimes Graves (see Longworth and Varndell 1996, plate 3). However, the consensus is that axes were not used for mining at Grimes Graves on any scale.

Reassessing the likely products of the Grimes Graves mines

The likely amount of flint available at the Grimes Graves mines is difficult to assess. Production has variously been estimated as about 40,000 tonnes (Mercer 1981, 112–13) or as lying between about 18,000 and 21,000 tonnes (Longworth and Varndell 1996, 85–9), with an estimated 12,800 tonnes used if a figure of 60 per cent extraction is assumed (Lech and Longworth 2000). Most articles written about Grimes Graves prior to Saville's 1981 report on the flint from Mercer's excavations (see below) had usually assumed that axes were the main product, and some publications still seem implicitly or explicitly to suggest that Grimes Graves was primarily producing axes.

Saville's report on the material from Mercer's excavations (which was published as the second volume of Mercer's Grimes Graves 1981 excavation report) is the only detailed modern typological analysis of flint from working floors at Grimes Graves to be published prior to that contained in this fascicule. His overall conclusion in this particular context was that there was no evidence for specialized production at all, axe production not being especially important (Saville 1981, 67–72). This certainly changed Mercer's own views. In the conclusions to his first volume, Mercer (1981, 112) recognized that the flint waste was very different to that found on the South Downs mines, but still noted that 'so unlikely is it that the enormous labour input involved in shaft excavation would have been expended simply to produce a normal domestic flint assemblage', and he still calculated production in terms of axes (see above). Shortly afterwards, in the introduction to Saville's report (1981, viii), Mercer had to admit: 'It is quite clear that the production of the 1971 shaft at Grimes Graves cannot be described as that of an axe factory.'

A change in attitude can also be perceived in the guide books to the site. The guide written by Rainbird Clarke (1963) just before the latest excavations and our analytical programme assumed that axe production 'was the purpose of the whole vast enterprise' (ibid., 23). The guide by Barbara Green (1993) is much more circumspect. In the section entitled 'What was produced at Grime's Graves?' (ibid., 10–12), she records that axe production is poorly represented on the excavated chipping floors and that discoidal knives were also there, albeit also poorly represented. But she still concludes from the evidence overall at the mine itself that axes and knives were likely to have been the main product, although suggesting that 'More detailed studies are needed of groups of implements from Grime's Graves, and of flint axes and other tools in museum collections before any real conclusions can be drawn about the products made from the flint extracted with such labour over such a long period'.

Overall it seems that in publications through the twentieth century, Grimes Graves was usually automatically equated with axe production, but latterly when further consideration became necessary, doubts set in.

There is not a great deal of evidence for the production on site of any specific item in any quantity and certainly none at all for processes such as polishing, rather suggesting that much of the material left the site in the form of roughly prepared cores or blanks to be finished elsewhere (Lech and Longworth 2000, figs 41–2). Burton (1980), however, noted that there was considerable variation between the various working floors investigated, citing the example of those published by Richardson (1920), which certainly *did* contain evidence of axe production. Overall some three hundred axes or axe roughouts, many having been broken during manufacture, have been recovered from Grimes Graves, and this is also strong evidence for their production at the site, confirmed by the recent analysis of a selection (see Tables 1 and 2). Healy (1991a and 1998) has pointed out that axeheads of the forms made at Grimes Graves are rare in East Anglia beyond industrial sites.

The distinctive working properties of the Grimes Graves *floorstone*

It is also necessary to consider possible reasons why Grimes Graves flint was only exploited in the later Neolithic as it seems unlikely that the local earlier Neolithic population was unaware of the distinctive flint outcropping in the Grimes Graves area. Elsewhere the early mines do seem to have concentrated on axe production, although other sources were used and it is possible that the Grimes Graves flint was perceived as unsuitable for axe production. Philip Harding's (1987) experiments making polished flint axes found that although the Grimes Graves *floorstone* was a joy to flake, it was much more resistant to polishing compared to flint from Wiltshire. Harding attributed part of this difference to the different grind stones he used, but the Grimes Graves flint does seem harder. The reason for this difference probably lies in the several per cent of calcium frequently encountered in other flints (Sieveking *et al.* 1972, Appendix A), but which is much reduced in Grimes Graves flint. This calcium is most likely to be in the form of calcium carbonate distributed through the flint which could significantly reduce the overall hardness. Thus in the Early and Middle Neolithic the hardness of Grimes Graves flint could have been regarded as an impediment in flint that was intended to be polished.

This was to change in the Late Neolithic, when there was a proliferation of elaborate, finely worked flint implement types, most of them made on flakes (Edmonds 1995, 96–105). For these items the superior flaking qualities could have made the Grimes Graves *floorstone* a very desirable material indeed, and once production had started it may have become popular for a wide range of flint artefacts. The appearance of the flint was no doubt also attractive in itself, but this could have been appreciated as an indication of superior mechanical qualities possessed

by the flint. The milkiness in flint from other sources is associated with the calcium content and its presence would significantly disrupt the micro-crystalline quartz structure, thereby weakening it. Inclusions of any sort are potential weakness points from which cracks could develop when subjected to shock.

It is worth recalling that some four thousand years later mining of the *floorstone* began again in the vicinity of Grimes Graves, this time for the production of gunflints, the industry being centred in Brandon. The selection of flint from the *floorstone* horizon for the gunflints was made on merit alone, the early nineteenth-century knappers being in total ignorance of the earlier industry. Gunflint production was established long before it was even recognized that the strange hollows out on the Brecklands were mines at all. Gunflint production came relatively late to East Anglia, but the Brandon gunflints rapidly became preferred over all others (Skertchley 1879; Forrest 1983). The quality was judged visually on the blackness of the flint and its freedom from inclusions. On both counts the *floorstone* scored well, and inclusion-free black gunflints sold at a premium, to such an extent that a minor industry developed staining flints that were slightly milky or had inclusions (Skertchley 1879, 25).

The most frustrating feature of the original project to provenance flint axes was that we could assign very few axes to Grimes Graves, the one mine we could characterize with some certainty. This led us to conclude in our 1983 paper that Grimes Graves probably produced a range of flint tools and weapons with axe production only on a minor scale.

The identification of artefacts of Grimes Graves flint

The only work directly to address some of the problems raised by our analytical work at Grimes Graves and in East Anglia is that of Frances Healy (1991a and 1998). In her 1991a paper, aptly titled 'The hunting of the floorstone', and the subsequent 1998 paper, she has discussed the whole problem of the sources of flint used in the East Anglian Neolithic and the role of Grimes Graves. In the former paper she succinctly sums up the problem at Grimes Graves thus: 'The removed output [from Grimes Graves], despite its large estimated size, remains obstinately close to invisible. The form in which most of it was taken from the site is unclear.' In the latter paper she is more positive: 'The record of the surrounding area [of Grimes Graves] thus seems to confirm Saville's conclusion that axeheads were an unimportant product at Grime's Graves, and suggests that the British Museum's flint analysis programme, for all its problems and limitations, may have been correct here too (Craddock *et al.* 1983).'

A great deal of field survey has taken place in East Anglia over the past thirty years, particularly on the fen edges, and large numbers of Neolithic (especially Late

Neolithic) and Early Bronze Age sites have been recorded. Based on her long experience with East Anglian flintwork, Healy distinguished flint coming from the gravel, till and other sources from that mined directly from the chalk. Furthermore, she tentatively suggested that the flint which retained its distinctive thick cortex may have come from Grimes Graves. On this basis she postulated that much of the Early and Middle Neolithic flintwork from the Norfolk fen edge was derived from secondary surface sources. In the Late Neolithic and Early Bronze Age flint from the chalk became more frequent in assemblages, but most of it derived from small, outcropping nodules, and very little could be regarded as possible *floorstone* material (Healy suggested 1 per cent). However, rather inconsistently, Healy elsewhere in the same article noted a large increase in retouched items in the Late Neolithic/Early Bronze Age fen-edge assemblages, especially arrowheads and knives, and suggested that these could be of Grimes Graves *floorstone*.

In the recent study of the flint collected from the fen edge in the Cambridge fenlands, especially in the vicinity of Soham, Edmonds *et al.* (1999, 67) found that in the Late Mesolithic and Early Neolithic the flintwork was all of 'secondary source flint', that is, from the glacial tills, etc. By contrast, in the Late Neolithic and Early Bronze Age, in addition to the secondary flint, black, primary flint from the chalk, sometimes with cortex still present, appears as a material in the assemblages. The latter assemblages are typified by the appearance of thumbnail scrapers, discoidal knives and tanged-and-barbed arrowheads, and these had often been made on multi-platform cores. As minimum estimates they suggested that 35 per cent of the flakes came from multi-platform cores and 20 per cent of these cores, where some cortex is preserved, were of primary chalk flint. Edmonds *et al.* make no comment on the source of the primary chalk flint, but even bearing in mind Healy's caveat about the small size of much of the material, the contemporary mines at Grimes Graves must be a strong contender for at least the larger pieces.

Turning to the Grimes Graves mines, Healy speculated on the reasons why the flint had been mined, noting that there was really no need to go to the trouble of deep mining for flint as a source of material for everyday items, including axes, and thereby questioned the whole *raison d'être* of the flint mines. But clearly the Late Neolithic people had gone to great lengths, not to say depths, to get the *floorstone* in quantity, although apparently it was not well represented in the contemporary East Anglian flint assemblages of everyday items (but see below, p. 154). Healy went on to suggest that perhaps the elusive *floorstone* was regarded as high-prestige material in itself and was disseminated as roughouts or as finished artefacts, and stated that 'The hypothetical transport of fine flint artefacts and/or blanks for them from Grimes Graves to the south-eastern fen edge and perhaps further

afield might be proved or disproved by flint analysis. If demonstrated it could be seen as part of the same pattern as the long-haul transport into the area, in the form of stone implements'. This pregnant suggestion has now been implemented.

Thus the work published over the last twenty years seems very generally to support our 1983 findings that not all axes came from the flint mines and not all mines had axes as their main product.

The new analytical programme

The samples
Returning to the problem of identifying artefacts of Grimes Graves flint away from the mine, Healy (1991a), Brown (1996) and others had suggested that the analytical programme should be extended to include a wider range of artefacts, and have even noted that some artefacts from the various East Anglian fen field surveys seemed to be of mined flint, possibly from Grimes Graves (see above). Following on these suggestions, it was decided to analyse a small selection of this material. The collections from the recent fenland project survey, however, were not available for study at the time (late 2001). Instead a small selection was made by Frances Healy, Gillian Varndell and Paul Craddock from the material collected earlier in the twentieth century, which forms part of the collections of the Castle Museum, Norwich.

The artefacts were selected partly on the basis of their appearance; those having a dense black colouration, some still with cortex attached, were considered as likely to have been mined from the chalk (plate 23). Another important practical criterion was the likelihood that it would be possible to drill a core of material free from surface contamination. Flint, for all its dense impermeable appearance, is in fact quite porous (Rottländer and Weymouth 1980/81), a property the nineteenth-century gunflint stainers were quick to exploit to their advantage at Brandon. Experiments by Patterson and Sollberger (1979) demonstrated that flint readily absorbs water, and studies by Andersen (1982) on Mesolithic flint artefacts found approximately three times as much water in the surface layers than was contained in the body of the flint. Thus buried flint will absorb the ground water and become contaminated with minerals in solution, which are typically those also found in the clay minerals that are important for provenancing the flint. Fortunately we were aware of this problem while carrying out the original project, and experiments carried out by us showed that the flint *beneath* the visible cortex or patina was still contaminated to a depth of about 2 or 3 mm (Cowell 1981a). After the core was taken, this material was broken from the drilled core with pliers and discarded. Thus any artefact that was less than about 5 mm thick was likely to be totally contaminated by ground water from its burial context. In practical terms, before a core of approximately

3–4 mm diameter could be taken that was certain to be free from contamination, the flint would have to be about 2 cm thick over a length of several centimetres. In reality, this precludes most flint artefacts except axes and other core tools, and some of the thicker flakes and artefacts made from them.

The fifteen items selected for the new analytical programme included bifacially worked pieces, large scrapers and flakes from Cranwich, Thetford St Peter and Two Mile Bottom (also in Thetford) in the Norfolk Breckland, and from Methwold and Feltwell further to the west (plate 23); and a fine polished axe of Late Neolithic type from Lound Run, Belton, Norfolk (Suffolk before 1974) (plate 24; NB this axe is not a part of the group found together at Lound Run and analysed in the previous project). Small items such as the thumbnail scrapers and arrowheads may well have been made from Grimes Graves flint, but as they are likely to have been contaminated throughout their thickness by ground water, it seems unlikely that it will ever be possible to provenance them analytically.

In addition to these artefacts, eleven flaked flint axes (plate 25) and two discoidal knives (plate 26) from Grimes Graves itself were also sampled. This was to provide a comparison with the composition of the twenty or so Grimes Graves flint artefacts and flakes, and the *in situ floorstone* in Pits 2, 11 and 15, analysed for the first project. It was also to check that these axes, apparently so rare in the archaeological record outside Grimes Graves, really were of Grimes Graves mined flint. Discoidal knives had been previously mentioned as another possible product (Holgate 1991, 38 and 48, and see above, p. 150), and two were included in the sample, once again to check that they were of Grimes Graves mined flint.

The analysis
The sampling and dissolution procedures were similar to those used in the previous studies (Sieveking *et al.* 1972; Craddock *et al.* 1983). Each artefact was drilled with a 6-mm water-cooled hollow-cored bit to remove a cylinder of flint. The tops of the samples, including any cortex, were removed with pliers and discarded. The samples were then cleaned with *aqua regia* (a mixture of concentrated nitric and hydrochloric acids), then de-ionized water and dried. This removed any contamination introduced by the sampling procedure. After weighing, each core sample was placed in a PTFE beaker and 10 ml of concentrated (48 per cent) hydrofluoric acid (Aristar grade) was added. The beakers were warmed on a hot plate and then left overnight to allow the samples to digest and dissolve. The beakers were then reheated to dryness to remove the excess hydrofluoric acid. To oxidize any organic material, 1 ml of concentrated nitric acid (Aristar grade) was then added and the beakers were evaporated to dryness again. Finally, 2 ml of concentrated (70 per cent) perchloric acid (Aristar grade) were added to each and the beakers

heated until the sample residues had fully dissolved. The solutions were then diluted to 60 ml with de-ionized water. A reagent blank was also prepared.

The solutions were analysed for eleven elements (Al, Ba, Ca, Fe, K, La, Li, Mg, Mn, Na and P) by ICP-AES (inductively coupled plasma atomic emission spectroscopy) using a Perkin-Elmer Optima 4300DV instrument. This is equipped for either axial or radial plasma viewing. All elements were measured in axial mode, which is generally more sensitive but typically has poorer precision than radial mode. In the previous studies eight elements (Al, Ca, Fe, K, Li, Mg, Na and P) were analysed, mostly by AAS (atomic absorption spectroscopy). The three additional elements, Ba, La and Mn, are more sensitive by ICP-AES and were included to provide more variables with which to compare the two sets of samples. Matrix-matched multi-element standards were used for calibration and the samples were processed in two batches for high or low calcium as it was found that there was some interference from calcium at high concentrations, particularly on the sodium and potassium measurements.

The current ICP-AES results are listed in Table 7. For comparison with other data, Table 8 shows the mean concentrations of the current results together with that of previous data for some of the relevant mine site groups, analysed by both AAS (Craddock *et al.* 1983) and ICP-AES (Thompson *et al.* 1986), and the *floorstone* flint layer from Pit 15 at Grimes Graves (Cowell *et al* 1980). It can be seen from Table 7 that the flint artefacts from the East Anglian sites are very similar in composition to the Grimes Graves site artefacts for all the elements quantified. Furthermore, when they are compared with the other British mine site data in Table 8, they are clearly closest to Grimes Graves in composition. This is emphasized by a plot of the concentrations of aluminium and potassium (two of the main discriminating elements) for the current data with selected mine site data, South Downs Group A, Easton Down, Peppard and Grimes Graves *floorstone* (Cowell *et al* 1980), in fig. 2. The plot shows almost complete coincidence of the two groups of the current data with that of the Grimes Graves *floorstone*, whereas the other mine site data are almost completely separated from them.

A statistical analysis of the data has also been carried out. The methodology used was equivalent to that employed in the classification of flint axes by Leese (Craddock *et al.* 1983). All the flint mine data from the 1983 paper were included, with the current data for the Grimes Graves axes being added to the original Grimes Graves group. A different analytical technique (AAS as opposed to ICP-AES) was of course used in the original study; however, Thompson has noted (Thompson *et al.* 1986) that there was no significant difference between his analyses of the mine site flints by ICP-AES and the original analyses by AAS. As in the 1983 study, the statistical method of quadratic discriminant analysis was applied with all data being log-transformed prior to analysis and using the same suite of elements (Al, Fe, Mg, K, Na, Li and P). Initially, to test the separation of the groups, the control group items were reclassified using the 'jack-knife' method where each member is treated as an unknown. This gave a success rate for reclassification of 77 per cent, which is similar to that obtained in the 1983 study. The East Anglian flakes and tools were then classified using the eleven groups of mine data as controls. Of the fifteen items, twelve were classified to Grimes Graves, one (BMGG 3) to Great Massingham, one (BMGG 10) to South Downs B (Cissbury etc.), and one (BMGG 5) was considered unclassifiable as it was assigned with almost equal probabilities to three mines (Grimes Graves, Great Massingham and South Downs B). Thus the majority appear to have been manufactured from flint derived from the Grimes Graves *floorstone*.

Discussion

Twelve of the thirteen flints from Grimes Graves have the distinctive composition, with the relatively high aluminium (422–656 ppm) and low calcium contents (although one had 12,000 ppm) already established for the flints from the mine in the previous project, and thus are almost certainly made from the mined flint. The exception is the axe 1973 475 (plate 27). It is possible that this piece could have been made from a local surface nodule that had been glacially deposited. However, beneath the patina the flint is black, similar to the other pieces of Grimes Graves flint, and the aluminium content of 391 ppm is only just outside the range of the others, suggesting on balance that it is likely also to be mined flint but of rather unusual composition.

Twelve of the fifteen Breckland and fen-edge flints assign to Grimes Graves. It could be argued that this apparent close association of so many flints with Grimes Graves might be because the composition of the Grimes Graves mined flint was fairly typical of East Anglian flint generally. Fortunately previous analytical programmes have shown this not to be the case (Cowell *et al.* 1980, Tables 2 and 3). The flint occurs in bands within the Cretaceous chalk, which in East Anglia tends to dip towards the east. Thus different horizons are exposed across the region and the individual horizons have differing composition. There is also some geographical variation in the composition of the individual horizons, but this is not pronounced. As noted above, the flints from Great Massingham, about 30 km north of Grimes Graves, and analysed as part of the previous project (Craddock *et al.* 1983) belong to a different geological zone and are very different from the Grimes Graves *floorstone*, but are more similar to the flints from the corresponding zone mined on the South Downs some 200 km distant.

The majority of the chalk in the vicinity of Grimes Graves tends to be buried under drift material, with only

minor outcrops of flint veins in valley sides, although these were apparently exploited in the remote past. Analyses by Cowell (Craddock and Cowell 2009, Table 3) on artefacts from the Neanderthal-period butchery site at Lynford Pit (Boismier 2002), previously collected by local archaeologist John Lord, show that they have a narrow composition range identical to that of the nearby Grimes Graves *floorstone*. These flints presumably came directly from exposed sections in the chalk, possibly at Grimes Graves itself. However, it is unlikely that surface exposures could have provided more than a tiny quantity of flint and thus, after the *floorstone* flint had been located, it could only have been properly exploited by mining. The flint sampled is therefore likely to have been obtained from Grimes Graves by mining, with a small possibility that some could have come from the putative mines at Great Melton, or at Swell Pit, Lynford and Buckenham Toft, Stanford, both in the general vicinity of Grimes Graves (Barber *et al.* 1999).

The composition of BMGG 3, 10 and 5, although assigning to Great Massingham, South Downs B or unassignable, are more likely to be from surface flints collected from East Anglia. Also, as noted above, the particular horizon exposed in the Great Massingham area geologically equates to the horizons mined in the South Downs mines.

The composition of the Cranwich biface, BMGG 8 (plate 28), is interesting as it has a high aluminium content compared with the Grimes Graves *floorstone*, whereas most flint artefacts have less. Although assigned to Grimes Graves, the aluminium content is more similar to that of the flint horizons beneath the *floorstone* as exemplified by the section at Taplin's Pit (see above, p. 146 and Cowell *et al.* 1980). As the chalk tilts up from west to east the chalk will have been eroded to a greater extent beneath what are now the fens, exposing the lower flint levels. Thus BMGG 8 could have come from a local gravel etc., derived from these exposed deeper layers. However, the appearance of the flint suggests that it is from a primary context. Thus this is possible evidence that the geologically deeper horizons may have been mined on occasion at Grimes Graves.

Conclusion

Grimes Graves flint was encountered across a range of artefacts that were large enough to be sampled, and furthermore, with the possible exception of the polished axe, none of the pieces was especially finely worked. Thus this admittedly very small and somewhat skewed sample provides no support for the suggestion that the Grimes Graves mined flint was intended for the production of a narrow range of specific items, or that it was even reserved for high-quality work. On the contrary, it seems that the Grimes Graves mines were the source of quality flint for general usage, including axe production.

As noted above, on the fen edge, flint which could

have come from Grimes Graves, sometimes retaining its cortex, seems only to occur among the Late Neolithic and Early Bronze Age assemblages. Healy suggested (1991b, 125) that perhaps the Late Neolithic marine incursions and Early Bronze Age peat growth would have rendered less and less accessible the flint-bearing deposits in the fenland basin used previously, encouraging the use of flint from other sources. The relative abundance in the collections of quite large pieces of flint that could

easily have been reworked to form smaller items such as arrowheads suggests that by the Late Neolithic, at least in the general vicinity of the mines in East Anglia, Grimes Graves flint was freely available. No analytical work has been done on comparable Late Neolithic material outside of East Anglia, but the observations of Edmonds *et al.* (1999) on the Cambridgeshire flint suggest that Grimes Graves mined flint was probably being disseminated over a much wider area.

BM no.	Norwich no.	Description	Provenance
GG 1	39.22 1.21 (18)	Scraper	Two Mile Bottom: site XXI
GG 2	1932.124. A2324	Polished axe	Lound Run
GG 3	153.929 Box 1624	Fabricator	Methwold: Warburton site 2a
GG 4	A1025 1.151 (in small box)	Flake	Methwold: sites 1, 3 and 4
GG 5	32.926.28 A982 1926.32	Plane	Cranwich
GG 6	32.926.28 A982 1926.32	Flake	Cranwich
GG 7	32.926.28 A982 1926.32	Scraper	Cranwich
GG 8	15 3 929 A979	Biface	Cranwich
GG 9	254 / 173 558 974 3	Flake	Cranwich
GG 10	16 8324 Box 984	Biface	Cranwich
GG 11	16.83 Box A978	Fabricator	Cranwich: site 76
GG 12	160.938 Small box A	Scraper	Two Mile Bottom
GG 13	A1029 153.929	Flake	Methwold
GG 14	39.22 A1060	Polished Biface	Thetford: St Peter
GG 28	A998 544 969 TL74259145	Biface	Feltwell
BM no.	**Grimes Graves no.**		
GG 15	1914 8-1 16	Axe	Pit 1
GG 16	1973 475	Axe	Pit XII, Floor D
GG 17	Balfour 1902	Axe	Brandon Park, surface find
GG 18	266	Axe	Pit 9 at 6'
GG 19	74 238	Axe	West Field F24 (4)
GG 20	1914 8-1 86	Discoidal knife	Floor 3C
GG 21	1924	Discoidal knife	Pit 10 at 4'6"
GG 22	366	Axe	Pit 10, Floor 3
GG 23	GG 74 (233)	Axe	West Field F18 (2)
GG 24	1914 8-1 32	Axe	Pit 2, layer 5
GG 25	GG 76 451	Axe	West Field F28 (5)
GG 26	GG 75 L 1022	Axe	1270/905 (topsoil)
GG 27	GG 75 L 1304	Axe	1270/900 O 15

Table 6 Descriptions of the flints selected and concordance between British Museum laboratory sample numbers and other identifiers (e.g. registration numbers, small find numbers, etc.).

East Anglian flint

BM no.	Type	Al	Ba	Ca	Fe	K	La	Li	Mg	Mn	Na	P
GG 1	Scraper	529	15.7	671	57	301	1.4	4.14	24.6	2.1	265	157
GG 2	Polished	574	9.5	370	86	258	0.8	4.44	24.2	< 0.1	303	97
GG 3	Fabricator	582	1.8	307	76	227	0.9	16.73	17.0	0.1	209	68
GG 4	Flake	671	2.1	645	75	283	1.6	5.38	21.7	< 0.1	285	139
GG 5	Plane	519	3.4	202	54	268	0.7	4.30	17.5	0.9	268	25
GG 6	Flake	524	2.7	321	96	248	0.8	4.52	19.5	0.1	238	67
GG 7	Scraper	598	5.9	433	69	267	0.7	4.85	18.6	< 0.1	286	131
GG 8	Biface	812	6.5	496	57	413	0.9	7.89	24.4	0.3	374	116
GG 9	Flake	519	8.2	272	63	241	0.8	4.48	17.0	0.1	260	91
GG 10	Biface	388	7.8	2032	67	201	1.1	12.99	25.5	1.2	197	54
GG 11	Fabricator	663	9.5	339	68	320	1.2	5.68	17.9	< 0.1	305	83
GG 12	Scraper	629	4.2	314	105	316	0.7	5.50	23.0	< 0.1	291	97
GG 13	Flake	701	4.6	533	69	319	1.0	7.65	18.8	0.2	338	160
GG 14	Polished	637	11.4	234	58	290	0.9	5.87	18.3	0.9	296	61
GG 28	Biface	488	3.2	342	78	227	0.8	4.18	19.7	< 0.1	241	81
	Mean	**589**	**6.4**	**501**	**72**	**279**	**1.0**	**6.6**	**21**	**0.4**	**277**	**95**
	s.d.	*99*	*3.8*	*431*	*14*	*50*	*0.2*	*3.5*	*3*	*0.6*	*44*	*38*

Grimes Graves flint

GG 15	Axe	489	2.0	12229	255	232	2.0	6.65	101.6	6.9	266	285
GG 16	Axe	391	2.3	2112	61	214	1.7	3.02	25.0	0.3	245	269
GG 17	Axe	484	9.0	268	51	256	1.1	3.98	17.7	< 0.1	274	84
GG 18	Axe	555	2.3	476	61	234	1.0	4.74	17.0	0.2	278	111
GG 19	Axe	423	2.6	839	84	201	1.2	3.12	20.7	< 0.1	226	214
GG 20	Discoidal knife	485	2.5	375	59	196	0.9	4.30	15.4	< 0.1	249	75
GG 21	Discoidal knife	425	2.1	356	57	190	0.8	3.55	14.9	< 0.1	224	72
GG 22	Axe	422	2.1	391	46	173	0.7	3.76	15.8	< 0.1	216	95
GG 23	Axe	696	3.8	431	64	301	1.1	6.23	19.2	< 0.1	332	94
GG 24	Axe	518	2.6	495	64	244	0.8	4.29	16.5	< 0.1	296	108
GG 25	Axe	489	2.0	434	55	220	0.9	4.18	15.9	< 0.1	270	117
GG 26	Axe	621	4.9	374	67	267	1.1	5.33	20.6	< 0.1	310	82
GG 27	Axe	552	9.0	2191	134	275	1.3	5.57	28.6	0.7	284	117
	Mean	**504**	**3.6**	**1613**	**81**	**231**	**1.1**	**4.5**	**25**	**0.7**	**267**	**133**
	s.d.	*83*	*2.4*	*3128*	*55*	*36*	*0.4*	*1.1*	*22*	*1.8*	*33*	*71*

Table 7 Analyses of flints from field collections in East Anglia (1–14 and 28), and of axes and discoidal knives from Grimes Graves (15–27).

Precision is generally in the range 2–4 per cent relative except for Mn, which is 5–10 per cent relative. The accuracy is expected to be similar. Concentrations are expressed in ppm.

Flint groups	Technique	Reference	Al	Ba	Ca	Fe	K	La	Li	Mg	Mn	Na	P
Grimes Graves and East Anglia													
Flakes, Norfolk sites	ICP-AES	Current data	589 ± 99	6.4	501	72	279 ± 50	1.0	6.6	21	0.4	277 ± 44	95
Axes, Grimes Graves	ICP-AES	Current data	504 ± 83	3.6	1613	81	231 ± 36	1.1	4.5	25	0.7	267 ± 33	133
Floorstone, Pit 15, Grimes Graves	AAS	Hughes *et al.* 1976	561 ± 102	nd	727	50	246 ± 30	nd	5.6	20.1	nd	267 ± 39	98
Grimes Graves, flint mine	ICP-AES	Thompson *et al.* 1986	510	2.6	420	62	210	nd	4.6	20	0.8	240	101
Grimes Graves, flint mine	AAS	Craddock *et al.* 1983	663 ± 115	nd	950	84	235 ± 31	nd	6	25	nd	288 ± 42	91
South Downs mines													
South Downs A	AAS	Craddock *et al.* 1983	183 ± 57	nd	3900	66	114 ± 27	nd	5	34	nd	175 ± 49	101
South Downs B	AAS	Craddock *et al.* 1983	247 ± 71	nd	6750	87	130 ± 43	nd	14	52	nd	159 ± 63	81
Cissbury, flint mine	ICP-AES	Thompson *et al.* 1986	240	< 0.1	1620	64	142	nd	1.3	28	0.7	171	38
Blackpatch, flint mine	ICP-AES	Thompson *et al.* 1986	270	6.4	7600	53	142	nd	7.8	56	3.5	141	59
Church Hill, flint mine	ICP-AES	Thompson *et al.* 1986	250	8.8	3150	44	128	nd	2.9	31	3	155	61
Other mines													
Peppard, flint mine	AAS	Craddock *et al.* 1983	472 ± 76	nd	2900	104	280 ± 37	nd	17	29	nd	287 ± 61	98
Peppard, flint mine	ICP-AES	Thompson *et al.* 1986	400	6.7	1680	71	210	nd	4.5	27	3.1	210	66
Easton Down, flint mine	AAS	Craddock *et al.* 1983	258 ± 67	nd	7500	46	142 ± 47	nd	13	55	nd	164 ± 62	119
Easton Down, flint mine	ICP-AES	Thompson *et al.* 1986	188	0.6	5900	26	110	nd	1.2	46	3.1	148	96

Table 8 Comparison of flint artefact and mine group compositions.

Table shows mean values and, where available, standard deviations for selected elements.
Concentrations are expressed in ppm.

VI Absolute chronology

J. Ambers

Over the past forty years a very large number of radiocarbon analyses have been produced for samples from Grimes Graves. All are listed here (Table 9), divided into contextual groups. They are quoted in the form recommended by Stuiver and Polach (1977), in radiocarbon years BP, corrected for isotopic variation as shown in the tables. Those results related to activity in the deep mines have already been listed in Fascicule 5 of the Grimes Graves Excavation Reports (Ambers 1996), and considered further in Ambers (1998) in the context of a number of fresh measurements, but are included here for completeness.

The majority of the measurements listed were made during the period 1961–86, with many of these being undertaken as part of a concentrated campaign of dating between 1972 and 1976. The 1972 project had an ambitious research design and was a concerted attempt to provide a detailed site chronology. However, reviewing the data from the benefit of a new century, it is apparent that the ambitions of this project were not matched by the abilities of the laboratory at that time and, in fact, some of the objectives might still not be achievable, even given modern technical advances. Much of the discussion in Fascicule 5 concerned the shortcomings of radiocarbon measurements made some twenty years or more ago. As might be expected there have been major changes in radiocarbon practice in the intervening period, both in terms of the techniques used and in approaches to sample selection. These improvements, and their implications, are discussed in some detail in Ambers (1996) and it seems redundant to repeat them here. It is, however, worth pointing out that a tendency by radiocarbon laboratories to overestimate the accuracy and precision of the results they produced, plus at times a lack of diligence in sample selection (most of the Grimes Graves dates were on antler picks, which must reflect human activity at the site, but a number were for unidentified charcoal samples, of uncertain age offset), must cast some doubt upon the reliability of many early radiocarbon measurements. As a consequence of these problems, it is not feasible to subject the pre-1980s Grimes Graves results to the types of Bayesian analysis which might solve some of the questions posed in the 1972 research design. Instead these figures can only safely be used to give a general chronology. In fact, at least one of the questions asked – the period of usage of a single deep mine, believed on archaeological and practical grounds to be in the order of a few years –

would probably be insoluble by radiocarbon even now, even given an ideal situation in which it were possible to generate a series of modern high-precision measurements on material taken from a clearly defined stratigraphic sequence with full Bayesian statistical analysis.

Following the publication of Fascicule 5, a selective programme of redating material from the deep mines was carried out (Ambers 1998) using only samples of high intrinsic integrity (identified to species where necessary) and modern measurement techniques, including the demonstrably high standards of quality control. These results are included in Table 9 and can be distinguished from the earlier group by having BM numbers above BM-3000. The success of this programme for the deep mines was followed by a similar redating exercise for material from the West Field.

Measurement methods

Only a brief summary of the methods used is given here; for full details of the methods the relevant datelists should be consulted. The samples listed in datelists III (Barker and Mackey 1961) and IV (Barker and Mackey 1963), together with BM-276, were measured by gas proportional counting of acetylene. Errors for these figures are based on counting statistics, together with additional errors of ± 80 years for possible isotopic variation and ± 100 years for natural atmospheric variation (de Vries effects) added in quadrature.

All other measurements were made by liquid scintillation counting of benzene in a succession of counters, using a modern standard of oxalic acid (NBS I or II). For results with BM numbers lower than 3000, errors are based on sample counting statistics alone, while for those with BM numbers higher than 3000, the errors are the counting error for the sample combined with an estimate of the errors contributed by the modern and background samples (this estimate includes both counting and non-counting errors, the latter being computed from differences in the overall count rates observed among the individual backgrounds and moderns).

Pretreatments used were similar throughout: for charcoal samples, hot acid and sometimes alkali washes, and for antler and bone, demineralization with dilute acid. The highly calcareous environment of Grimes Graves makes any humic acid contamination unlikely.

In common with most liquid scintillation laboratories, the $\delta^{13}C$ values quoted here are for the carbon dioxide gas used to produce the benzene sample counted. They are produced with the intention of giving a counting correction, including both natural fractionation and that induced in chemical processing in the laboratory, in order to provide the correct date. They are not designed or intended to give an accurate reflection of the $\delta^{13}C$ value of the total bone collagen. They can therefore only be used as a very general indication of dietary input, or of possible contamination.

Nomenclature

The table includes three sets of double measurements (BM-1000a and -1000b, BM-1052a and -1052b, and BM-1056a and -1056b). Unfortunately these suffixes were not used consistently. Of the three pairs, only BM-1000a and -1000b represent true replicates, prepared from the separate samples of the same raw materials. The other pairs were produced by recounting of the same sample benzene at different times, and are therefore not true replicates.

Calibration (figs 118a–e and 119)

Calibrated age ranges were generated from the INTCAL 98 curve (Stuiver *et al.* 1998), using OxCal v3.10 (Bronk Ramsey 1995). For this reason the calibrated ranges differ slightly from those given in Fascicule 5, where the 1986 calibration curves were used. Calibrated age ranges are quoted in the form recommended by Mook (1986).

Results and discussion

Pre-Neolithic features

Only two figures fall into this group, both measured over thirty years ago. The errors on these figures may well be underestimated, but despite this, these results indicate some early human activity on the site during the seventh or eighth millennium BC.

Deep mines

Two groups of radiocarbon results exist for the deep mines: the original measurements made on a wide suite of materials, and subject to the limitations discussed above; and the more recently measured group, for which care was taken to choose only from samples known to come from secure contexts (preferably where a photographic record exists) and to be short-lived materials (all are of antler). These are identified by sample numbers over 3000. There is considerable variation in the first group, with some materials evidently being intrusive to the Neolithic workings, although the most extreme outliers can be explained in terms of the nature of the samples involved; from Mercer's excavations, BM-1097 comes from deposits of Middle Bronze Age midden material in the top of the Mercer 1972 shaft; BM-779 comes from a deposit of charcoal on an old ground surface; and BM-780 is from a charcoal spread underlying the

first of two successive Iron Age burials in the top fill of the 1971 shaft. Despite this variation there is a clear concentration of activity in the mid-third millennium BC. While not indicating a significant change in the date of mining at the site, the second group suggest a much tighter grouping, more in accord with the archaeological interpretation, than the previous results (in fact, the results are statistically indistinguishable within individual shafts). Using the Bayesian analysis available through the OxCal programme it is possible to go much further in interpreting these figures. To do this involves assuming that the use of each shaft represents a single phase, and that the events dated by the radiocarbon results are fairly uniformly chronologically distributed through that phase. In the circumstances of the deep mines both of these assumptions seem eminently reasonable. Modelling the figures for the individual shafts as uniform phases, it is then possible to use the OxCal programme to calculate the period of usage of Greenwell's Pit. Quoting all ranges at the 68 per cent confidence level, this gives an estimate of 2580–2470 cal BC for the first dated event and 2550–2400 cal BC for the last, with a span of use within 0–120 years. While there are only three measurements from Pit 15, and the model is therefore less reliable, the equivalent figures are 2630–2490 cal BC for the first dated event and 2555–2465 cal BC for the last, with a span of use within 0–120 years. Greenwell's Pit, Pit 15 and Pit 11 are all, in fact, groups of pits not all of which would need to have been worked simultaneously.

Area A; chipping floor

These dates fall into a similar range to those for the deep mines.

West Field

As with the deep mines, two groups of radiocarbon results exist for the West Field: the original 1970s measurements subject to the limitations discussed above, and the more recently measured group of short-lived samples (all but one are of antler; the only charcoal sample used has been identified as *Pinus* sp, and is thus extremely unlikely to be of any appreciable intrinsic age) known to come from secure contexts, measured under modern conditions. When the whole suite of radiocarbon dates from the West Field is considered, a very long period of use across the second and third millennia BC seems to be indicated. However, as with the deep mines (see Ambers 1998 and above), selection and careful redating of only short-life material from secure contexts suggests a much more compact age range. Using the Bayesian analysis capability of the OxCal programme (see Bronk Ramsey 1995 for an explanation of this technique) gives a 68 per cent confidence that activity in those areas included in the redating began between 2610 and 2300 cal BC and ended between 2010 and 1670 cal BC. Unfortunately, using the data available it is not possible to determine with certainty

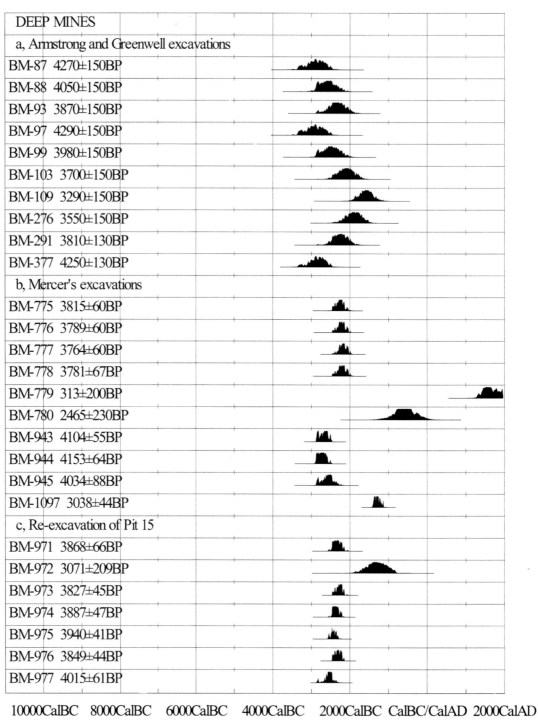

Fig. 118 a–e: Calibrated age ranges for archaeological materials from Neolithic and later periods.

BM-978 3865±44BP						
BM-979 3820±46BP						
BM-980 3736±58BP						
BM-986 3845±44BP						
BM-996 3890±42BP						
BM-997 3960±56BP						
BM-998 3992±45BP						
BM-1000a 4051±109BP						
BM-1000b 4022±57BP						
BM-1001 3868±56BP						
BM-1002 3882±45BP						
BM-1003 3949±42BP						
BM-1011 3952±44BP						
BM-1051 3887±56BP						
BM-1052a 4114±45BP						
BM-1052b 3954±43BP						
BM-1053 3834±50BP						
BM-1054 3904±36BP						
BM-1056a 3838±42BP						
BM-1056b 3740±48BP						
BM-1057 3924±47BP						
BM-1058 3876±48BP						
BM-1059 3977±47BP						
BM-1260 4037±62BP						
BM-1262 3900±54BP						
BM-3007 4060±90BP						
BM-3087 4010±40BP						
BM-3090 4010±70BP						
d, Re-excavation of Pit 11						
BM-981 3874±47BP						
BM-982 4090±58BP						

10000CalBC 8000CalBC 6000CalBC 4000CalBC 2000CalBC CalBC/CalAD 2000CalAD

Calibrated date

BM-983 3761±48BP						
BM-984 3902±58BP						
BM-985 4010±59BP						
BM-987 3671±75BP						
BM-3068 3890±40BP						
e, Re-excavation of Greenwell's Pit						
BM-1027 3855±36BP						
BM-1028 3922±38BP						
BM-1029 3859±53BP						
BM-1044 3922±86BP						
BM-1045 3949±41BP						
BM-1046 3797±52BP						
BM-1047 3974±45BP						
BM-1048 3880±38BP						
BM-1049 3884±43BP						
BM-1050 3893±44BP						
BM-1068 3784±50BP						
BM-1261 3853±71BP						
BM-2377 4060±90BP						
BM-2380 3810±60BP						
BM-3009 4060±90BP						
BM-3010 3960±45BP						
BM-3088 3980±60BP						
BM-3089 3960±60BP						
f, Re-excavation of Pit 2						
BM-1020 3844±221BP						
BM-1069 3896±141BP						
g, Pit 3A						
BM-1060 3863±86BP						

10000CalBC   8000CalBC   6000CalBC   4000CalBC   2000CalBC   CalBC/CalAD   2000CalAD

Calibrated date

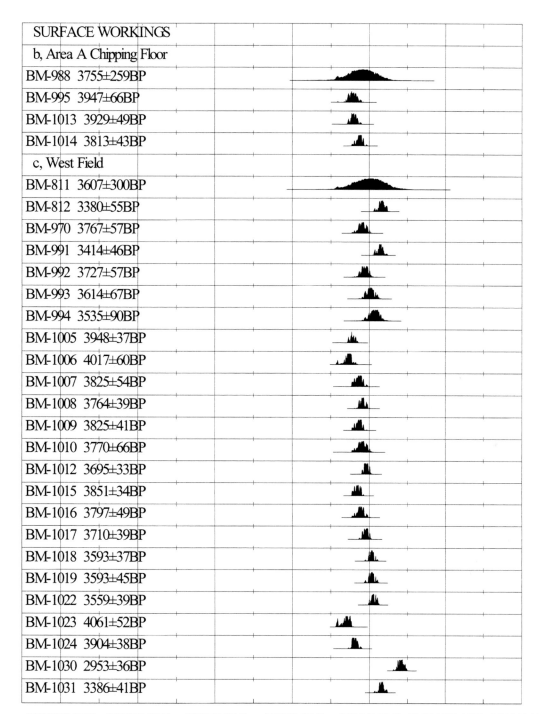

SURFACE WORKINGS

b, Area A Chipping Floor

BM-988 3755±259BP	
BM-995 3947±66BP	
BM-1013 3929±49BP	
BM-1014 3813±43BP	

c, West Field

BM-811 3607±300BP	
BM-812 3380±55BP	
BM-970 3767±57BP	
BM-991 3414±46BP	
BM-992 3727±57BP	
BM-993 3614±67BP	
BM-994 3535±90BP	
BM-1005 3948±37BP	
BM-1006 4017±60BP	
BM-1007 3825±54BP	
BM-1008 3764±39BP	
BM-1009 3825±41BP	
BM-1010 3770±66BP	
BM-1012 3695±33BP	
BM-1015 3851±34BP	
BM-1016 3797±49BP	
BM-1017 3710±39BP	
BM-1018 3593±37BP	
BM-1019 3593±45BP	
BM-1022 3559±39BP	
BM-1023 4061±52BP	
BM-1024 3904±38BP	
BM-1030 2953±36BP	
BM-1031 3386±41BP	

10000CalBC 8000CalBC 6000CalBC 4000CalBC 2000CalBC CalBC/CalAD 2000CalAD

Calibrated date

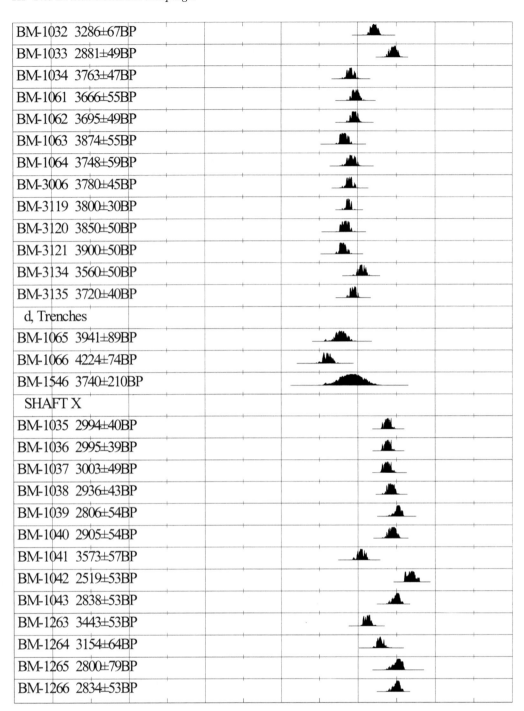

BM-1032 3286±67BP							
BM-1033 2881±49BP							
BM-1034 3763±47BP							
BM-1061 3666±55BP							
BM-1062 3695±49BP							
BM-1063 3874±55BP							
BM-1064 3748±59BP							
BM-3006 3780±45BP							
BM-3119 3800±30BP							
BM-3120 3850±50BP							
BM-3121 3900±50BP							
BM-3134 3560±50BP							
BM-3135 3720±40BP							
d, Trenches							
BM-1065 3941±89BP							
BM-1066 4224±74BP							
BM-1546 3740±210BP							
SHAFT X							
BM-1035 2994±40BP							
BM-1036 2995±39BP							
BM-1037 3003±49BP							
BM-1038 2936±43BP							
BM-1039 2806±54BP							
BM-1040 2905±54BP							
BM-1041 3573±57BP							
BM-1042 2519±53BP							
BM-1043 2838±53BP							
BM-1263 3443±53BP							
BM-1264 3154±64BP							
BM-1265 2800±79BP							
BM-1266 2834±53BP							

10000CalBC 8000CalBC 6000CalBC 4000CalBC 2000CalBC CalBC/CalAD 2000CalAD

Calibrated date

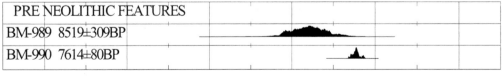

PRE NEOLITHIC FEATURES					
BM-989 8519±309BP					
BM-990 7614±80BP					

14000CalBC   12000CalBC   10000CalBC   8000CalBC   6000CalBC   4000CalBC

Calibrated date

Fig. 119 Calibrated age ranges for archaeological materials from pre-Neolithic features.

if the period of use of the two areas overlapped or not (although on archaeological grounds it is likely to have done so, and the radiocarbon results do not contradict this), but activity in the West Field appears to have continued for a considerable period after work ceased in those of the deep mines so far excavated.

Shaft X

The majority of the Shaft X results indicate a concentration of Bronze Age activity in the early part of the second millennium and at the very end of the first millennium BC. Three outliers to this group suggest Neolithic/earlier Bronze Age material was introduced along with the later Bronze Age midden material dumped within the shaft.

Future work

Since the work described here was carried out, further advances have been made both in techniques of radiocarbon measurement and approaches to statistical analysis. Since large quantities of material from the Grimes Graves excavations suitable for radiocarbon dating remain in storage, it is hoped that further analysis may answer some of the chronological questions raised here. A start has been made on this work, with ten dates being commissioned from the Centrum voor Isotopen Onderzoek Rijksuniversiteit Groningen and the Scottish Universities Environmental Research Centre (Healy pers. comm.).

BM no.	Material	Ref. *Radiocarbon*	Pit no./ feature	Context/ cutting	Find no.	⋆^{13}C (‰)	Results BP	Possible calibrated age range(s) calendar years BC unless otherwise stated	
								68% probability	95% probability
DEEP MINES									
a Armstrong and Greenwell excavations									
87	Charcoal	1961, 3, 41	Pit 15	Shaft at 14 ft			4270 ± 150	3090–2600	3350–2450
88	Antler	1961, 3, 41	Pit 15	Shaft at 11 ft			4050 ± 150	2880–2450 or 2420–2400	3050–2100
93	Antler	1963, 5, 106	Pit 10				3870 ± 150	2600–2050	2900–1900
97	Antler	1963, 5, 106	Pit 12				4290 ± 150	3300–3200 or 3100–2600	3400–2450
99	Antler	1963, 5, 106	Pit 14				3980 ± 150	2900–2800 or 2700–2200	2900–2000
103	Antler	1963, 5, 106	Pit 11				3700 ± 150	2300–1880	2550–1650
109	Antler	1963, 5, 106	Pit 8				3290 ± 150	1770–1400	2000–1100
276	Antler	1969, 11, 286	Pit 12				3550 ± 150	2130–2080 or 2050–1680	2350–1500
291	Antler	1969, 11, 286	Greenwell's Pit	Gallery 3			3810 ± 130	2460–2130 or 2090–2040	2650–1800
377	Antler	1969, 11, 286	Pit 12, repeat of BM-97, above				4250 ± 130	3020–2600	3350–2450
b Mercer excavations									
775	Charcoal	1976, 18, 32	1971 shaft	Gallery 3 backfill			3815 ± 60	2400–2380 or 2350–2190 or 2170–2140	2470–2130 or 2080–2040
776	Charcoal	1976, 18, 32	1971 shaft	Hearth in centre of pit floor			3789 ± 60	2330–2130 or 2080–2060	2460–2030
777	Charcoal	1976, 18, 32	1971 shaft	Entrance to Gallery 1			3764 ± 60	2290–2120 or 2090–2040	2410–1970
778	Charcoal	1976, 18, 33	1971 shaft	Top of shaft fill			3781 ± 67	2310–2130 or 2090–2040	2460–2030

Table 9 Radiocarbon results for archaeological materials from Grimes Graves.

779	Charcoal	1976, 18, 33		On old ground surface			313 ± 200	AD 1400–1950	AD 1317–1352 or AD 1388–1950
780	Charcoal	1976, 18, 33		Top fill of shaft			2465 ± 230	850–200	1200 BC–AD 100
943	Antler	1976, 18, 33	1971 shaft	Beside hearth in centre of pit floor			4104 ± 55	2860–2810 or 2750–2720 or 2700–2570	2880–2490
944	Antler	1976, 18, 33	1971 shaft	Gallery 1 (floor)			4153 ± 64	2880–2620	2890–2570 or 2520–2500
945	Antler	1976, 18, 33	1971 shaft	Gallery 3 (floor)			4034 ± 88	2860–2810 or 2700–2460	2900–2300
1097	Charcoal		1972	Deposits in top of Mercer 1972 shaft			3038 ± 44	1390–1210	1410–1130
c Re-excavation of Pit 15									
971	Charcoal	1979, 21, 43	Pit 15 1	Gallery	219	−25.8	3868 ± 66	2460–2280 or 2250–2210	2500–2140
972	Charcoal	1979, 21, 43	Pit 15 D3	Gallery	253	−27.4	3071 ± 209	1550–1000	1900–800
973	Antler	1979, 21, 43	Pit 15 A1	Gallery	7	−24.2	3827 ± 45	2400–2380 or 2350–2200	2460–2140
974	Antler	1979, 21, 43	Pit 15 C2	Gallery	60	−24.1	3887 ± 47	2460–2300	2470–2200
975	Antler	1979, 21, 43	Pit 15 B1	Gallery	105	−24.1	3940 ± 41	2550–2540 or 2490–2400 or 2380–2340	2570–2520 or 2500–2300
976	Antler	1979, 21, 43	Pit 15 G1	Gallery	128	−23.0	3849 ± 44	2460–2450 or 2410–2200	2470–2200
977	Antler	1979, 21, 43	Pit 15 F2	Gallery	209	−24.5	4015 ± 61	2630–2460	2900–2300
978	Antler	1979, 21, 43	Pit 15 D2	Gallery	228	−25.0	3865 ± 44	2460–2280 or 2250–2230	2470–2200
979	Antler	1979, 21, 43	Pit 15 J1	Gallery	231	−25.0	3820 ± 46	2400–2380 or 2340–2190 or 2160–2140	2460–2140
980	Antler	1979, 21, 43	Pit 15 D1	Gallery	109	−24.8	3736 ± 58	2270–2250 or 2210–2030	2310–1950
986	Charcoal	1979, 21, 43	Pit 15 J1	Gallery	236	−25.9	3845 ± 44	2410–2370 or 2350–2200	2460–2190 or 2160–2140
996	Antler	1979, 21, 43	Pit 15 B3	Gallery	30	−23.6	3890 ± 42	2460–2310	2470–2200
997	Antler	1979, 21, 43	Pit 15 C1	Gallery	47	−24.9	3960 ± 56	2570–2520 or 2500–2400 or 2380–2350	2620–2280
998	Antler	1979, 21, 43	Pit 15 E2	Gallery	216	−23.0	3992 ± 45	2580–2460	2630–2400 or 2380–2340
1000a	Antler	1979, 21, 43	Pit 15 G	Shaft base	124	−23.2	4051 ± 109	2860–2810 or 2760–2720 or 2700–2460	2900–2300
1000b	Antler	1979, 21, 43	Pit 15 G	Shaft base	124	−23.2	4022 ± 57	2620–2460	2900–2350
1001	Antler	1979, 21, 43	Pit 15 E	Gallery	246	−23.3	3868 ± 56	2460–2280 or 2250–2210	2470–2190 or 2170–2140
1002	Antler	1979, 21, 43	Pit 15 E1	Gallery	116	−21.2	3882 ± 45	2460–2300	2470–2200
1003	Antler	1979, 21, 43	Pit 15 B2	Gallery	20	−22.5	3949 ± 42	2560–2540 or 2500–2400 or 2380–2350	2580–2300
1011	Antler	1979, 21, 43	Pit 15 D2	Gallery	261	−22.5	3952 ± 44	2560–2530 or 2500–2400 or 2380–2350	2580–2300

1051	Antler	1979, 21, 43	Pit 15 B1	Gallery	103	−23.2	3887 ± 56	2460–2300	2500–2190
1052a	Antler	1979, 21, 43	Pit 15 B2	Gallery	23	−22.9	4114 ± 45	2860–2810 or 2750–2720 or 2700–2580	2880–2570 or 2520–2500
1052b	Antler	1979, 21, 43	Pit 15 B2	Gallery	23	−22.9	3954 ± 43	2560–2530 or 2500–2400 or 2380–2350	2580–2300
1053	Antler	1979, 21, 43	Pit 15 A/B	Gallery	31	−23.3	3834 ± 50	2400–2380 or 2350–2200	2460–2140
1054	Antler	1979, 21, 43	Pit 15 C2	Gallery	61	−22.2	3904 ± 36	2470–2340	2480–2280 or 2250–2210
1056a	Antler	1979, 21, 43	Pit 15 D1	Gallery	110	−23.8	3838 ± 42	2400–2380 or 2350–2200	2460–2190 or 2170–2140
1056b	Antler	1979, 21, 43	Pit 15 D1	Gallery	110	−23.8	3740 ± 48	2210–2030	2290–2020 or 2000–1980
1057	Antler	1979, 21, 43	Pit 15 D1/J1	Gallery	238	−23.0	3924 ± 47	2470–2310	2570–2520 or 2500–2280 or 2250–2210
1058	Antler	1979, 21, 43	Pit 15 E1	Gallery	119	−22.9	3876 ± 48	2460–2290	2470–2200
1059	Antler	1979, 21, 43	Pit 15 F1	Gallery	207	−22.6	3977 ± 47	2580–2450 or 2420–2400	2620–2310
1260	Antler	1979, 21, 43	Pit 15 D4	Gallery	1514	−22.5	4037 ± 62	2830–2820 or 2660–2650 or 2630–2460	2900–2350
1262	Antler	1979, 21, 43	Pit 15 D4	Gallery	1516 and 1523	−24.7	3900 ± 54	2470–2300	2560–2540 or 2500–2200
3007	Antler	*Archaeometry* 41, 186	Pit 15 C2	Gallery	60	−23.8	4060 ± 90	2860–2810 or 2700–2470	2900–2350
3087	Antler	*Archaeometry* 41, 186	Pit 15 B1	Gallery	103	−23.4	4010 ± 40	2570–2515 or 2500–2470	2630–2450
3090	Antler	*Archaeometry* 41, 186	Pit 15 B3	Gallery	30	−20.4	4010 ± 70	2840–2820 or 2670–2650 or 2630–2450 or 2420–2400	2900–2300

d Re-excavation of Pit 11

981	Antler	1979, 21, 44	Pit 11 A	Gallery	333	−22.8	3874 ± 47	2460–2290	2470–2200
982	Antler	1979, 21, 44	Pit 11 B/E	Gallery	322	−21.0	4090 ± 58	2860–2810 or 2740–2720 or 2700–2570 or 2520–2500	2880–2470
983	Antler	1979, 21, 44	Pit 11 D	Gallery	332	−21.7	3761 ± 48	2280–2250 or 2230–2130 or 2080–2040	2340–2020
984	Antler	1979, 21, 44	Pit 11 E	Gallery	316	−23.1	3902 ± 58	2470–2300	2560–2520 or 2500–2200
985	Antler	1979, 21, 44	Pit 11 F	Gallery	341	−23.0	4010 ± 59	2620–2460	2900–2300
987	Charcoal	1979, 21, 44	Pit 11 B/E	Gallery	324	−26.0	3671 ± 75	2190–2180 or 2150–1940	2300–1750
3008	Antler	*Archaeometry* 41, 186	Pit 11	Gallery		−23.3	3890 ± 40	2460–2310	2470–2200

e Re-excavation of Greenwell's Pit

1027	Antler	1979, 21, 43	Greenwell III[2]	Gallery	567	−23.0	3855 ± 36	2460–2200	2460–2200
1028	Antler	1979, 21, 44	Greenwell IV	Gallery	578	−19.5	3922 ± 38	2470–2340	2560–2540 or 2500–2290

1029	Antler	1979, 21, 44	Greenwell C	Gallery	647	−22.4	3859 ± 53	2460–2280 or 2250–2200	2470–2190 or 2170–2140
1044	Antler	1979, 21, 44	Greenwell IV	Gallery	711	−22.3	3922 ± 86	2560–2520 or 2500–2280 or 2250–2230	2700–2100
1045	Antler	1979, 21, 44	Greenwell C	Gallery	668	−23.3	3949 ± 41	2560–2540 or 2500–2400 or 2380–2350	2580–2300
1046	Antler	1979, 21, 44	Greenwell C	Gallery	679	−20.3	3797 ± 52	2310–2140	2460–2120 or 2100–2040
1047	Antler	1979, 21, 44	Greenwell C	Gallery	683	−22.6	3974 ± 45	2580–2450 or 2420–2400	2620–2610 or 2590–2310
1048	Antler	1979, 21, 44	Greenwell IVc	Gallery	705	−21.6	3880 ± 38	2460–2300	2470–2200
1049	Antler	1979, 21, 44	Greenwell IIb	Gallery	900	−22.1	3884 ± 43	2460–2300	2470–2200
1050	Antler	1979, 21, 44	Greenwell A	Gallery	923	−21.7	3893 ± 44	2460–2310	2480–2200
1068	Antler	1979, 21, 44	Greenwell A	Gallery	933	−22.1	3784 ± 50	2300–2130	2410–2030
1261	Antler	1979, 21, 44	Greenwell III³a	Gallery	832	−21.4	3853 ± 71	2460–2200	2550–2000
2377	Charcoal	1987, 29, 181	Greenwell	Hearth on old ground surface sealed by upcast		−23.9	4060 ± 90	2860–2810 or 2700–2470	2900–2350
2380	Antler	1987, 29, 181	Greenwell	On old ground surface sealed by upcast		−23.0	3810 ± 60	2400–2380 or 2350–2140	2460–2130 or 2090–2040
3009	Antler	*Archaeometry* 41, 186	Greenwell IV	Gallery	578	−21.4	4060 ± 90	2860–2810 or 2700–2470	2900–2350
3010	Antler	*Archaeometry* 41, 186	Greenwell IVc	Gallery	705	−22.7	3960 ± 45	2570–2520 or 2500–2400 or 2380–2350	2580–2300
3088	Antler	*Archaeometry* 41, 186	Greenwell A	Gallery	923	−22.3	3980 ± 60	2580–2400 or 2370–2350	2850–2800 or 2700–2250
3089	Antler	*Archaeometry* 41, 186	Greenwell IIb	Gallery	900	−21.7	3960 ± 60	2570–2520 or 2500–2400 or 2380–2350	2630–2280 or 2250–2210

f Re-excavation of Pit 2

1020	Antler	1979, 21, 44	Pit 2 A/B	Gallery	1005	−23.0	3844 ± 221	2650–1950	2900–1600
1069	Antler	1979, 21, 44	Pit 2 A/B	Gallery	1007	−22.0	3896 ± 141	2580–2140	2900–1950

g Pit 3 A

1060	Antler	1979, 21, 45	Pit 3 A layer 10			−23.5	3863 ± 86	2580–2140	2900–1950

SURFACE WORKINGS

a Pre-Neolithic features

990	Charcoal	1979, 21, 43	F1 hearth	880/910		−24.9	7614 ± 80	6590–6380	6640–6250
989	Charcoal	1979, 21, 43	F5 hearth	900/870		−21.6	8519 ± 309	8200–7000	8300–6600

b Area A chipping floor

988	Charcoal	1979, 21, 45		1255/905		−25.0	3755 ± 259	2600–1750	2900–1500
995	Charcoal	1979, 21, 45		1267/906		−25.3	3947 ± 66	2570–2520 or 2500–2340	2620–2200
1013	Charcoal	1979, 21, 45	L6 baulk	1255/905		−27.0	3929 ± 49	2490–2310	2570–2280 or 2250–2210
1014	Charcoal	1979, 21, 45		1266/900		−25.8	3813 ± 43	2340–2190 or 2170–2140	2460–2130

c West Field

811	Charcoal	1979, 21, 45		1000/905		−27.2	3607 ± 300	2500–1600	2900–1200
812	Antler	1979, 21, 45		1000/910		−26.6	3380 ± 55	1750–1600 or 1550–1540	1880–1840 or 1780–1520
970	Antler	1979, 21, 44	F3 at 2.15m (lower fill)	950/820		−24.9	3767 ± 57	2290–2130 or 2090–2040	2410–2370 or 2350–2020 or 2000–1980
991	Charcoal	1979, 21, 45	F2 hearth	900/870		−24.1	3414 ± 46	1860–1840 or 1770–1630	1880–1600 or 1560–1530
992	Antler	1979, 21, 44	F5 (24)	950/820		−23.2	3727 ± 57	2200–2030	2300–1950
993	Antler	1979, 21, 44	F6 (4)	950/820		−23.5	3614 ± 67	2120–2090 or 2040–1880 or 1840–1830	2200–2170 or 2150–1770
994	Charcoal	1979, 21, 45	F7 (8)	950/820		−25.1	3535 ± 90	2010–2000 or 1980–1740	2150–1600
1005	Charcoal	1979, 21, 44	F12 (11)	950/820		−24.7	3948 ± 37	2570–2520 or 2500–2340	2620–2200
1006	Charcoal	1979, 21, 45	F38 chipping	950/820		−25.1	4017 ± 60	2630–2460	2900–2300
1007	Antler	1979, 21, 44	F6 (1)	950/820		−23.3	3825 ± 54	2400–2380 or 2350–2190 or 2160–2140	2470–2130
1008	Antler	1979, 21, 44	F24 (4)	950/820		−23.1	3764 ± 39	2280–2250 or 2230–2130 or 2080–2060	2300–2030
1009	Antler	1979, 21, 44	F7 (10)	950/820		−20.6	3825 ± 41	2400–2380 or 2340–2200	2460–2140
1010	Antler	1979, 21, 44	F14 (25)	950/820		−21.5	3770 ± 66	2300–2120 or 2090–2040	2460–1980
1012	Antler	1979, 21, 45	F19 (1)	950/820		−22.9	3695 ± 33	2140–2030	2200–1970
1015	Antler	1979, 21, 44	F51	950/820		−22.2	3851 ± 34	2410–2370 or 2350–2200	2460–2200
1016	Antler	1979, 21, 44	F11 (12)	950/820	141	−20.6	3797 ± 49	2300–2140	2460–2120 or 2100–2040

1017	Antler	1979, 21, 44	F16 (7)	950/820		−23.1	3710 ± 39	2200–2180 or 2150–2030	2210–1970
1018	Antler	1979, 21, 45	F23 (1)	950/820	124	−21.7	3593 ± 37	2010–2000 or 1980–1880	2040–1870 or 1850–1780
1019	Antler	1979, 21, 44	F4 (3)	950/820		−23.2	3593 ± 45	2020–1880	2130–2080 or 2040–1770
1022	Charcoal	1979, 21, 45	F13 (3)	950/820		−24.9	3559 ± 39	1960–1870 or 1850–1780	2030–1750
1023	Charcoal	1979, 21, 45	F18 (2)	950/820		−24.3	4061 ± 52	2840–2810 or 2670–2470	2870–2810 or 2760–2460
1024	Charcoal	1979, 21, 45	F36 (7)	950/820		−18.6	3904 ± 38	2470–2340 or 2320–2310	2490–2280 or 2250–2210
1030	Charcoal	1979, 21, 45	F106 (8)	940/940		−25.8	2953 ± 36	1260–1080 or 1060–1050	1300–1020
1031	Charcoal	1979, 21, 45	F108 (1)	940/940		−24.9	3386 ± 41	1740–1620	1860–1840 or 1770–1520
1032	Charcoal	1979, 21, 45	F112 (3)	940/940		−20.1	3286 ± 67	1680–1490	1740–1410
1033	Charcoal	1979, 21, 45	F121 (2)	940/940		−25.6	2881 ± 49	1190–1180 or 1150–970 or 950–940	1260–1240 or 1220–920
1034	Charcoal	1979, 21, 45	F124 (2)	940/940		−25.8	3763 ± 47	2290–2130 or 2080–2040	2340–2030
1061	Antler	1979, 21, 44	F105 (39)	940/940	1372	−22.0	3666 ± 55	2140–1950	2200–1880
1062	Antler	1979, 21, 44	F34 (3)	950/820		−22.9	3695 ± 49	2200–2180 or 2150–2020 or 2000–1980	2280–2250 or 2210–1920
1063	Antler	1979, 21, 44	F28 (? 21)	950/820		−22.1	3874 ± 55	2460–2290	2490–2190 or 2170–2140
1064	Antler	1979, 21, 45	F32 (4)	950/820	1224	−22.8	3748 ± 59	2280–2250 or 2230–2030	2350–1960
3006	Antler	*Archaeometry* 41, 186	F6	950/820		−22.2	3780 ± 45	2290–2130	2400 – 2380 or 2350–2030
3119	Antler	*Archaeometry* 45, 534	F5 (24)	950/820		−22.7	3800 ± 30	2290–2190 or 2160–2140	2400–2380 or 2340–2130
3120	Antler	*Archaeometry* 45, 534	F6 (4)	950/820		−21.0	3850 ± 50	2460–2200	2470–2190 or 2170–2140
3121	Antler	*Archaeometry* 45, 534	F7 (10)	950/820		−20.6	3900 ± 50	2470–2300	2560–2540 or 2500–2200
3134	Antler	*Archaeometry* 45, 534	F105 (39)	940/940		−22.8	3560 ± 50	2010–2000 or 1980–1870 or 1850–1770	2030–1740
3135	Charcoal (*pinus* sp)	*Archaeometry* 45, 534	F124 (2)	940/940		−25.0	3720 ± 40	2200–2030	2280–2250 or 2230–1970

d Trenches

1065	Charcoal	1979, 21, 45	Trench 3 occupation debris, ogs	1274/1022		−24.6	3941 ± 89	2570–2290	2900–2800 or 2700–2100
1066	Charcoal	1979, 21, 45	Trench 2 knapping episode	1195/945		−24.7	4224 ± 74	2910–2840 or 2820–2670	3020–2950 or 2930–2570
1546	Bone (*equus* sp)	1982, 24, 232	Trench 3	1273/1019.5		−21.4	3740 ± 210	2500–1850	2900–1600

SHAFT X

1035	Charcoal	1979, 21, 45	(14) phase II	1270/900		−25.5	2994 ± 40	1370–1360 or 1310–1130	1390–1080
1036	Charcoal	1979, 21, 45	(19) phase II	1270/900		−25.5	2995 ± 39	1370–1360 or 1310–1130	1390–1080
1037	Charcoal	1979, 21, 46	(9) phase II	1270.5/905.5		−21.4	3003 ± 49	1370–1340 or 1320–1160 or 1140–1130	1400–1050
1038	Charcoal	1979, 21, 46	(5) phase II	1270.5/905.5		−24.8	2936 ± 43	1260–1240 or 1220–1050	1300–1000
1039	Charcoal	1979, 21, 45	(20) phase II	1270/900		−25.0	2806 ± 54	1020–840	1130–830
1040	Charcoal	1979, 21, 45	(20a) phase II	1270/900		−25.0	2905 ± 54	1210–1000	1260–920
1041	Charcoal	1979, 21, 45	(19a) phase II	1270/900		−25.2	3573 ± 57	2020–1870 or 1850–1780	2130–2080 or 2040–1740
1042	Charcoal	1979, 21, 45	(19b) phase II	1270/900		−24.7	2919 ± 53	1210–1010	1300–930
1043	Charcoal	1979, 21, 46	(19c) phase II	1270/900		−24.8	2838 ± 53	1110–1100 or 1070–900	1210–830
1263	Charcoal	1979, 21, 46	(4) phase II	1270.5/905.5		−24.8	3443 ± 53	1880–1680	1920–1610
1264	Charcoal	1979, 21, 46	(10) phase III	1270.5/905.5		−24.9	3154 ± 64	1520–1380 or 1340–1320	1600–1560 or 1530–1260
1265	Charcoal	1979, 21, 46	(4) phase II	1270.5/905.5		−24.2	2800 ± 79	1050–830	1210–800
1266	Charcoal	1979, 21, 46	(6) phase?	1275.5/905.5		−24.7	2834 ± 53	1050–900	1210–1180 or 1160–830

VII Summary and conclusions

While the precise spatial limits of human activity at Grimes Graves have yet to be finally established, present evidence suggests that it extends over a minimum of 20 hectares. Already by the conclusion of Armstrong's work in 1939 it had become clear that mining activity extended well beyond the limits of the visible mine field that he had originally surveyed in 1914. His Pits 3–7, 13 and 14 lay to the north, while Pits 8–12 were sited in the West Field. Mercer established in 1972 that a masked pit lay to the east of the shaft he had begun to explore the previous year, although the 1971 shaft was to show perhaps that *floorstone* capable of being viably worked was running out in this direction. Further south the presence of Grimshoe, a mound that appears to incorporate mined material which had not, as was the norm on the site, been thrown back into a worked-out shaft, may again mark the extent of deep mining in this direction. The Museum's own explorations demonstrated the presence of at least one masked pit beyond the south-eastern border *viz.* Shaft X, together with two further probable pits: Y and Z; a probable fourth discovered by the phosphate survey (see above, p. 36, sampling point L4); and a fifth in Area C (Longworth *et al.* 1988, 36). The likelihood that Armstrong's Black Hole represented the top of a further shaft suggests that other masked pits extend beyond the visible mine field further along the southern border to the west. Deep sand dunes further to the south and east, however, make additional identification, at least in this direction, difficult. To the north-west a shallow cable trench recorded by Frances Healy in 1982–3 (1985b) showed indications of further buried features, potentially mines, in the area between Pits 9 and 15. In the West Field the resistivity survey and subsequent exploratory trenches dug by Sieveking have demonstrated that mining activity here, although often shallow, was both widespread and intensive, extending certainly over a triangular area between Pits 8 and 12 in the north to Pit 11 to the south. More recently, a ground-penetrating radar survey carried out by English Heritage in 2007 (Linford *et al.* 2009) has shown activity immediately north of the visible mine field and around the head of the dry valley near the current access route. In the same year an electrical resistivity survey carried out by Geocarta (Favard and Dabas 2007) in the area of the West Field confirmed the extensive nature of mining in that part of the site.

The extent of modern exploration

From the ground survey that he had undertaken in 1914 Armstrong judged that some 366 deep mines lay within the 16½ acres (6.68 ha) of the visible mine field, and that many smaller mines lay in the 17½ acres (7.08 ha) where no surface indication remained (Armstrong 1927, 91). The re-examination of Greenwell's Pit and Pit 15, which revealed many more shafts than were visible from the ground, showed that the average distance between shafts in the area of Greenwell's Pit was a little over 7 m and, in the case of Pit 15, approximately 6 m. The true number of deep mines may well be in excess of 400. Of these, only the workings of Greenwell's Pit, Pits 1 and 2, Pit 15 and Mercer's 1971 shaft have been explored to any great extent, while the 1971 shaft remains the only intact deep mine to have been explored in its entirety by modern methods. To the further thirteen mines to the north and west of the deep mines explored by Armstrong can now be added the split-level mines, 3A to the north and F105 in the West Field excavated by Sieveking, together with the numerous small mines revealed by the West Field cuttings. The earthwork survey carried out by English Heritage, published in 1999 and reproduced here (fig. 120), has quite literally thrown into relief the scale and complexity of the workings. Although more of the surface of the site has been examined by trenching (see p. 44 above) and by exploration of areas of flint reduction, even now too little has been explored to modern standards to offer any coherent picture of how the mine field actually developed. It remains probable, however, that development moved from the known to the unknown, i.e. from areas where the *floorstone* had been successfully extracted to adjoining areas, but whether this process began in one place or at different loci we cannot say. Given that the chalk cover increases as one moves east and south across the site, the most likely hypothesis is that the deepest mines and those most costly in terms of time and effort along the southern and eastern borders of the field would have been among the latest to be tackled within the Deep Mine Field.

Prehistoric episodes on the site

Despite the heat and fury of debate earlier in the twentieth century, the earliest human presence on the site is attested by a single handaxe redeposited in the upper filling of Shaft X (see fig. 122 and Appendix 5) and two features: Feature 5 900/870 and Feature 1 880/910 containing hearth material, in the north-west of the site, episodes

Fig. 120 Ground survey carried out by English Heritage. © Crown copyright. NMR.

associated with ^{14}C dates of 8200–7000 BC (BM-989) and 6590–6380 BC (BM-990). Nor is there evidence for anything other than a minor temporary occupation in the earlier part of the Neolithic, evidenced by a small quantity of Middle Neolithic Bowl sherds, of which the only significant group comes from a single feature, Feature 2 880/910, and three leaf-shaped arrowheads. Equally, the contexts of the small number of sherds of Peterborough Ware and Beaker recovered suggest only a minor involvement with the site of communities using these types of pottery. Sherds of Collared Vessel and associated fragments of clay spindle whorls, weights and other fired clay artefacts attest to the presence, at least in the West Field, of some occupation in the Early Bronze Age. While the concentration lying in the shallow depression Feature 108 940/940 indicates perhaps a short-stay camping episode, most of the evidence comes from the tops of deeper features. Results from English Heritage's current programme of new radiocarbon determinations may provide fresh evidence for the active mining of flint in this area during this or subsequent phases of the Bronze Age.

Rich deposits of Middle Bronze Age midden material from Armstrong's Black Hole, Mercer's 1971 and 1972 excavations, and Shaft X show that during this phase a fairly heavy occupation of farmers practising primarily a dairying economy had occurred apparently close to the south-eastern boundary of the site (Longworth *et al.* 1988, 28, Table 2; Legge 1992), although the extensive phosphate survey failed to locate any permanent settlement. Yet the quantity of midden material argues for such a settlement to have been in existence at no great remove. Analysis of the associated flintwork (Herne 1991), however, revealed that much was based on the opportunistic reuse of flint, both *wallstone* and *floorstone*, which had already been mined.

Too little has been recovered to suggest much interest in the site during the Iron Age (Rigby 1988, 105ff.), although the two burials recovered by Mercer in the top of his 1971 shaft clearly document a presence (Mercer 1981, 16ff.).

From the combined evidence provided by pottery, lithic artefacts and ^{14}C determinations, there is therefore strong evidence that the actual mining of flint at Grimes Graves in the deeper mines was undertaken during the Late Neolithic and confined to that period. Pottery recovered shows that the only identifiable group involved during that period were Grooved Ware users.

Activity in the West Field appears on present evidence to have begun before deep mining had ceased, but to have continued on for some time, exploiting the residual *floorstone* that survived in the area at no great depth, and whatever could be scavenged from the remains of earlier flint-processing sites surviving elsewhere on the surface. The extent to which undisturbed deposits were exploited by way of more explicit mines such as Feature 105 remains to be established.

Methods of exploitation

An important contribution made by the Museum's research programme was the confirmation and refinement of earlier observations as to the methods used to win the flint from the ground. In Fascicule 5 the detailed evidence recovered by our Dutch colleagues from the Prehistoric Flint Mines Working Group of the Dutch Geological Society, Limburg Section, particularly their re-examination of Greenwell's Pit, demonstrates in astonishing detail the way in which the amount of *floorstone* from the base of the shaft could be increased more than eleven times by a careful strategy of opening up radial galleries and niching. Here in the deep mines there can be no doubt that we are in the presence of miners with great expertise, intent upon maximizing the amount of flint recovered, but taking great care to ensure their own safety and minimizing the labour by removing the least amount of spoil from the mine by methodical backfilling as the work progressed. Craftsmanship coupled with basic applied economics are in evidence. The conclusion reached from analysis of the data recovered from Greenwell's Pit was that such a mine could have been dug and completely exploited in a period of ± ninety-three days. Even accepting wide margins of error, such a figure suggests exploitation of the deep mines is likely to have persisted over a considerable period. Taking a figure of 400 shafts and assuming (a) continuity of activity, (b) work throughout the year, (c) up to two mines being worked at the same time, since there are hints that this sometimes was the case, and (d) an average of ninety-three days for exploitation of each mine, a minimum figure would emerge for exploitation of the area covered by the visible mine field of eight mines a year for fifty years. If only two shafts were opened each year then we would be talking of a period of some 200 years. Since the extensive phosphate survey undertaken on and to the south of the site failed to pick up the remains of any occupation site of any scale, present evidence would support the suggestion of limited mining spread over an extended period of time.

The variables involved are perhaps too great to offer more than a general feeling for the active life of the mine field, but with the revised ^{14}C determinations now available for Greenwell's Pit and Pit 15 it seems likely that for a period of perhaps 50–200 years the Deep Mine Field was being exploited and that this period lay in the middle of the third millennium BC. With techniques presently available it now seems an impossible task to attempt either to date the life of the Deep Mine Field more precisely or to establish the way in which it developed. Ambers's judgement that 'the aims of the project were in advance of what was technologically possible at the time' (1996, 101) still stands.

Beyond the deep mines the picture is somewhat different. The split-level mines such as 3, 3A and Feature 105 show adaptation of mining techniques to local requirements. Here utilizable flint could be extracted at two levels: in the upper cryoturbated zone and in a remnant *floorstone* layer itself. Depths were not great and the use of bone picks suggests a different tradition of mining to that employed in the deep mines (see p. 74). By their very nature the split-level mines combined extraction with an element of prospection, seeking out the lower seam of flint. In the West Field one feature, Feature 7, may represent a shaft dug simply for prospection, but its nature suggests rather a natural feature whose potential to yield information about the underlying deposits has been seized and exploited. Elsewhere exploitation has been by simple shaft and peripheral niching down to where nodules of *floorstone* could be recovered. Over much of the West Field this amounted to little more than digging pits, sometimes overlapping, seldom needing to be more than 2 m deep. Such work would have required little of the mining skills in evidence in the deep mines and could have been carried out over time on an opportunistic basis by elements of many communities. The artefacts recovered, however, offer little in the way of further insight about those carrying out this work.

Evidence of utilization

If the date of the flint mines at Grimes Graves was the most contentious topic of the first half of the twentieth century, then what was made from the flint excavated has come to be the main issue of the recent past. Some attempt has been made to quantify the potential amount of *floorstone* that could have been won from the Deep Mine Field. An estimate of 17,955 metric tonnes was calculated, based on the degree of exploitation achieved in the Greenwell Pit system, i.e. 84 per cent (Longworth and Varndell 1996, 89). Felder, however, has cautioned that a present-day figure of 60 per cent might be a safer assumption. If so, then the total potential flint capable of being utilized could have been in the region of 12,825 metric tonnes.

Although any attempt to assess artefact production must rely heavily on assumption and estimation, some effort must now be made. As noted earlier (p. 117), in the middle decades of the last century 'flint mines' and 'axe factories' were taken to be more or less synonymous terms. Evidence from the Sussex mines seemed to amply justify this usage and it was perhaps only natural that the same interpretation was assumed to be applicable to the largest of the known mine sites – Grimes Graves. Saville, in his comprehensive report on the flint assemblages recovered from Mercer's excavations (1981), rightly took exception to this, implying as it did that axe production was either the only or prime product, providing the very *raison d'être* for mining to have taken place on the site. Evidence across the site points to a range of artefacts being produced, but since the axe/adze and discoidal knife figure prominently, it is perhaps prudent not to underestimate the importance of these products. Richardson (1920) had already noted that in some

areas there was clear evidence for axe manufacture. But the most compelling argument for this is simply to compare the number of axe/adze roughouts recovered from Grimes Graves (at least 321) with the number of axes (from whatever flint source) from known sites of the same age. The comparison is admittedly hampered by the continuing lack of convincing published occupation sites of Late Neolithic date in southern England, but what evidence does survive suggests a relative sparsity of recognizable axe forms discarded at any of these locations. Thus at the great henge sites such as Durrington Walls, Marden and Mt Pleasant, the number of axes recovered amount to four, zero and eleven respectively, while at sites more suggestive of settlement use, such as Hunstanton and Tattershall Thorpe, the numbers are one and zero, and the Hunstanton axe was a stray find (Healy pers. comm.; recent excavations at Durrington Walls have not changed this picture, only one small sliver of polished flint axe having been found to date: Parker Pearson pers. comm.). Yet at all these sites the need for axes and adzes both to fell and shape the timbers is undeniable, even if the latter like the former task occurred off site. The number of axe/adze roughouts from Grimes Graves is not far short of the number of axes recorded from the area of the River Thames of all periods (Adkins and Jackson 1978, with recent additions). The number recovered from Grimes Graves therefore stands out as significantly high and the simplest explanation would be to accept that axe manufacture along with discoidal knives was a major component in the utilization of the flint mined from the site. This is further supported by Lech's analysis of the chipping floors (see p. 116 above), which demonstrates that at least in these contexts the vast majority of flakes recovered are what you would expect from the reduction process employed in the production of these types of implement.

It must be stressed that it is easy to inflate both the number of successful artefacts made and the likely survival rate of individual axes. One of the more important contributions to knowledge gained from a greater understanding of flint technology and how the material was actually worked has been the realization that the number of finished implements likely to have been produced has in the past been wildly overestimated. Some idea of the actual loss of potentially utilizable flint is offered in the model set out in fig. 121, together with alternative trajectories for an axe to survive and be recognizable in the archaeological record. No percentages have been attempted to quantify this risk analysis, but simply on *a priori* grounds it can be assumed that for the bulk of functional percussive tools such as the axe made from a relatively frangible material like flint, chances of survival in an intact, unreworked state are likely to have been slim unless some degree of curation has taken place.

Once the *floorstone* had been extracted from the seam in which it lay, the process of utilization began. Some loss

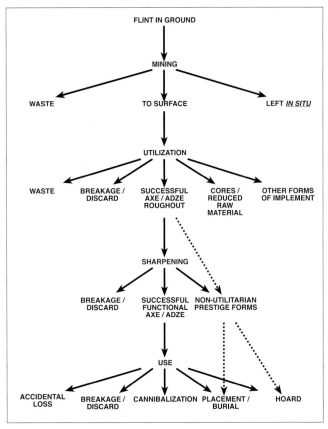

Fig. 121 Model for flint loss.

would occur immediately through the process of breaking up the nodules for transportation to the surface, and large intractable pieces were discarded at this stage. Initial reduction of blocks selected for further working seems to have taken place already in the mines and a proportion may have been set aside at this stage for transportation away from the site. Some support for the suggestion that flint was leaving the site as raw material, as suggested by Healy (1998, 231), has also come from the second flint analysis programme (see above p. 145), while at the site of Soham it can be noted that 35 per cent of flakes from multi-platform cores and about 20 per cent of the cores themselves seemed to be of flint derived from the chalk – although not of course necessarily from Grimes Graves (Edmonds *et al.* 1999, 67). Evidence from the 1972–4 chipping floor examined in Area A and the chipping floor in the top of Feature 112 in the West Field confirms, however, that in these areas at least blocks which had already been prepared elsewhere were now worked towards roughout form. Although relatively few implements survive in their final form on the chipping floors, this is to be expected if the flint knappers were skilled at their job. Indeed, negative evidence could be misleading: the relative absence of advanced forms of roughout for axe, adze and discoidal knife may be a measure of the success rate rather than suggesting that the production of these was not a major aim of the reduction process.

If we accept Felder's suggestion, based on modern mining experience, of a 60 per cent recovery rate yielding 12,825,000 kg, then taking the data set published for axes from the Thames, excluding Scandinavian forms and broken examples, we can try to estimate the weight of the original blanks from which these were made. To do this we can take the experimental evidence produced by Harding (1987) and Moloney (1988). Harding put the actual weight loss due to polishing at 2 per cent (and for partial polish we have taken a 1 per cent notional loss). Moloney, working with non-flint lithic materials, suggested a loss of 86 per cent before polishing from the original chosen blank (cf. 70–85 per cent loss estimated for an axe from Loosberg and an experimental axe made by Weiner from Dutch flint: Felder *et al.* 1998). Based on the weights of the complete axes, the average weight of an axe from the Thames was 374 g and the average of the original blank would have been 2.716 kg. The potential number of axe blanks from Grimes Graves would therefore have been 12,825,000 ÷ 2.716 = 4,722,018. If we suppose, for the sake of argument, that only as much as 50 per cent of the potential flint was available for axe manufacture due to other calls, including the processes leading up to the creation of the blank and utilization for non-axe manufacture, then this number would be reduced to 2,361,009. Based on these figures, if output were spread over 50 years, the number of axes produced per year would have been 47,220; if over 100, the number would have been 23,610; and if over 200 the number would have been 11,805.

As a check on these figures, a sample of 469 examples was taken from the corpus of flint axes compiled by Pitts (housed in Swindon, NMR MWP01 Pitts, M. Neolithic Stone Axes) and this produced an average axe weight of 354 g, giving an average blank weight of 2.529 kg. In this connection it can be noted that no piece in the assemblage studied and deemed to be in the process of becoming an axe roughout proved greater than this notional average blank weight. Using these figures, total axe output would have been marginally greater at 2,535,587. Over 50 years the number would have been 50,711; over 100 years, the number would have been 25,356; and over 200 years, the number would have been 12,678.

These figures are, of course, only assessed on the utilization of the *floorstone* recovered from the deep mines. More artefacts were certainly made from the small quantities of *wallstone* recovered during the sinking of the shafts, and a few more would have been made from flint from those pits of the West and North Fields that may have been open at the same date. While these would undoubtedly increase the numbers proposed, they would be unlikely to do so by any great order of magnitude.

It has been noted that there is little or no evidence for the polishing of manufactured artefacts on the Grimes Graves site. Production of axes, chipped to their final form but unpolished, has four advantages. Firstly, as noted by Pitts (1996, 314), once the flint blank has been reduced to more or less its final form much of the danger of accidental breakage has been eliminated. Secondly, as Olausson (1983, 63) has argued, the quality and fault-free nature of the product is more readily apparent in an unpolished state. Thirdly, a massive reduction in weight has taken place between blank and roughout state, amounting to perhaps as much as 86 per cent (Moloney 1988, 60), making transport a very much more viable task. Fourthly, the time-consuming and laborious task of polishing – up to eight hours for the cutting edge and thirty hours for a complete axe (Harding 1987) – is transferred to a future more convenient occasion and venue, or more likely, to the actual end user.

Little in the way of convincing data exists either for the likely population count during the late Neolithic in southern England or for the rate of axe destruction during use (but see Olausson 1983). An approximate position can, however, be suggested:

No. of years of mining	Potential production of axes per year	Axe-using population		
		200	**250**	300
		Axes per person per year		
50	50,000	250	200	166
100	25,000	125	100	83
200	**12,500**	62.5	**50**	42
250	10,000	50	40	33

Table 10 Hypothetical range for axe production given varying years over which flint might have been extracted and differing estimates of axe-using population.

If, for the sake of argument, we assume a modest axe-wielding population of 250 and a total average output from Grimes Graves of say 12,500 axes per year over a period of 200 years, a supply of 50 axes (or one a week) per person per year, the resulting figures do not seem excessive for a woodworking culture known to have been capable of felling and trimming trees up to 1.06 m in diameter (e.g. Durrington Walls, Southern Circle, Wainwright and Longworth 1971, 206), as well as splitting and shaping timbers once felled. These figures are based on the assumption that up to 50 per cent of the worked flint went into the production of axe/adzes subsequent to the production of the blank. Any lesser percentage, due, for example, to a greater quantity of flint leaving the site as basic raw material, would of course further reduce the number produced but still leave the form as a significant component of output.

The flint analysis programme has thrown up the problem of recognizing these products off site. On site there is clear evidence that much decortication of the raw material mined took place. Much of this was obviously a preliminary stage, as Lech has shown, for further working on the chipping floors. Even if raw material rather than specific implements was leaving the site, the removal of cortex would be a logical step to take to reduce weight and to eliminate obvious waste, thus providing a better return for time and energy expended in transportation. Visual examination is at the best of times unreliable and shorn of cortex an attribution to Grimes Graves becomes impossible. Even with cortex surviving the product can only be considered as possibly made of Grimes Graves flint. Any meaningful attribution must therefore rely on scientific analysis. In the case of discoidal knives the difficulty lies simply in the type of analysis at present at our disposal. This requires robust sampling, confined, even when permission can be obtained, to pieces with a thickness greater than 2 cm. Analysis of most discoidal knives beyond an early roughout stage is therefore ruled out. The failure to find axes in any quantity off site made from Grimes Graves flint, however, requires further examination.

A simplistic argument would be to see almost the entire output from the site being dedicated to use on the site itself. Yet flint and stone axes played only a peripheral role in the actual mining process. They simply met the need to fell woodland in the immediate vicinity of the shaft, to be worked together with shaping timber for ladders, platforms and any other wooden constructions required to assist the process of raising the flint to the surface, as well as minor cosmetic shaping within the mine galleries themselves. Axes employed in these tasks would *per se* have represented only a small proportion of those apparently produced. It must be remembered, too, that if employed on site, these must have been used unpolished or polished off site, for there is no evidence for polishing on site and only a single example of a broken polished flint axe (from Shaft X) has so far been recovered.

If axes were leaving the site but have failed to be picked up in any quantity in the sampling programme, then other explanations must be entertained. Three are offered:

a That the vast majority of axes sampled are not of contemporary (Late Neolithic) date but belong to an earlier period. This in turn would imply that the mechanism by which axes made from other sourced flint came to be available for random discovery must have changed over time. It has always seemed improbable that the large number of unbroken axes recovered in the countryside by chance discovery were the product of casual loss. While simple loss may have occurred occasionally, deliberate placement is likely to account for the majority. If the belief system which led to this phenomenon changed over time, the apparent rarity of Late Neolithic axe finds would be explained.

b That the axes made from Grimes Graves flint were accorded a different status and therefore did not fall into the same taphonomic context which allowed comparable contemporary axes of other flint to be discovered.

c   That the quality of Grimes Graves flint was such that the vast majority of axes once broken were cannibalized and once broken down would become invisible to the type of analysis used in the programme described in Chapter V above.

Explanation (a) certainly seems to apply, since two thirds of the axes sampled were attributed to the South Downs group of mines and are likely to belong to an earlier phase of the Neolithic. Explanation (c) seems highly likely and perhaps subsumes (b), for the sheer quantity of flint extracted from the site predicates the unlikelihood that axes were not being made even if blocks rather than finished implements were leaving the site, especially when change in the environment would have made other sources less accessible in East Anglia (Waller 1994). Two assiduous field walkers working over about 20 acres of land around Kessingland, Suffolk, have picked up thirty-eight fragments of polished flint implements, four of which are cores and the rest struck flakes and fragments. They were chiefly collected from flint scatters (Padfield and Courtauld pers. comm.). While it cannot be demonstrated that any are of Grimes Graves flint, it supports existing evidence for the practice of working down polished implements.

The problem is at the least a European one. The chiefly calcareous plains of Basse-Normandie were a focus for flint extraction during the Neolithic. At Bretteville-le-Rabet, Calvados, at least 20,000 extraction pits are estimated over a minimum of 40 ha and the product appears to have been almost exclusively axes. A newly discovered extraction site at Ri on the Plaine d'Argenten, Orne, covers 30 ha (Marcigny pers. comm.). An ongoing survey of collections in the region by Jean Desloges suggests that stone axes predominate, and that even right in the middle of the zone of flint-bearing rock the proportion of flint to stone axes is no more than 50:50 (Desloges pers. comm.). South-east of the Paris Basin (Pays d'Othe and Pays de l'Yonne) is another flint-mining region where the product was predominantly axes (Affolter and de Labriffe 2007). Some blades and flakes were produced, but these seem to have been principally for local consumption. It has not been possible to track the axes away from the locale. While this could be accounted for in various ways (patterns of research, the consumption of most of the output locally), the problem has not been satisfactorily resolved. One possible answer is that over a certain distance from source the axes were treated as reserves of raw material, thus transforming their status (ibid., 20).

One further point is perhaps worth making. While the assumption is that axes made at Grimes Graves were essentially functional implements, the presence of a product such as the axe discovered by Armstrong in Floor

85 points to the manufacture also of items clearly beyond the scale of the merely utilitarian. Yet these prestige objects, too, remain largely unrecognized and for the present are likely to remain difficult to detect, not least for the simple reason that present sampling requirements would not justify the damage to the specimen.

Mining and the community

Given the area of Grimes Graves that has so far been examined and the information thus gained, we are of course in no position to extrapolate that the entire area of the deep mines was exploited by a single group or segment of society, still less that the mine field was developed by means of some preconceived plan of exploitation. It would be equally unwise to assume that the whole enterprise was driven by some single ritual intent or, conversely, that ritual played no part in its development. At one extreme it could be argued that the actual process of extracting the flint was the most important element in a hierarchy of ritual activity, or that the flint itself as a manifestation of the difficulties of procurement was the key element of ritualistic belief. At the other extreme, a simplistic economic model would see the flint procured and the procurement process in a system of values where the *floorstone* was prized not only for its innate qualities but also in acknowledgement of the difficulties met in its extraction. But rarity and danger are often embodied in ritual values and a more balanced view would see the *floorstone* being imbued inextricably with both economic and ritual significance.

In economic terms the *floorstone* (and to a lesser extent the *topstone* and *wallstone*) offers value in two different markets: firstly, to the flint knapper in ease of manufacture, then as an item for exchange or functional use. Despite certain weaknesses, in particular the presence of some natural cleavage planes, the *floorstone* does represent a high-quality, easily processed raw material, which because of its tabular form is less wasteful than flint in irregular nodules or weakened by post-depositional thermal action. It is less simple to assess the value placed on the product. Two ways of approaching this might be to discover how far the products were traded and, secondly, to see if any have been demonstrably 'curated'. Unfortunately, as we have seen, both lines of enquiry have proved difficult to follow.

What seems incontrovertible is that the group(s) working the deep mines must themselves have been supported by their community for periods of up to three months at a time and perhaps on a more regular long-term basis. This support in turn must have extended beyond simply subsistence to the organized collection and supply of the antlers needed to make the essential mining tool, the pick (Clutton-Brock 1984). It seems likely that the miners were supplemented by others engaged in working the mined flint, and in transporting the raw material and finished products from the site.

The scale and duration of the work in the deep mines, and the type of subsequent treatment of the mined flint involving the initial decortication of much of the raw material prior to ongoing reduction, as exemplified by the 1972–4 chipping floor, implies more than an *ad hoc* casual approach but rather an integration of this work into the life of one or more Late Neolithic communities over an extended period of time. In contrast, the less skilled and less intensive shallow mining in the West Field could have satisfied the needs of other groups who may have been excluded or did not possess the necessary skills to work the deep mines. Unfortunately no primary dating evidence for this activity has so far been recovered, although the ^{14}C dates suggest that much of this may have occurred after the floruit of the Deep Mine Field.

The degree to which Grimes Graves flint was used for the creation of objects of prestige remains difficult to assess (Healy 1991a). The quality of the *floorstone* must have been a major attraction, as it was in historic times, for the ease with which it could be worked, at least when freshly mined. The quantity recovered, however, would limit the rarity value *per se*, although the skill needed in its safe extraction suggests a group of highly skilled if not semi-professional miners, who were presumably in limited supply. The raw material would therefore have had high value in its own right, but the highest value must have accrued from the craftsmanship which produced objects of outstanding quality, not least in an aesthetic sense (Healy 1998, 233), this conversion taking place away from the extraction site. It would be hard to view items such as the axe recovered by Armstrong from Floor 85 (plate 17) or the broken discoidal knife from the 1972–4 chipping floor (fig. 111a) as anything other than objects of actual or potential prestige. Against this the range and variety of implements in the course of manufacture across the site, not always made from the finest flint and on occasion utilizing both *wall-* and *topstone*, indicate that a major portion of the flint extracted was destined for less exalted use. It may be that the term 'prestige' has been used in the past to cover too broad a spectrum of behaviours and that more precision needs to be applied to its use.

Postscript

The research campaign begun by the Museum in 1972 was the product of a feeling of great optimism generated not only by the new chronological horizons established for the Neolithic by ^{14}C in the 1960s, but also by an array of new geophysical and analytical techniques that seemed to offer a greater ability to shed light upon many of the questions surrounding the mines which had so stubbornly resisted resolution. With the passage of more than thirty years it is now possible to see that some of the hopes were doomed to failure and many still remain to be achieved by methods and techniques yet to be pioneered.

It might be useful in conclusion to summarize some of the questions still outstanding:

1   How did the mine field develop? A much larger sample from the area of the deep mines is required to yield primary dating samples from actual mining episodes. Given the prohibitively expensive cost of excavating a single mine and the stringent requirements now imposed by health and safety legislation, the opportunity for multiple sampling seems remote. The ability of ^{14}C to place individual mines into a sequential series remains a hope for the future.

2   Where were the miners living? Phosphate analysis demonstrated the ability to establish the presence of occupation if this was of sufficient intensity (Bronze Age episodes) but may struggle to pinpoint shorter episodes, such as seasonal camp sites. The technique equally cannot be expected to distinguish between different chronological horizons (Neolithic, Bronze Age or even Modern). Failure to locate the source of the Bronze Age middens deposited in several of the filled-in mine shafts is troubling, since this cannot have been at far remove. The failure may be due to looking in the wrong place, although a dairying economy of the type which Legge (1992) has demonstrated must have had need of a secure source of water and, in an otherwise dry area, proximity to the River Little Ouse seems inevitable. A further possibility is that the type of occupation present was of a form which could be missed by the interval chosen for the soil phosphate grid.

3   What was made from the flint extracted? Lech's work has helped to demonstrate and confirm the range of products made, but much remains to be done to quantify the numerical importance of each product within the total output. Since the vast majority of the products left the site, the ability to answer this question requires the supplementary evidence that only the dispersed products can provide.

4   How far were the products of Grimes Graves flint extraction dispersed? Present analytical techniques require sample sizes which prohibit sampling of much of the material available for study. Less demanding forms of analysis therefore need to be developed and deployed.

5   The discovery of a much greater range of Late Neolithic settlement evidence would offer at least the potential to assess what role Grimes Graves flint played in the life of the communities of the period and its spatial importance.

Discoidal knives

G. Varndell

Technique

These appear to have been made chiefly on flakes of variable thickness, many of these cortical (fig. 112c). Sometimes the shape of the flake has determined the ultimate shape of the knife. Well-shaped, thick cortical flakes were often chosen as needing little further work after removal of the cortex and trimming of the outline. Steep peripheral removals often formed the first stage in removing the cortex.

At certain stages of the reduction process, roughouts for discoidal knives might resemble Levallois cores. Cleal (1984, 151) notes that tortoise cores in eastern England 'only seem to occur in Grooved Ware-associated industries, and are likely to have been used for the production of blanks for transverse arrowheads'. Healy, writing of the Breckland (1998, 226), also comments on the 'Levallois-like' technique used for transverse arrowheads as well as 'much larger flakes, some of which served as blanks for discoidal knives or even axeheads'. Manby (1974, 83) also observed the presence of prepared Levallois-like cores in flint assemblages associated with Grooved Ware in northern England. Levallois-like cores and flakes do appear to have been used at Grimes Graves in discoidal knife production, although not exclusively (see fig. 89b).

Durden (1995, 430), in her discussion of discoidal knives in the north of England, argues against the claim that they were always made on flakes, positing that these would have been quite thin: thus it would have been 'inefficient to flake the ventral surface which would already be smooth if it was then going to be polished' – and most appear to be bifacially worked. At Grimes Graves, when discoidal knives were being fashioned on flakes, work on the dorsal surface was frequently more advanced at the point of abandonment than work on the ventral surface, which was sometimes restricted to the removal of the bulb and a few flakes (fig. 111b). Further work here appears to have occurred at a consistently later stage. Even in the case of a 'good' bulbar surface where the piece is already well thinned (or made on a thin flake), attempts might be made to remove thin flakes ventrally. Worked-down cores could also have been used at Grimes Graves in the production of discoidal knives. Some of the cores characteristic of later Neolithic assemblages would readily lend themselves to such secondary use. Durden (ibid., 430) suggests that the under-representation of tortoise cores in one of her assemblages could result from their secondary working into knives. She also suggests that some large cortical flakes may have been used for the same purpose.

Some early-stage reduction was carried out by removing long flakes, leaving long parallel scars (fig. 112a). Some of the thicker blanks have been reduced in this way on both faces, with the flake scars at right angles to each other. There is, however, some ambiguity, and some of these may simply be cores.

There are relatively few near-finished examples and none bears any trace of grinding or polishing (two fine polished examples in the Museum's collections from Bermondsey and Yorkshire are featured in plates 29 and 30). Healy (1998, 227) has remarked on the fact that flaked axeheads and discoidal knives are commoner in the Breckland, while ground ones are commoner on the fen edge. A find in Two Mile Bottom, Thetford, included some effectively finished but unpolished discoidal knives and a couple of possible axe roughouts made on flint which to the eye resembles Grimes Graves flint (Robins 2002). The collection remains in private hands.

One of the Grimes Graves knives (fig. 111a), found in two halves in two separate years (one of the pieces was in a baulk), must have been nearing completion when a thinning blow caused it to break across in a hinge fracture. Some were abandoned because of flaws in the flint; fissures and fossil inclusions are common. Thin layers of calcite, possibly picking out fissures, occur frequently and evidently caused the flint to shear during knapping. The calcite was then treated as cortex and removed. Some were begun on unlikely-looking material regardless of the seemingly evident future difficulties. Some appear to have been reworked from broken axe roughouts, and some from worked-down cores; however, because one is dealing mainly with abandoned, unfinished artefacts it is often difficult to predict the final outcome and there remain grey areas: the knappers themselves might only have decided on the future shape of the piece at a relatively late stage in reduction. Blanks such as that figured by Lech (fig. 79b) could equally well have been worked into a discoidal knife or a small axe. It may be difficult to distinguish between discoidal knife roughouts and some types of core, and in some cases these could be one and the same.

Taphonomy, context and date

Clark's paper of 1928 noted 133 disc knives. For the county of Norfolk, Healy's 1980 gazetteer indicates about 80 excluding Grimes Graves; her published 1996 gazetteer for a limited area of the fen edge and a small area of Breckland brought the total to nearly 100. From Grimes Graves alone the British Museum has over 200 roughouts in its collections, in various stages of completion. Even allowing for some uncertainty about the earlier-stage roughouts, this adds significantly to the number of such artefacts that may be associated directly with Grooved Ware activity. Their post-production history, however, adds little to our knowledge of them. Most finds are from flint scatters. However, they have been cached with axes. At Great Baddow, Essex, a sub-triangular example, finely flaked and edge-polished, was placed with five flint axeheads (one flaked only, the others ground to various degrees) and one of greenstone. A disturbed hoard from Banham, Norfolk (Gurney 1990, fig. 2), contained an edge-polished discoidal knife of similar shape, two polished flint axeheads, and – interestingly – a weathered greenstone axe and a part-polished stone macehead. It is possible that these were cached tool sets or work in progress (Pitts 1996, 341). If the Great Baddow items had been deliberately placed in the ground as they were found – the flint axes packed blade up, side by side and on top of the other two items – one could argue special deposition. However, the same effect could result from having been buried in an organic container now perished. The Grooved Ware ring-ditch at Tye Field, Lawford, produced one fragment of a polished-edge discoidal knife (Healy 1985a, 199, F29), but the roughout referred to by Wainwright and Longworth (1971, 260) is not identified as such in the report. The absence of discoidal knives from major henge sites is notable. These sites are thus not a context for their use, or they were disposed of off site. Recognizable (polished) fragments of stone and flint axes are relatively frequent finds, sometimes forming part of placed deposits in pits (for example at Barrow Hills, Radley, Oxfordshire, where Grooved Ware Pit 2082 contained a Grooved Ware body sherd, antler fragments and worked flint including the butt end of a reworked axe) (Barclay and Halpin 1999, 94 and fig. 4.46). Roe (1999, 228) has remarked on the frequent occurrence in Grooved Ware pits of fragments of axes of Group I greenstone 'or other greenstone of probable south-western origin'.

Manby (1974, 86) describes the frequent occurrence of thick, all-over or edge-polished disc knives as surface finds in East Yorkshire and the Peak District, with rather fewer from Lincolnshire and the Pennines. One from Carnaby Top 12 was the only example from a Grooved Ware site in the north. However, although they have not been found at northern Grooved Ware sites, Manby remarks on the similar distribution of the polished flake/blade knives known from hoards and burials. The question of prestige goods, their manufacture, use and disposal is too large to address here. The combining of selected 'special' items for deposition and the complexity of patterning has long been recognized and will remain a rich source of debate, particularly in the light of the early dates for Peterborough pottery. It does appear that the North of England may have had its own production and distribution network. In her paper on specialized flintwork of the later Neolithic on the Yorkshire Wolds, Durden (1995) describes how some of these artefacts, including disc knives, fine oblique arrowheads and polished axes, were made locally from local flint.

To conclude, the available evidence points to association with Grooved Ware, but secure contexts remain elusive. Over eighty years ago Clark, facing an even greater dearth of information, favoured a Beaker attribution, chiefly on the grounds of distribution (1928, 52ff.). Their non-appearance in Beaker graves with 'warrior' gear was explained by classing the disc knife as a woman's implement.

Function

In Clark's view disc knives were poor for cutting and better for scraping, although useful for cutting and preparing thin materials such as hides (Clark 1928, p. 44). This seems to be a fair enough suggestion. The question remains, as with axes, how far polishing might improve the tool's performance for a particular job and how far it added to its perceived value.

Typology

There is nothing in the Grimes Graves assemblage which deviates from Clark's basic classification (ibid., p. 41). In the catalogue of discoidal knives from Grimes Graves archived at the British Museum, basic geometric descriptors are used where it is possible to define a shape; the shapes tend to grade into each other and corners can be more or less angular or rounded. The range is: a) mitriform, b) trapezoid, c) rectangular, d) triangular, e) discoid and f) ovoid, with truncated versions of the last two. At a more basic level the knives may be three-sided, four-sided or rounded. The size range is quite large; there is a small ovoid example 61 mm long which is at an advanced stage of manufacture (cat. 77), a small advanced discoid 69 mm in diameter (fig. 111d), a near-finished rectangular piece (cat. 86/7) (fig. 111a), which is 136 mm long, and a very large roughout (cat. 187) (fig. 111c) 165 mm in diameter where the edge shaping suggests that the intention was to produce a large discoid.

APPENDIX 2
Gunflints
(fig. 116r and s)

G. Varndell

Post-excavation study of the flint artefacts from the British Museum excavations in the West Field revealed the presence of a type (in some numbers) conforming to no known prehistoric tool form but with a notable internal morphological consistency within certain parameters. These were almost always from superficial layers in West Field dug features and chipping floors.

Morphology
The shape of these artefacts varies from rectangular to horseshoe-shaped. Typically the size range varies from about 55 x 45 mm for the larger examples to about 40 x 30 mm for the smaller ones.

At the proximal end, where a bulb of percussion is present, this is normally prominent. Any point of percussion is similarly marked. Bulbar scars occasionally occur. Where the platform is present it is sometimes complex (faceted); where absent it may be snapped or trimmed.

At the distal end there is frequently evidence of premature termination in the form of a hinge or step fracture. Sometimes this edge is modified.

Where edges have been modified this often manifests itself on the dorsal surface; typically one edge has been retouched to give approximately a 45-degree angle, the other an obtuse angle. The proximal end of the dorsal surface may bear a marked negative bulb.

While these are features that regularly recur, the treatment of the struck flake does vary, apparently being adapted to the morphology of the blank. Patination and flint colour are variable.

Interpretation
Over sixty such artefacts were identified from the upper levels of features and chipping floors alone in the West Field. The pronounced bulbs and points of percussion present on many of these indicate the use of a metal hammer, the hinge and step fractures at least a hard hammer. The iron naturally present in Grimes Graves flint renders the detection of metal tool marks in the laboratory extremely difficult.

Further research of the available literature, and a visit to Thetford Museum, suggest that they belong to a variety of 'wedge' gunflints – although they are not typical of the classic wedge gunflint in the collections at Thetford and illustrated in the works consulted. Museums have possibly concentrated on collecting the well-known products of the Brandon workshops: beautifully regular, black 'platform' gunflints, and to a lesser extent the more typical of the wedge variety which preceded them.

History
Much of the early literature on the subject is frustrating to anyone with an interest in the detail of knapping technology and *chaîne opératoire* – archaeologists, in other words. However, the work of Sydney Skertchley remains extremely useful and his paper, subtitled (in part) '... and the connexion between Neolithic art and the gunflint trade' (1879) contains many relevant observations.

Gunflints evolved from strike-a-lights. Lovett remarked how closely the latter 'resemble the Stone-Age implement known as a Scraper' (1887, 209). Wedge-type gunflints could be produced on an *ad hoc* basis. De Lotbinière (1977) describes this as 'do-it-yourself' technology, and suggests that they were made on field flint, which was not as good as mined flint. He describes the wedge type as a semicircular flake with a wedge profile, the thin edge being the firing edge; the sides were trimmed straight. The 'heel' often had a convex trim as did (sometimes) the firing edge, but the flint would be 'turned over' for this. The bulb could be reduced but this was rare.

De Lotbinière (1980) identifies the period 1660–1785 as that during which the transition to craft-produced gunflints occurred. By 1790 Brandon knappers were manufacturing the familiar 'platform' type of gunflint and supplying the army; these flints were made on *floorstone*, much of it from the Lingheath mines about 12 miles from Brandon (Goodwin 1983).

The Grimes Graves gunflints
One of the initial problems with firmly identifying these as gunflints was posed by the frequent hinge fractures at the distal end. The assumption was that these were discards, because the hinge fracture would have precluded their use, a typical wedge gunflint having, literally, the thin end of the wedge as the striking edge. If this were so it was difficult to see why the side edges were sometimes carefully trimmed. In this matter I am most grateful to Simon Cleggett for much helpful discussion. His report (Cleggett 2000) on caches of gunflints from Portsmouth

has brought a new perspective to the subject. His *species three* (wedge flints, on average slightly smaller than the Grimes Graves population) was probably used in the Sea Service musket 'based on the earlier Brown Bess that served from 1720 until the 1840s'. Typologically the species can be traced back as far as 1575 (ibid., 39*)*. According to Cleggett (pers. comm.), the hinge fractures in the Grimes Graves examples would not have rendered the flints useless.

It is clear from Thetford Museum's collection of wedge gunflints that size varied according to the gun, those destined for use in cannon being much larger. It is difficult to say what purpose the Grimes Graves examples were to serve; sporting guns must be among the possibilities.

The type did turn up in the early excavations on the site, but the possibility that they were anything but prehistoric did not occur to the excavators. Smith (1915, 199, fig. 76) describes a 'side-scraper with facetted butt' from the Tumulus Pit, 'which might have been disturbed ground'. The piece, squarish in shape, had, as well as a faceted butt, a prominent bulb and retouch along one edge. The author remarks: 'These three features have frequently been noticed in this Report, and are found also in the Northfleet industry'. These characteristics are used as confirmation of a Mousterian date.

Not a few similar pieces survive in the Armstrong collection. Forty-six were counted from Pit 12 alone, almost exclusively from Floor B. Armstrong (1932, 60–61, figs 6 and 7) notes that the Floor B industry was 'characterised by the production of small square ended flakes, mostly bearing hinge fractures and all having pronounced bulbs' – recalling, to his mind, the Clactonian.

Pit 12 is a masked pit some 18 ft deep at the extreme east side of the West Field (Longworth and Varndell 1996, 73). The shaft fill comprised chalk rubble and sand. Various chipping horizons were incorporated, the uppermost being Floors A and B. Floor A was a thin spread across the whole pit mouth, described by Armstrong as being 'much mixed with compacted chalky rubble and infiltrated humus from the 6 inch covering of humus which overspread the whole area'. Floor B has the appearance of a scoop immediately beneath Floor A; it was 3 ft 9 in thick at the centre and contained mostly 'small flakes and worn out cores'. Floor C beneath included sherds from a Peterborough bowl – probably redeposited – and sherds from a Bronze Age Bucket-shaped Vessel (ibid., 73). Armstrong noted that the flint debris of Floor B was closely compacted, such that it 'resembled a tip of road metal'.

There is nothing to suggest, despite Armstrong's view to the contrary, that Floors A and B should not represent much later activity, Floor B being perhaps a dump of debris from an intensive gunflint-knapping episode. Floor A is so thin and superficial that it is best regarded as a disturbed, perhaps redeposited context.

The Pit 12 flints may be fresh and black, or patinated and a mottled blue-grey. That they are by and large consistently a little bigger than those from the West Field may be significant in terms of their use: perhaps this was one knapping episode with a particular type and size of gun in mind. The West Field, with its mobile deposits and history of disturbance by prehistoric activity, by medieval ploughing and by rabbits, might have provided a very good source for raw material used in the *ad hoc* knapping of gunflints.

Prehistoric pottery: a supplement

I. Longworth

Since publication of the pottery in Fascicule 2 (Longworth *et al.* 1988), a further small quantity of pottery has come to light, the most important being a group of Neolithic Bowl sherds from 880/910 as well as additional Grooved Ware and Bronze Age sherds. The following table therefore amends the previous entries (ibid., 12 and 23).

Middle Neolithic Bowl

880/910 2 and Feature 2: 54 sherds from layer 2 and 26 sherds from Feature 2.

Grooved Ware

950/820 Feature 28: 1 sherd from layer 5 and 1 sherd from an internally decorated bowl from layer 12.

940/940 Feature 108: 2 sherds from layer 1.

Early Bronze Age		
Context	**Total**	**Of these: Collared Vessel**
Feature 28, layer 14	1	1
Feature 33, layer 1	21	21
Feature 105, layer 1	9	9
Feature 108, layer 1	240	57
Feature 112, layer 2	10	7
Feature 112, layer 3	7	7
Feature 114, layer 3	8	8
880/910, Feature 2, layer 1	2	-
900/870, Feature 2, layer 2	7	-
940/950, layer 2	1	1
Middle Bronze Age		
		Bucket-shaped Vessel
880/910, Feature 2, layer 1	1	1
880/910, Feature 2, layer 2	21	21

Table 11 Neolithic and Bronze Age pottery recovered during British Museum excavations additional to that listed in Fascicule 2.

APPENDIX 4
The handaxe
(fig. 122)

N. Ashton

A small flint handaxe was excavated from Shaft X, layer 10, 1275/900. It is 94 mm in length, 65 mm wide, 23 mm thick and weighs 129 g. The piece is in fresh condition, but has a white patination on both sides, and on one face has small round pittings, indicative of damage by frost. The patination and damage both suggest that the artefact lay exposed on a land surface for some considerable time. There is a small, more recent break on one lateral edge, although how recent is unclear.

The handaxe has been worked on both faces through soft-hammer flaking, although a remnant of cortex has been left on one face, and cortex has been retained at the butt. Slight problems in knapping are evident through a hinge fracture on each face. There are slight s-twists on both lateral edges, although one of these may have been fortuitously created through the knapping problems.

Typologically the piece would be classified by Bordes (1961) as a cordiform, by Wymer (1968) as a cordate or flat-butted cordate (Types J or N), and by Roe (1968) as pointed. Although similar pieces have been recovered from sites dating from the earliest Lower Palaeolithic in Britain (at least 500,000 years ago) to the latest Middle Palaeolithic (some 40,000 years ago), cordiform and sub-triangular handaxes are particularly associated with the later Middle Palaeolithic (60–40,000 years ago) (White and Jacobi 2002).

This suggestion is given added weight by the nature of the handaxes from the recently excavated site of Lynford, 4 km to the north. The handaxes were associated with the remains of mammoth and recovered from organic sediments in a former river channel of the River Wissey. The site has been dated by radiocarbon and OSL

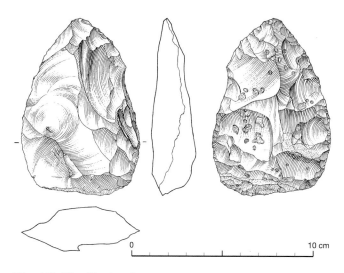

Fig. 122 The flint handaxe.

(optically stimulated luminescence) to about 55,000 years ago (Schreve 2006). Here, the handaxes tend to be cordiform and sub-triangular in shape, and the Lynford piece certainly falls within the range of variation. The possibility should be considered that the Grimes Graves handaxe originated from Lynford, where suitable raw material was readily available, and was brought by hand to Grimes Graves. The association of the handaxe with deposits forming the latest phase of the silting up of Shaft X, and pre-dating the dumping of midden material during the Middle Bronze Age, might suggest that this was during the Late Neolithic, when perhaps it was picked up as an object of curiosity.

Bibliography

Adkins, R. and Jackson, R. 1978. *Neolithic Stone and Flint Axes from the River Thames – an illustrated corpus.* British Museum Occasional Papers, 1, London.

Affolter, J. and de Labriffe, P.-A. 2007. 'Mais où sont passées les haches en silex?' in Besse, M. (ed.), *Sociétés Néolithiques: des faits archéologiques aux fonctionnements socio-économiques. Actes du 27e Colloque Interrégional sur le Neolithique. Cahiers d'archéologie romande*, 108, 13–22. Lausanne.

Ambers, J. 1996. 'Radiocarbon analyses from the Grimes Graves mines' in Longworth, I. and Varndell, G., *Excavations at Grimes Graves, Norfolk, 1972–1976. Fascicule 5*, 100–108. British Museum Press, London.

Ambers, J.C. 1998. 'Dating Grimes Graves'. *Radiocarbon*, 40 (1), 591–600.

Ambers, J. and Bowman, S. 1998. 'Radiocarbon measurements from the British Museum: datelist XXIV'. *Archaeometry*, 40 (2), 413–37.

Ambers, J., Matthews, K. and Bowman, S. 1987. 'British Museum radiocarbon measurements XX'. *Radiocarbon*, 29 (1), 271–8.

Andersen, H.H. 1982. 'A study of water uptake in flint'. *PACT*, 7.2, 447–58.

Armstrong, A.L. 1921a. 'The discovery of engravings upon flint crust at Grime's Graves, Norfolk.' *Antiquaries Journal*, 1 (2), 81–6.

Armstrong, A.L. 1921b. 'Flint-crust engravings, and associated implements, from Grimes' Graves, Norfolk'. *Proceedings of the Prehistoric Society of East Anglia*, 3 (3), 434–43.

Armstrong, A.L. 1922. 'Further discoveries of engraved flint-crust and associated implements at Grimes' Graves'. *Proceedings of the Prehistoric Society of East Anglia*, 3 (4), 548–58.

Armstrong, A.L. 1923. 'Discovery of a new phase of early mining at Grimes' Graves, Norfolk. Preliminary Report'. *Proceedings of the Prehistoric Society of East Anglia*, 4 (1), 113–25.

Armstrong, A.L. 1924a. '(1) Further researches in the primitive flint mining area; (2) Discovery of an Early Iron Age site of Halstatt Culture'. *Proceedings of the Prehistoric Society of East Anglia*, 4 (2), 182–93.

Armstrong, A.L. 1924b. 'Further excavations upon the engraving floor (floor 85), Grimes' Graves'. *Proceedings of the Prehistoric Society of East Anglia* 4 (2), 194–202.

Armstrong, A.L. 1927. 'The Grime's Graves problem in the light of recent reseaches'. *Proceedings of the Prehistoric Society of East Anglia*, 5 (2), 91–136.

Armstrong, A.L. 1932. 'The Percy Sladen Trust Excavations, Grime's Graves, Norfolk. Interim Report 1927–32'. *Proceedings of the Prehistoric Society of East Anglia*, 7 (1), 57–61.

Armstrong, A.L. 1934. 'Grime's Graves, Norfolk. Report on the excavation of Pit 12'. *Proceedings of the Prehistoric Society of East Anglia*, 7 (3), 382–94.

Armstrong, A.L. Armstrong Papers. (Armstrong Mss., British Museum).

Ashwin, T. 1996. 'Neolithic and Bronze Age Norfolk'. *Proceedings of the Prehistoric Society*, 62, 41–62.

Bakels, C.C. 1978. *Four Linearbandkeramik Settlements and their Environment: A Paleoecological Study of Sittard, Stein, Elsloo and Hienheim.* Analecta Praehistorica Leidensia, 11. Universitaire Pers Leiden, Leiden.

Bamford, H.M. 1982. *Beaker Domestic Sites in the Fen Edge and East Anglia.* East Anglian Archaeology, 18. Norfolk Archaeological Unit, Gressenhall.

Barber, M., Field, D. and Topping, P. 1999. *The Neolithic Flint Mines of England.* English Heritage, London.

Barclay, A. and Halpin, C. 1999. *Excavations at Barrow Hills, Radley, Oxfordshire. Volume 1: the Neolithic and Bronze Age monument complex.* Oxford Archaeological Unit, Thames Valley Landscapes, 11. Eynsham.

Barker, H. and Mackey, J. 1961. 'British Museum Radiocarbon Measurements III'. *Radiocarbon*, 3, 39–45.

Barker, H. and Mackey, J. 1963. 'British Museum Radiocarbon Measurements IV'. *Radiocarbon*, 5, 104–8.

Barrett, J., Bradley, R. and Green, M. 1991. *Landscape, Monuments and Society: the prehistory of Cranbourne Chase.* Cambridge University Press, Cambridge.

Begg, C. and Lucas, G. 1997. 'Archaeological investigations at Owl End Road, Bury, Cambridgeshire'. *Cambridge Archaeological Unit Report*, 241. Cambridge.

Bell, G.H., Davidson, J.N. and Scarborough, H. 1968. *Textbook of Physiology and Biochemistry.* Livingstone, Edinburgh.

Bethell, P. and Máté, I. 1989. 'The use of soil phosphate analysis in archaeology: a critique' in Henderson, J. (ed.), *Scientific Analysis in Archaeology and its Interpretation.* Oxford University Committee for Archaeology Monograph 19, 1–29. Oxford.

Binford, L.R. 1963. 'A proposed attribute list for the description and classification of projectile points' in White, A.M., Binford, L.R. and Papworth, M.L. (eds), *Miscellaneous Studies in Typology and Classification.* Anthropological Papers, 19, 193–221. University of Michigan, Ann Arbor.

Boismier, B. 2002. 'Lynford Quarry: a Neanderthal butchery site'. *Current Archaeology*, 16.2, no. 182, 53–8.

Booth, A. St. J. and Stone, J.F.S. 1952. 'A trial mine at Durrington, Wiltshire.' *Wiltshire Archaeological Magazine*, 54, 381–8.

Bordes, F. 1961. *Typologie du Paléolithique Ancien et Moyen*. Institut de Préhistoire de l'Université de Bordeaux, Bordeaux.

Borkowski, W., Migal, W., Saɫaciński, S. and Zalewski, M. 1991. 'Possibilities of investigating Neolithic flint economies as exemplified by the banded flint economy'. *Antiquity*, 65, 607–27.

Bostyn, F. and Lanchon, Y. 1998. *Jablines: le Haut Château*. Fondation de la Maison des Sciences et de l'Homme, Paris.

Bradley, R. and Edmonds, M.E. 1993. *Interpreting the Axe Trade*. Cambridge University Press, Cambridge.

Bronk Ramsey, C. 1995. 'Radiocarbon calibration and the analysis of stratigraphy: the program OxCal'. *Radiocarbon*, 37 (2), 425–30.

Brown, A. 1996. 'Use and non-use: aspects of the prehistoric exploitation of the fen-edge at Isleham' in Hall, D. (ed.), *The Fenland Project, no. 10: Cambridgeshire Survey, Isle of Ely and Wisbech*. East Anglian Archaeology, 79, 202–12.

Buck, C.E., Cavanagh, W.G. and Litton, C.D. 1992. 'Tools for the interpretation of soil phosphate data from Archaeological surveys' in Spoerry, P. (ed.), *Geoprospection in the Archaeological Landscape*. Oxbow Monograph, 18, 75–87. Oxford.

Burton, J. 1980. 'Making sense of waste flakes. New methods for investigating the technology and economics behind chipped stone assemblages'. *Journal of Archaeological Science*, 7 (2), 131–48.

Burton, J. 1984. 'Quarrying in a tribal society'. *World Archaeology*, 16 (2), 234–47.

Burton, J. 1987. 'Exchange pathways at a stone axe factory in Papua New Guinea' in Sieveking, G. de G. and Newcomer, M.H. (eds), *The Human Uses of Flint and Chert*, 183–91. Cambridge University Press, Cambridge.

Cahen, D. 1987. 'Refitting stone artefacts: why bother?' in Sieveking, G. de G. and Newcomer, M.H. (eds), *The Human Uses of Flint and Chert*, 1–9. Cambridge University Press, Cambridge.

Care, V. 1979. 'The production and distribution of Mesolithic axes in southern England'. *Proceedings of the Prehistoric Society*, 45, 93–102.

Catt, J.A. 1986. 'The nature, origin and geomorphological significance of the clay-with-flints' in Sieveking, G. de G. and Hart, M.B. (eds), *The Scientific Study of Flint and Chert*, 151–9. Cambridge University Press, Cambridge.

Clark, A.J. 1996. *Seeing Beneath the Soil: prospecting methods in archaeology*. 2nd edn, Batsford, London.

Clark, J.G.D. 1928. 'Discoidal polished flint knives – their typology and distribution'. *Proceedings of the Prehistoric Society of East Anglia*, 6, 40–54.

Clark, J.G.D. 1952. *Prehistoric Europe. The Economic Basis*. Methuen, London.

Clark, J.G.D. and Piggott, S. 1933. 'The Age of the British Flint Mines'. *Antiquity*, 7, 166–83.

Clarke, R.R. 1963. *Grime's Graves, Norfolk*. HMSO, London.

Clarke, W.G. (ed.) 1915. *Report on the Excavations at Grime's Graves, Weeting, Norfolk, March–May 1914*. Prehistoric Society of East Anglia, London.

Clarke, W.G. 1917. 'Are Grime's Graves Neolithic?' *Proceedings of the Prehistoric Society of East Anglia*, 2 (3), 339–49.

Clarke, W.G. 1921. 'The Grime's Graves Fauna'. *Proceedings of the Prehistoric Society of East Anglia*, 3 (3), 431–3.

Clayton, C.J. 1986. 'The chemical environment of flint formation in Upper Cretaceous chalk' in Sieveking, G. de G. and Hart, M.B. (eds), *The Scientific Study of Flint and Chert*, 43–54. Cambridge University Press, Cambridge.

Cleal, R. 1984. 'The Later Neolithic in Eastern England' in Bradley, R. and Gardiner, J. (eds), *Neolithic Studies. A review of some current research*. British Archaeological Reports, British Series, 133, 135–58. Oxford.

Cleal, R. 1999. 'Introduction: the what, where, when and why of Grooved Ware' in Cleal, R. and MacSween, A. (eds), *Grooved Ware in Britain and Ireland*, Neolithic Studies Group Seminar Papers 3, 1–8. Oxbow, Oxford.

Cleggett, S. 2000. *The Gunflint from Gunwharf Quays, Portsmouth*. Report for Gifford and Partners Ltd, Southampton.

Clough, T.H. McK. and Green, B. 1972. 'The petrological identification of stone implements from East Anglia'. *Proceedings of the Prehistoric Society*, 38, 108–55.

Clutton-Brock, J. 1984. *Excavations at Grimes Graves, Norfolk, 1972–1976. Fascicule 1. Neolithic antler picks from Grimes Graves, Norfolk, and Durrington Walls, Wiltshire: a biometrical analysis*. British Museum Press, London.

Clutton-Brock, J. and Burleigh, R. 1991. 'The skull of a Neolithic horse from Grime's Graves, Norfolk, England' in Meadow, R.H. and Uerpmann, H.-P. (eds), *Equids in the Ancient World*, vol. 2, 242–9. Wiesbaden.

Coles, J.M. and Hibbert, F.A. 1968. 'Prehistoric roads and tracks in Somerset, England: 1. Neolithic'. *Proceedings of the Prehistoric Society*, 34, 238–58.

Collet, H., Hauzeur, A. and Lech, J. 2008. 'The prehistoric flint mine complex at Spiennes (Belgium) on the occasion of its discovery 140 years ago' in Allard, P., Bostyn, F., Giligny, F. and Lech, J. (eds), *Flint Mining in Prehistoric Europe: interpreting the archaeological records*. British Archaeological Reports, International Series, 1891, 41–78. Oxford.

Conway, J.S. 1983. 'An investigation of soil phosphorus distribution within occupation deposits from a Romano-British hut group'. *Journal of Archaeological Science*, 10, 117–28. Oxford.

Cook, J. and Dumont, J. 1987. 'The development and application of microwear analysis since 1964' in Sieveking, G. de G. and Newcomer, M.H. (eds), *The Human Uses of Flint and Chert*, 53–61. Cambridge University Press, Cambridge.

Cook, S.F. and Heizer, R.F. 1965. *Studies on the Chemical Analysis of Archaeological Sites*. University of California Publications in Anthropology, 2. Berkeley.

Corbett, W.M. 1973. *Breckland Forest Soils*. Soil Survey Special Survey, no. 7. Harpenden.

Cowell, M.R. 1981a. 'The distribution of trace elements in some Cretaceous chalk flint from N.W. Europe'. D.I.C. thesis, Geology Department, Imperial College, London.

Cowell, M.R. 1981b. 'The archaeological and geochemical implications of trace element distributions in some English, Dutch and Belgian flints' in Engelen, F.H.G. (ed.), *Third International Symposium on Flint, 24–27 Mei 1979*, Staringia 6, 81–4. Nederlandse Geologische Vereniging, Maastricht.

Cowell, M.R., Ferguson, J. and Hughes, M.J. 1980. 'Geochemical variation in East Anglian flint with particular reference to Grimes Graves flint mines' in Slater, E.A. and Tate, J.O. (eds), *Proceedings of the 16th International Symposium on Archaeometry and Archaeological Prospection, Edinburgh 1976*, 80–89. National Museum of Antiquities of Scotland, Edinburgh.

Craddock, P.T. 1984. 'The soil phosphate survey at the Cat's Water subsite, Fengate 1973–77' in Pryor, F., *Excavations at Fengate, Peterborough, England: the fourth report*. Northamptonshire Archaeological Society Monograph, 2, Appendix 4, 259 and microfiche pp. 234–41.

Craddock, P.T. and Cowell, M.R. 2009. 'Finding the floorstone' in Freestone, I.C. and Rehren, Th. (eds), *Mine to Microscope: essays in honour of Mike Tite*, 21–39. University College London Press, London.

Craddock, P.T., Cowell, M.R., Leese, M.N. and Hughes, M.J. 1983. 'The trace element composition of polished flint axes as an indicator of source'. *Archaeometry*, 25 (2), 135–64.

Craddock, P.T., Gurney, D., Pryor, F. and Hughes, M.J. 1985. 'The application of phosphate analysis to the location and interpretation of archaeological sites'. *Archaeological Journal*, 142, 361–76.

Cunliffe, B. 1973. 'Chalton, Hants: the evolution of a landscape'. *Antiquaries Journal*, 53, 173–90.

Cziesla, E., Eickoff, S., Arts, N. and Winter, D. (eds) 1990. *The Big Puzzle: international symposium on refitting stone artefacts*. Studies in Modern Archaeology, 1. Holos-Verlag, Bonn.

De Lotbinière, S. 1977. 'The story of the English gunflint'. *Journal of the Arms and Armour Society*, 9, 32–53.

De Lotbinière, S. 1980. 'Gunflint enquiry'. *Kent Archaeological Review*, 59, 198–201.

Douglas, M. 1990. Foreword in Mauss, M., *The Gift. The form and reason for exchange in archaic societies*, vii–xviii. Routledge, London.

Durden, T. 1995. 'The production of specialised flintwork in the later Neolithic: a case study from the Yorkshire Wolds'. *Proceedings of the Prehistoric Society*, 61, 409–32.

Dzieduszycka-Machnikowa, A. and Lech, J. 1976. *Neolityczne zespoły pracowniane z kopalni krzemienia w Sąspowie*. [English summary: The Neolithic workshop assemblages from the flint mine of Sąspów]. Polskie Badania Archeologiczne, 19. Zakład Narodowy imiena Ossolińskich, Wrocław.

Edmonds, M. 1995. *Stone Tools and Society*. Batsford, London.

Edmonds, M., Evans, M. and Gibson, D. 1999. 'Assembly and collection – lithic complexes in the Cambridgeshire Fenlands'. *Proceedings of the Prehistoric Society*, 65, 47–82.

Eidt, R.C. and Woods, W.I. 1974. *Abandoned Settlement Analysis: theory and practice*. Field Test Associates, Milwaukee.

Evans, J. 1872. *Ancient Stone Implements, Weapons and Ornaments of Great Britain*. Longman, Green, Reader and Dyer, London.

Favard, A. and Dabas, M. 2007. *Grimes Graves, Norfolk. Report on geophysical surveys, March 2007*. Report archived with English Heritage.

Felder, P.J. 1981. 'Prehistoric flint mining at Ryckholt St. Geertruid (Netherlands) and Grimes Graves (England)' in Engelen, F.H.G. (ed.), *Third International Symposium on Flint, 24–27 Mei 1979*, Staringia 6, 57–62. Nederlandse Geologische Vereniging, Maastricht.

Felder, P.J. (Sjeuf), Rademakers, P. Cor M. and de Grooth, M.E. Th. (eds) 1998. *Excavations of Prehistoric Flint Mines at Rijckholt-St-Geertruid (Limburg, The Netherlands) by the Prehistoric Flint Mines Working Group of the Dutch Geological Society, Limburg Section*, Archäologische Berichte 12. Selbstverlag der Deutschen Gesellschaft für Ur und Frügeschichte, Bonn.

Fiedorczuk, J. 2006. *Final Paleolithic Camp Organisation as Seen from the Perspective of Lithic Artefacts Refitting*, ed. R. Schild. Institute of Archaeology and Ethnology, Polish Academy of Sciences, Warsaw.

Firth, R. 1956. *Elements of Social Organisation*. Watts, London.

Firth, R. 1965. *Primitive Polynesian Economy*. Routledge and Kegan Paul, London.

Forrest, A.J. 1983. *Masters of Flint*. Lavenham Press, Lavenham, Suffolk.

Gardiner, J.P. 1984. 'Lithic distributions and Neolithic settlement patterns in central southern England' in Brown, A.G. and Gardiner, J.P. (eds), *Neolithic Studies: a review of some research*. British Archaeological Reports, British Series, 133, 15–40. Oxford.

Gardiner, J.P. 1987. 'Tales of the unexpected: approaches to the assessment and interpretation of museum flint collections' in Brown, A.G. and Edmonds, M.R. (eds), *Lithic Analysis and Later Prehistory*. British Archaeological Reports, British Series, 162, 49–63. Oxford.

Gardiner, J.P. 1990. 'Flint procurement and Neolithic axe production on the South Downs: a re-assessment'. *Oxford Journal of Archaeology*, 9 (2), 119–40.

Garrow, D. 2006. *Pits, Settlement and Deposition during the Neolithic and Early Bronze Age in East Anglia*. British Archaeological Reports, British Series, 414. Oxford.

Gijn, A.L. van 1990. *The Wear and Tear of Flint. Principles of functional analysis applied to Dutch Neolithic assemblages*. Analecta Praehistorica Leidensia, 22. Leiden.

Goodwin, C. 1983. *Flint*. Norfolk Museums Service Information Sheet, Norfolk Museums Service.

Green, B. 1993. *Grime's Graves*. English Heritage, London.

Green, H.S. 1980. *The Flint Arrowheads of the British Isles*. British Archaeological Reports, British Series, 75. Oxford.

Greenwell, Revd W. 1870a. 'On the opening of Grime's Graves in Norfolk'. *Journal of the Ethnological Society of London*, n.s. 2, 419–39.

Greenwell, Revd W. 1870b. 'Grime's Graves'. Paper read to the seventeenth annual meeting of the Wiltshire Archaeological and Natural History Society, Salisbury. Private publication.

Grooth, M.E.Th. de 1991. 'Socio-economic aspects of Neolithic flint mining: a preliminary study'. *Helinium*, 31 (2), 153–89.

Grooth, M.E. Th. de 1995. 'The organisation of chert exploitation in southeastern Bavaria during the Neolithic'. *Archaeologia Polona*, 33, 163–72.

Grooth, M.E. Th. de 1997. 'The social context of Neolithic flint mining in Europe' in Schild, R. and Sulgostowska, Z. (eds), *Man and Flint: proceedings of the VIIth International Flint Symposium Warszawa-Ostrowiec Świętokrzyski, September 1995*, 71–5. Institute of Archaeology and Ethnology, Polish Academy of Sciences, Warsaw.

Guilford, J.P. 1965. *Fundamental Statistics in Psychology and Education*. 4th edn, McGraw-Hill, New York.

Gurney, D. 1985. *Phosphate Analysis of Soils: a guide for the field archaeologist*. Institute of Field Archaeologists Technical Paper, 3.

Gurney, D. 1990. 'Archaeological finds in Norfolk 1989'. *Norfolk Archaeology*, 41 (1), 96–106.

Hamond, F.W. 1983. 'Phosphate analysis of archaeological sediments' in Reeves-Smith, T. and Hamond, F. (eds), *Landscape and Archaeology in Ireland*. British Archaeological Reports, 116, 47–80. Oxford.

Hansen, P.V. and Madsen, B. 1983. 'Flint axe manufacture in the Neolithic: an experimental investigation of a flint axe manufacture site at Hastrup Vænget, East Zealand'. *Journal of Danish Archaeology*, 2, 43–59.

Harding, P. 1987. 'An experiment to produce a ground flint axe' in Sieveking, G. de G. and Newcomer, M.H. (eds), *The Human Uses of Flint and Chert*, 37–42. Cambridge University Press, Cambridge.

Healy, F. 1980. 'The Neolithic in Norfolk'. Unpublished PhD thesis, University of London.

Healy, F. 1984. 'Farming and field monuments: the Neolithic in Norfolk' in C. Barringer (ed.), *Aspects of East Anglian Prehistory (twenty years after Rainbird Clarke)*, 77–140. Geo Books, Norwich.

Healy, F. 1985a. 'The struck flint' in Shennan, S.J., Healy, F. and Smith, I.F., 'The excavation of a ring-ditch at Tye Field, Lawford, Essex'. *Archaeological Journal*, 142, 177–207.

Healy, F. 1985b. 'Recent work at Grimes Graves, Weeting-with-Broomhill'. *Norfolk Archaeology*, 39 (2), 175–81.

Healy, F. 1987. 'Flint and stone in Neolithic Britain'. *Lithics*, 8, 27–8.

Healy, F. 1991a. 'The hunting of the floorstone' in Schofield, A.J. (ed.), *Interpreting Artefact Scatters: contributions to ploughzone archaeology*. Oxbow Monograph, 4, 29–37. Oxford.

Healy, F. 1991b. 'Appendix 1. Lithics and pre-Iron Age pottery' in Silvester, R.J., *The Fenland Project no. 4: the Wissey Embayment and the Fen Causeway, Norfolk*. East Anglian Archaeology, 52, 116–39.

Healy, F. 1993. 'Artefacts 1. Lithic material' in Healy, F., Cleal, R.M.J. and Kinnes, I., 'Excavations on Redgate Hill, Hunstanton, 1970 and 1971'. East Anglian Archaeology, 57, 28–39.

Healy, F. 1996. *The Fenland Project no. 11: the Wissey Embayment: evidence for Pre-Iron Age settlement accumulated prior to the Fenland Project*. East Anglian Archaeology, 78.

Healy, F. 1998. 'The surface of the Breckland' in Ashton, N., Healy, F. and Pettitt, P. (eds), *Stone Age Archaeology. Essays in honour of John Wymer*. Oxbow Monograph, 102, 225–35. Oxford.

Healy, F., Cleal, R.M.J. and Kinnes, I. 1993. 'Excavations on Redgate Hill, Hunstanton, 1970 and 1971' in Bradley, R., Chowne, P., Cleal, R.M.J., Healy, F. and Kinnes, I., *Excavations on Redgate Hill, Hunstanton, Norfolk, and at Tattershall Thorpe, Lincolnshire*. East Anglian Archaeology, 57, 1–77.

Herne, A. 1991. 'The flint assemblage' in Longworth, I., Herne, A., Varndell, G. and Needham, S., *Excavations at Grimes Graves, Norfolk, 1972–1976. Fascicule 3*, 21–93. British Museum Press, London.

Herz, N. and Garrison, E.G. 1998. *Geological Methods for Archaeology*. Oxford University Press, New York.

Hesse, P.R. 1971. *A Textbook of Soil Chemical Analysis*. Murray, London.

Holgate, R. 1988. 'Further investigations at the later Neolithic domestic and Napoleonic "camp" at Bullock Down, near Eastbourne, East Sussex'. *Sussex Archaeological Collections*, 126, 21–30.

Holgate, R. 1991. *Prehistoric Flint Mines*. Shire Publications, Princes Risborough, Buckinghamshire.

Holgate, R. 1995. 'Neolithic flint mining in Britain'. *Archaeologia Polona*, 33, 133–61.

Holmes, W.H. 1919. *Handbook of Aboriginal American Antiquities. Part I: Introductory. The Lithic Industries*. Government Printing Office, Washington, DC.

Hughes, M.J., Cowell, M.R. and Craddock, P.T. 1976. 'Atomic absorption techniques in archaeology'. *Archaeometry*, 18.1, 19–36.

Kahn, R.L. and Cannell, Ch. F. 1957. *The Dynamics of Interviewing. Theory, technique and cases*. Wiley, New York.

Kendall, Revd H.G.O. 1920a. 'Grime's Graves: Floors 47 to 59'. *Proceedings of the Prehistoric Society of East Anglia*, 3 (2), 290–305.

Kendall, Revd H.G.O. 1920b. 'Windmill Hill, Avebury and Grimes Graves: cores and choppers'. *Proceedings of the Prehistoric Society of East Anglia*, 3 (2), 192–9.

Kendall, Revd H.G.O. 1925. 'Arrowheads at Grimes Graves'. *Proceedings of the Prehistoric Society of East Anglia*, 5 (1), 64–6.

Lambert, J. 1997. *Traces of the Past: unravelling the secrets of archaeology*. Addison Wesley, Reading, Massachusetts.

Lech, J. 1975. 'Neolithic flint mine and workshops at Sąspów near Cracow' in Engelen, F.H.G. (ed.), *Second International Symposium on Flint, 8–11 Mei 1975*, Staringia 3, 70–71. Nederlandse Geologische Vereniging, Maastricht.

Lech, J. 1980. 'Flint mining among the early farming communities of central Europe'. *Przegląd Archeologiczny*, 28, 5–55.

Lech, J. 1981. 'Flint mining among the early farming communities of Poland' in Engelen, F.H.G. (ed.), *Third International Symposium on Flint, 24–7 Mei 1979*, Staringia 6, 39–45. Nederlandse Geologische Vereniging, Maastricht.

Lech, J. 1983. 'Flint mining among the early farming communities of Central Europe. Part II: the basis of research into flint workshops'. *Przegląd Archeologiczny*, 30, 47–80. Wrocław.

Lech, J. 1991. 'The Neolithic-Eneolithic transition in prehistoric mining and siliceous rock distribution' in Lichardus, J. (ed.), *Die Kupferzeit als Historische Epoche*, 557–74. Dr Rudolf Habelt GMBH, Bonn.

Lech, J. 1997. 'Remarks on prehistoric flint mining and flint supply in European archaeology' in Ramos-Millan, A. and Bustillo, A. (eds), *Siliceous Rocks and Culture*, Monográfica Arte y Arqueología, 611–37. Granada.

Lech, J. and Longworth, I. 1995. 'A Late Neolithic chipping-floor on the Grimes Graves flint mines site: preliminary results from a study of the Grooved Ware assemblage recovered during the 1972–74 excavations'. *VIIth International Flint Symposium, Warszawa-Ostrowiec Świętokrzyski, 4–8 September 1995. Abstracts*, 29–30. Warsaw.

Lech, J. and Longworth, I. 2000. 'Kopalnia krzemienia Grimes Graves w świetle nowych badań'. [English summary: The Grimes Graves flint mine site in the light of new research]. *Przegląd Archeologiczny*, 48, 19–73. Wrocław.

Lech, J. and Longworth, I. 2006. 'The Grimes Graves flint mine site in the light of two Late Neolithic workshop assemblages: a second approach' in Körlin, G. and Weisgerber, G. (eds), *Stone Age–Mining Age*. Der Anschnitt, Zeitschrift für Kunst und Kultur im Bergbau, Beiheft 19, 413–22. Bochum.

Legge, A.J. 1981. 'The agricultural economy' in Mercer, R.J., *Grimes Graves, Norfolk. Excavations 1971–72*, 79–103. D.O.E. Research Report, 11. HMSO, London.

Legge, A.J. 1992. *Excavations at Grimes Graves, Norfolk, 1972–1976. Fascicule 4. Animals, environment and the Bronze Age economy*. British Museum Press, London.

Lévi-Strauss, C. 1973. *Tristes Tropiques*. Jonathan Cape, London.

Linford, N., Martin, L. and Holmes, J. 2009. *Grimes Graves, Norfolk: report on geophysical survey, October 2007*. English Heritage Research Department Report Series, no. 64-2009.

Longworth, I. and Cleal, R. 1999. 'Grooved Ware gazetteer' in Cleal, R. and MacSween, A. (eds), *Grooved Ware in Britain and Ireland*. Neolithic Studies Group Seminar Papers, 3, 177–206. Oxbow, Oxford.

Longworth, I., Ellison, A. and Rigby, V. 1988. *Excavations at Grimes Graves, Norfolk, 1972–1976. Fascicule 2. The Neolithic, Bronze Age and Later pottery*. British Museum Press, London.

Longworth, I., Herne, A., Varndell, G. and Needham, S. 1991. *Excavations at Grimes Graves, Norfolk, 1972–1976. Fascicule 3. Shaft X: Bronze Age flint, chalk and metal working*. British Museum Press, London.

Longworth, I. and Varndell, G. 1996. *Excavations at Grimes Graves, Norfolk, 1972–1976. Fascicule 5. Mining in the deeper mines*. British Museum Press, London.

Lovett, E. 1887. 'Notice of the gunflint manufactory at Brandon, with reference to the bearing of its process upon the modes of flint-working practised in prehistoric times'. *Proceedings of the Society of Antiquaries of Scotland*, 21, 206–12.

Madsen, B. 1984. 'Flint axe manufacture in the Neolithic: experiments with the grinding and polishing of thin-butted flint axes'. *Journal of Danish Archaeology*, 3, 47–62.

Malinowski, B. 1922. *Argonauts of the Western Pacific. An account of native enterprise and adventure in the archipelagos of Melanesian New Guinea*. George Routledge and Sons, London.

Manby, T.G. 1974. *Grooved Ware Sites in the North of England*. British Archaeological Reports, 9. Oxford.

Mauss, M. 1990. *The Gift. The form and reason for exchange in archaic societies*. Routledge, London.

McBryde, I. 1984. 'Kulin greenstone quarries: the social contexts of production and distribution for the Mt William site'. *World Archaeology*, 16 (2), 267–85.

McBryde, I. 1997. '"The landscape is a series of stories". Grindstones, quarries and exchange in Aboriginal Australia: a Lake Eyre case study' in Ramos-Millan, A. and Bustillo, A. (eds), *Siliceous Rocks and Culture*, Monográfica Arte y Arqueología, 42, 587–607. Granada.

Mercer, R.J. 1981. *Grimes Graves, Norfolk. Excavations 1971–72*. D.O.E. Research Report, 11. HMSO, London.

Mercer, R.J. 1987. 'A flint quarry in the Hambledon Hill Neolithic enclosure complex' in Sieveking, G. de G. and Newcomer, M.H. (eds), *The Human Uses of Flint and Chert*, 159–63. Cambridge University Press, Cambridge.

Millet-Richard, L.-A. 2006. 'Settlements and flint workshops in the Grand Pressigny region: hypotheses about the knappers of livres de beurre' in Körlin, G. and Weisgerber, G. (eds), *Stone Age–Mining Age*. Der Anschnitt, Zeitschrift für Kunst und Kultur im Bergbau, Beiheft 19, 423–32. Bochum.

Moloney, N. 1988. 'Experimental biface manufacture using non-flint lithic materials' in MacRae, R.J. and Moloney, N. (eds), *Non-flint Stone Tools and the Palaeolithic Occupation of Britain*. British Archaeological Reports, 189, 49–65. Oxford.

Mook, W.G. 1986. 'Business meeting: recommendations and resolutions adopted by the twelfth international radiocarbon conference'. *Radiocarbon*, 28, 799.

Mortimore, R.N. and Wood, C.J. 1986. 'The distribution of flint in the English chalk, with particular reference to the "Brandon Flint Series" and the high Turonian flint maximum' in Sieveking, G. de G. and Hart, M.B. (eds), *The Scientific Study of Flint and Chert*, 7–20. Cambridge University Press, Cambridge.

Murphy, J. and Riley, J.P. 1962. 'A modified single solution method for the determination of phosphate in natural waters'. *Analytica Chimica Acta*, 27, 31–6.

Newcomer, M.H. 1971. 'Some quantitative experiments in handaxe manufacture'. *World Archaeology*, 3 (1), 85–94.

Newcomer, M.H. and Sieveking, G. de G. 1980. 'Experimental flake-scatter patterns: a new interpretative technique'. *Journal of Field Archaeology*, 7 (3), 345–52.

Olausson, D.S. 1983. 'Lithic technological analysis of the thin-butted flint axe'. *Acta Archaeologica*, 53, 1–87.

Owen, A., Jenkins, D. and Kelso, W.I. 2001. 'Sampling strategies for phosphorus in archaeological sites' in Millard, A. (ed.), *Archaeological Sciences '97. Proceedings of the conference held* in *Durham 2nd–4th September 1997*, British Archaeological Reports, 939, 170–77. Oxford.

Patterson, L.W. and Sollberger, J.B. 1979. 'Water treatment of flint'. *Lithic Technology*, 8, 50–51. University of Texas, Center for Archaeological Research.

Peake, A.E. 1915. 'The Grime's Graves excavations, 1914' in Clarke, W.G. (ed.), *Report on the Excavations at Grime's Graves, Weeting, Norfolk, March–May 1914*, 10–134. Prehistoric Society of East Anglia, London.

Peake, A.E. 1916. 'Recent excavations at Grime's Graves'. *Proceedings of the Prehistoric Society of East Anglia*, 2 (2), 268–319.

Peake, A.E. 1917. 'Further excavations at Grime's Graves'. *Proceedings of the Prehistoric Society of East Anglia*, 2 (3), 409–36.

Peake, A.E. 1919. 'Excavations at Grime's Graves during 1917'. *Proceedings of the Prehistoric Society of East Anglia*, 3 (1), 73–93.

Pelegrin, J. and Richard, A. (eds) 1995. *Les Mines de Silex au Néolithique en Europe: avancées récentes*. Comité des Travaux Historiques et Scientifiques, Documents Préhistoriques, 7.

Piggott, S. 1954. *The Neolithic Cultures of the British Isles.* Cambridge University Press, Cambridge.

Pitts, M. 1996. 'The stone axe in Neolithic Britain'. *Proceedings of the Prehistoric Society*, 62, 311–71.

Potts, P. 1987. *A Handbook of Silicate Rock Analysis*. Blackie, London.

Provan, D.M.J. 1971. 'Soil phosphate analysis as a tool in archaeology'. *Norwegian Archaeological Review*, 4, 37–50.

Pryor, F. 1984. *Excavations at Fengate, Peterborough, England.* Northamptonshire Archaeological Society Monograph, 1.

Ramos-Milan, A. and Bustillo, A. (eds), *Siliceous Rocks and Culture*, Monográfica Arte y Arqueología. Granada.

Rappaport, R.A. 1968. *Pigs for the Ancestors. Ritual in the Ecology of a New Guinea People.* Yale University Press, New Haven.

Reeves-Smith, T. and Hamond, F. (eds) 1983. *Landscape and Archaeology in Ireland*. British Archaeological Reports, 116. Oxford.

Richardson, D. 1920. 'A new celt-making floor at Grimes Graves'. *Proceedings of the Prehistoric Society of East Anglia*, 3 (2), 243–58.

Rigby, V. 1988. 'The Late Prehistoric, Roman and Later Wares' in Longworth, I., Ellison, A. and Rigby, V., *Excavations at Grimes Graves, Norfolk, 1972–1976. Fascicule 2*, 100–10. British Museum Press, London.

Robins, P. 2002. 'A Late Neolithic flint hoard at Two Mile Bottom, near Thetford, Norfolk'. *Lithics*, 23, 29–31.

Roe, D.A. 1968. 'British Lower and Middle Palaeolithic hand-axe groups'. *Proceedings of the Prehistoric Society*, 34, 1–82.

Roe, F. 1999. 'Stone axes' in Barclay, A. and Halpin, C., *Excavations at Barrow Hills, Radley, Oxfordshire. Volume I: the Neolithic and Bronze Age monument complex*, 228–33. Oxford Archaeological Unit, Thames Valley Landscapes, 11.

Rosehill, the Hon. Lord 1871. 'Note of Excavations at "Grimes Graves", Norfolk'. *Proceedings of the Society of Antiquaries of Scotland*, 8, 419–28.

Rottländer, R.C.A. and Weymouth, J. 1980/81. 'Über das Ionentauschverhalten von Feuersteinen'. *Acta Praehistorica et Archaeologica*, 11/12, 35–6.

Rowell, D.L. 1994. *Soil Science: methods and applications.* Longman, Harlow.

Rudebeck, E. 1998. 'Flint extraction, axe offering and the value of cortex' in Edmonds, M. and Richards, C. (eds), *Understanding the Neolithic of North-western Europe*, 312–27. Cruithne Press, Glasgow.

Russell, M. 2000a. *Flint Mines in Neolithic Britain.* Tempus, Stroud.

Russell, M. 2000b. 'Of flint mines and fossil men: the Lavant Caves'. *Oxford Journal of Archaeology*, 19.1, 105–8.

Sandars, H.W. 1910. 'On the use of the deer-horn pick in the mining operations of the ancients'. *Archaeologia*, 62, 101–24.

Saville, A. 1981. 'The flint assemblage' in Mercer, R.J., *Grimes Graves, Norfolk. Excavations 1971–72*, vol. 2, 1–182. D.O.E. Research Report, 11. HMSO, London.

Schild, R. 1980. 'Introduction to dynamic technological analysis of chipped stone assemblages in Schild, R. (ed.), *Unconventional Archaeology. New approaches and goals in Polish archaeology*, 57–85. Zakład Narodowy imienia Ossolińskich, Wrocław.

Schmid, E. 1980. 'Der Silex-Bergbau bei Veaux-Malaucène in Südfrankreich' in Weisgerber, G., Slotta, R. and Weiner, J. (eds), *5000 Jahre Feuersteinbergbau: Die Suche nach dem Stahl der Steinzeit*, 166–78, Der Anschnitt, Deutsches Bergbau Museum, Bochum.

Schreve, D.C. 2006. 'The taphonomy of a Middle Devensian (MIS 3) vertebrate assemblage from Lynford, Norfolk, UK, and its implications for Middle Palaeolithic subsistence strategies'. *Journal of Quaternary Science*, 21 (5), 543–56.

Sherratt, A. 1994. 'The transformation of early agrarian Europe: the Later Neolithic and Copper Ages 4500–2500 BC' in Cunliffe, B. (ed.), *The Oxford Illustrated Prehistory of Europe*, 167–201. Oxford University Press, Oxford.

Sieveking, G. de G. 1979. 'Grimes Graves and prehistoric European flint mining' in Crawford, H. (ed.), *Subterranean Britain*, 1–43. John Baker, London.

Sieveking, G. de G. 1980. 'GB 13 Weeting Village, "Grimes Graves", Norfolk' in Weisgerber, G., Slotta, R. and Weiner, J. (eds), *5000 Jahre Feuersteinbergbau: Die Suche nach dem Stahl der Steinzeit*, 528–40. Der Anschnitt, Deutsches Bergbau Museum, Bochum.

Sieveking, G. de G., Bush, P., Ferguson, J., Craddock, P.T., Hughes, M.J. and Cowell, M.R. 1972. 'Prehistoric flint mines and their identification as sources of raw material'. *Archaeometry*, 14 (2), 151–76.

Sieveking, G. de G., Craddock, P.T., Hughes, M.J., Bush, P. and Ferguson, J. 1970. 'Characterization of Prehistoric flint mine products'. *Nature*, 228 (5268), 251–4.

Sieveking, G. de G., Longworth, I.H., Hughes, M.J., Clark, A.J. and Millett, A. 1973. 'A new survey of Grimes Graves'. *Proceedings of the Prehistoric Society*, 39, 182–218.

Sieveking, G. de G. and Newcomer, M.H. (eds) 1987. *The Human Uses of Flint and Chert*. Cambridge University Press, Cambridge.

Sillitoe, P. 1998. *An Introduction to the Anthropology of Melanesia: culture and tradition*. Cambridge University Press, Cambridge.

Silvester, R.J. 1991. *The Fenland Project no. 4: the Wissey Embayment and the Fen Causeway, Norfolk*. East Anglian Archaeology, 52.

Skertchley, S.B.J. 1879. 'On the manufacture of gunflints, the method of excavating for flint, the age of Palaeolithic man, and the connexion between Neolithic art and the gunflint trade'. *Memoirs of the Geological Survey of England and Wales*. HMSO, London.

Smith, R.A. 1912. 'On the date of Grime's Graves and Cissbury flint mines'. *Archaeologia*, 63, 109–58.

Smith, R.A. 1915. 'The flint implements' in Clarke, W.G. (ed.), *Report on the Excavations at Grime's Graves, Weeting, Norfolk, March–May, 1914*, 147–207. Prehistoric Society of East Anglia, London.

Smith, R.A. 1931. *The Sturge Collection. An illustrated selection of flints from Britain bequeathed in 1919 by W. Allen Sturge*. British Museum, London.

Smolla, G. 1987. 'Prehistoric flint mining: the history of research – a review' in Sieveking, G. de G. and Newcomer, M.H. (eds), *The Human Uses of Flint and Chert*, 127–9. Cambridge University Press, Cambridge.

Spoerry, P. (ed.) 1992. *Geoprospection in the Archaeological Landscape*. Oxbow Monographs, 18. Oxford.

Strathern, A.M. 1969. 'Stone axes and flake tools: evaluations from two New Guinea Highlands societies'. *Proceedings of the Prehistoric Society*, 35, 311–29.

Strathern, A. 1971. *The Rope of Moka: big-men and ceremonial exchange in Mount Hagen, New Guinea*. Cambridge University Press, Cambridge.

Stuiver, M. and Polach, H.J. 1977. 'Discussion: reporting of ^{14}C data'. *Radiocarbon*, 19 (3), 355–63.

Stuiver, M., Reimer, P.J., Bard, E., Beck, J.W., Burr, G.S., Hughen, K.A., Kromer, B., McCormac, G., van der Plicht, J. and Spurk, M. 1998. 'INTCAL 98 radiocarbon age calibration'. *Radiocarbon*, 40 (3), 1041–84.

Taçon, P. 1991. 'The power of stone: symbolic aspects of stone use and tool development in western Arnhem Land, Australia'. *Antiquity*, 65, 192–207.

Thomas, J. 1991. *Rethinking the Neolithic*. Cambridge University Press, Cambridge.

Thomas, J. 1996. *Time, Culture and Identity: an interpretive archaeology*. Routledge, London.

Thompson, M., Bush, P. and Ferguson, J. 1986. 'Flint source determination by plasma spectrometry' in Sieveking, G. de G. and Hart, M.B. (eds), *The Scientific Study of Flint and Chert*, 243–7. Cambridge University Press, Cambridge.

Tilley, C. 1994. *A Phenomenology of Landscape: places, paths and monuments*. Berg, Oxford.

Tite, M.S. and Mullins, C. 1971. 'Enhancement of the magnetic susceptibility of soils on archaeological sites'. *Archaeometry*, 13.2, 209–19.

Topolski, J. 1976. *The Methodology of History*. Polish Scientific Publishers and D. Reidel, Warsaw–Dortrecht–Boston.

Topping, P. 1997. 'Structured deposition, symbolism and the English flint mines' in Schild, R. and Sulgostowska, Z. (eds), *Man and Flint: proceedings of the VIIth International Flint Symposium Warszawa-Ostrowiec Świętokrzyski, September 1995*, 127–32. Institute of Archaeology and Ethnology, Polish Academy of Sciences, Warsaw.

Varndell, G. 1991. 'The Worked Chalk' in Longworth *et al.*, *Excavations at Grimes Graves, Norfolk, 1972–1976. Fascicule 3*, 94–153. British Museum Press, London.

Varndell, G. 2004. 'The Great Baddow Hoard and discoidal knives: more questions than answers' in Gibson, A. and Sheridan, A. (eds), *From Sickles to Circles: Britain and Ireland at the time of Stonehenge*, 116–22. Tempus, Stroud.

Varndell, G. 2005. 'Seeing things: A.L. Armstrong's flint-crust engravings from Grimes Graves' in Topping, P. and Lynott, M. (eds), *The Cultural Landscape of Prehistoric Mines*, 51–62. Oxbow, Oxford.

Wainwright, G.J. and Longworth, I.H. 1971. *Durrington Walls: excavations 1966–1968*. Society of Antiquaries of London Research Report, 29. London.

Walker, R. 1992. 'Phosphate survey: method and meaning' in Spoerry, P. (ed.), *Geoprospection in the Archaeological Landscape*. Oxbow Monograph, 18, 61–73. Oxford.

Waller, M. 1994. *The Fenland Project no. 4: Flandrian environmental change in Fenland*. East Anglian Archaeology, 70.

Weiner, J. 2003. 'As time goes by – forty years later: a visit at the Neolithic mining area of Veaux-Malaucène, Dept. Vaucluse, Provence, France' in Stollner, T., Körlin, G., Steffens, G. and Clerny, J. (eds), *Man and Mining*, 513–25. Der Anschnitt, Deutsches Bergbau Museum, Bochum.

Weisgerber, G., Slotta, R. and Weiner, J. (eds) 1980. *5000 Jahre Feuersteinbergbau: Die Suche nach dem Stahl der Steinzeit*. 3rd edn (1999), Der Anschitt, Deutsches Bergbau Museum, Bochum.

White, M.J. and Jacobi, R.M. 2002. 'Two sides to every story: Bout Coupé handaxes revisited'. *Oxford Journal of Archaeology*, 21 (2), 109–33.

Whittle, A. 1995. 'Gifts from the earth: symbolic dimensions of the use and production of Neolithic flint and stone axes'. *Archaeologia Polona*, 33, 247–59.

Whittle, A. 1996. *Europe in the Neolithic: the creation of new worlds*. Cambridge University Press, Cambridge.

Wymer, J.J. 1968. *Lower Palaeolithic Archaeology in Britain as Represented by the Thames Valley*. John Baker, London.

Zeitlin, R.N. 1987. 'A sociocultural perspective on the spatial analysis of commodity and stylistic distributions' in Sieveking, G. de G. and Newcomer, M.H. (eds), *The Human Uses of Flint and Chert*, 173–81. Cambridge University Press, Cambridge.

Plate 1 Phosphate survey: setting out the 50-m grid.

Plate 2 Feature 32: *floorstone in situ.*

Plate 3 Feature 34: a feature excavated to full depth.

Plate 4 Feature 118: an area of flint-knapping debris.

Plate 5 The 1972–4 chipping floor under excavation.

Plate 6 The 1972–4 chipping floor under excavation.

Plate 7 Nodule of *wallstone*.

0 ⊢————————⊣ 10 cm

Plate 8 Nodule of *floorstone*.

Plate 9

Plate 10

Plate 9–11 First Group: category
F.I. Example of primary stage of axe
preparation; three views.

Plate 11

0   10 cm

0   10 cm

Plate 12 Second Group, without microflakes and chips.

Plate 13 Second Group, microflakes and chips.

0 _____ 10 cm

Plate 14 Hammerstones.

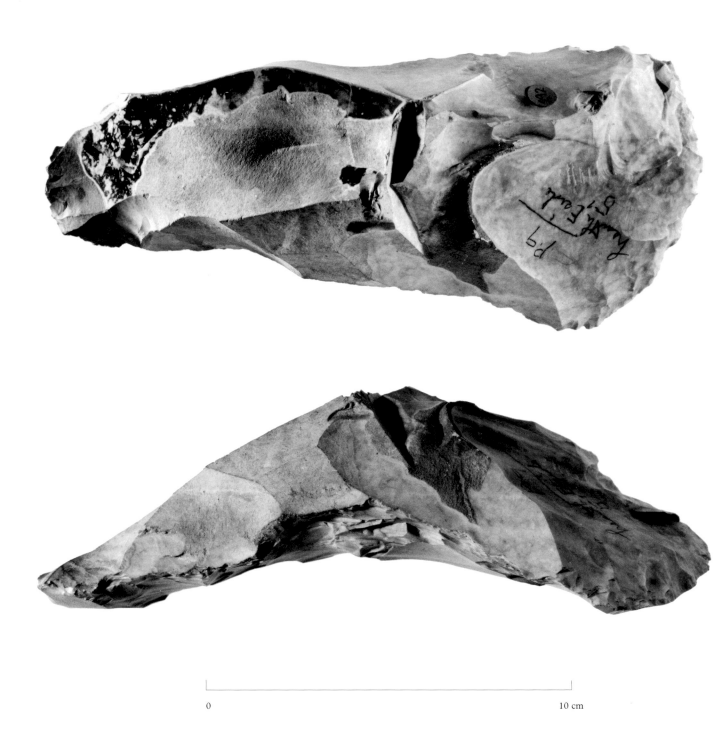

Plate 15 Flint adze, front and side views.

Plate 16 Flint axe with polish on butt.

0   10 cm

Plate 17 Flint axe of size and finish suggesting prestige status.

Plate 18 Flint axe of Type 9.

Plate 19 Stone axe, Greenwell's Pit.

Plate 20 Stone axe, Floor 15.

0   10 cm

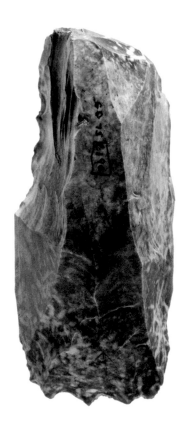

Plate 21 Flint scraper (plane), front and side views.

0   10 cm

Plate 22 Rubbing stone, Feature 105.

Plate 23 Selection of artefacts sampled for analysis and found to be of Grimes Graves flint.

0   10 cm

Plate 24 Polished axe from Lound Run, Suffolk.

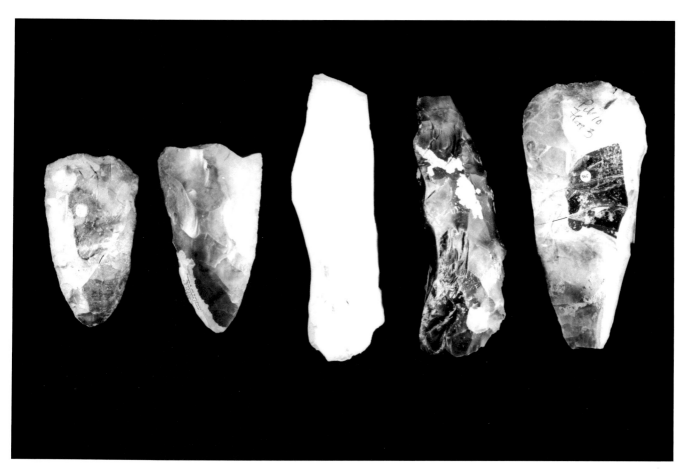

Plate 25 Selection of axes in various stages of production.

0   10 cm

Plate 26 Two discoidal knives from Grimes Graves.

Plate 27 Axe found at Grimes Graves but with composition atypical of the site.

Plate 28 Biface of Grimes Graves flint, possibly from a deeper geological horizon than *floorstone*.

0   10 cm

Plate 29 Polished discoidal knife, Bermondsey.

Plate 30 Polished discoidal knife, Yorkshire.